ALAN SUES
A Funny Man

love and peace
Alan Sues

A Biography
By Michael Gregg Michaud

Alan Sues: A Funny Man
By Michael Gregg Michaud
© 2016, ALL RIGHTS RESERVED
No part of this book may be reproduced in any form or by any means, electronic, mechanical, digital, photocopying, or recording, except for inclusion of a review, without permission in writing from the publisher or Author.

Published in the USA by:
BearManor Media
P O Box 71426
Albany, Georgia 31708
www.bearmanormedia.com

ISBN: 978-1-62933-098-3
BearManor Media, Albany, Georgia
Printed in the United States of America
Book design by Robbie Adkins, www.adkinsconsult.com

"Years from now, when you talk about this—and you will—be kind."
Robert Anderson, *Tea and Sympathy*

Alan Sues in Singin' in the Rain, *1986*

Program

FOREWORD	vii
Act 1, Scene 1	1
1926-1946 "The truth just isn't funny."	
Act 1, Scene 2	26
1946-1954 "I washed my hair in the toilet bowl, and realized I had finally arrived in New York."	
Act 1, Scene 3	57
1954-1962 "I'm a better sketch artist than a stand-up."	
Act 2, Scene 1	96
1962-1968 "What's a Laugh-in?"	
Act 2, Scene 2	124
1968-1972 "Camp is great, but I don't think it's necessary to lay heavy on the homo jokes."	
Act 2, Scene 3	175
1972-1976 "This role is definitely a career move."	
Act 3, Scene 1	220
1976-1986 "You could play gay if it was funny and not sexual, but you couldn't be gay."	
Act 3, Scene 2	252
1986-1991 "People still think I'll jump out of a cake."	
Act 3, Scene 3	278
1991-2011 "This is no fun."	
Alan Sues, Playwright	318
ACKNOWLEDGEMENTS	365

Alan Sues, Patricia (Eng) Faure, and the author. 2003

FOREWORD

Alan Sues was a part of my life—close at home and from afar—for more than thirty-seven years.

He was complicated, intelligent, observant, generous, thoughtful, unaffected, shy, frugal, lonely, outrageous, crotchety, impatient, and very funny. Besides being friends, we worked on many writing projects together, including a screenplay, a couple of film treatments, his one-man show, and his standup material. Countless conversations and interviews informed this biography beginning in 1975 on the porch of Alan's cottage overlooking Lake Wesserunsett at Lakewood Theater in Skowhegan, Maine, during his appearance in the musical *Sugar*. In his last years Alan remained guarded about his "personal indiscretions," but he wanted me to complete this book about his life and times, and career.

Funny is a generic word – subjective, and a cliché. In Alan's case, his sense of funny was rooted in exposing the wit of the everyday, and the absurdity of chance. Finding the humor in living helped him maneuver through his complicated life.

Alan entertained me and made my life better. Being in his company was always an adventure. With no effort, he could turn a simple night out at a restaurant into a master class in comedy.

Whether for an audience of ten thousand or an audience of two, Alan loved to perform. He could be a very charming host, and he was proud of his lovely, comfortable home. He liked my sister, and always enjoyed her visits. One afternoon, we had cheese and crackers and Cabernet ("Not necessarily in that order," he would say) on the back patio, and he sang and danced a soft-shoe routine for her and her friend who was visiting from out of town. In the final months of his life, my sister was one of the few people he received at home. Not long before his death, my sister dropped in. "How are you?" he asked her. "I'm good," she said. "Well, *I'm* not," he cracked. "But you look good," she said, and added, "getting old sucks shit." Alan guffawed, turned to me and said, "I like her! Does she play football?"

Alan was an excellent cook. Through the years, besides seeking out the newest restaurants in town, we spent many hours in the kitchen, cooking and talking about food. One evening, I poached pears, a fruit that we both loved. Every Christmas thereafter, he sent me a box of fresh pears. He never forgot. But with every gift came a playful slap on the hand. "The only way you're going to poach pears again is if I give you the damn pears," he'd say.

It seems only fitting that I share the poached pear recipe that he so loved. Before every show, patrons have a go at the snack bar. Here's something to eat while you're reading Alan's story.

POACHED PEARS À LA SUES

1 Bottle of Moscato (white preferable, but red works), or Riesling
2 cups of simple syrup
1 teaspoon of ground cinnamon
2 tablespoons of honey
1 teaspoon of ground ginger
1 teaspoon of pure vanilla extract
6 firm Anjou pears, peeled

In a large saucepan, combine wine, simple syrup, cinnamon, honey, ginger and vanilla extract. Bring the mixture to a simmer, stirring frequently to prevent burning, until the honey is melted. Add the pears and simmer 15–20 minutes, turning the pears occasionally until they are tender. Remove the pears and set aside to cool. Simmer the syrup 15–20 minutes longer until thickened and reduced by half. Be careful not to burn. Drizzle pears with the syrup reduction, and serve with vanilla ice cream.

Act 1
Scene 1

1926–1946 "The truth just isn't funny."

"I was born on a ferry boat," Alan Sues explained. "My mother was going to a party, and was crossing San Francisco Bay. It was before the Golden Gate Bridge was even built. It was foggy and all the cars started rocking and a car bumped ours and—plop—a baby! I ruined her green satin dress. She never forgave me."

Performers often create and propagate mythologies about their lives. Alan was a master of personal reinvention. "The truth just isn't funny," he'd say.

Actually, Allen (Alan) Grigsby Sues was born on March 7, 1926, in bucolic Ross, California. The small town suburb of San Francisco is located fifteen miles north of Sausalito in Marin County. Ross, defined by farmland, tree-covered hills, and creeks, had a population of less than five hundred people at that time.

Alan's mother's premature labor prompted a Caesarean section, and he was kept in an incubator for several months. "She was expecting a girl," Alan said. "She was knitting pink sweaters and booties for months. *That's* probably why she never forgave me."

Alice Murray Sues had been a secretary, and a "professional shopper," as Alan described her. "She bought $35 hats and $64 dresses on a $32.50 weekly salary during the Depression. She may have *caused* the Depression," he joked. Her excessive shopping was exceeded only by her excessive drinking. When she was confined to the house while Alan was in the incubator, a Catholic priest visited her daily. "It was the closest she ever came to religious practice," Alan mused. "She liked the priest because he was the only person she met who could keep up with her drinking!"

Alan was surrounded by a large family. His maternal grandmother lived nearby, and his aunts, uncles and cousins congregated at her house. "There was a terrible draught," Alan recalled. "My grandmother lived outside of town in a creaky old house that sat in the middle of fields of dusty dirt. When the wind blew, you couldn't find the place. It looked like a scene from *The Grapes of Wrath*. Actually, my grandmother looked like Pa Joad."

Alan's parents were married on June 16, 1924. "I really don't know how my mother and father met," he said, "but I'd always thought it was in an alley. I never saw any affection between them. I think the only way she got pregnant was because my father rolled around in his sleep."

Alan's father, Melvin G. Sues was a native of San Francisco. In 1921, he began working as a radio salesman at the H. Earl Wright Company. Several years later, he became the sales manager for the Leo J. Mayberg Company in San Francisco, distributors for RCA Victor radios.

"My father's nickname was Pete for some reason," Alan recalled. "He didn't seem to mind, but *I* did. I was called Son of a Pete by all my friends."

Pete was a towering, stoic man of German descent. He was a hard drinker with a terrible temper. Although Pete was a good provider, he was emotionally distant from his family. "The whole idea of *family* was foreign to me," Alan said. "We had meals together,

A rare tender moment at the beach with Alan and his father, Pete. 1930

but my father didn't say a word. He would read the paper or a book or a business report at the table. And we could not disturb him."

Alice played the part of an "apron-wearing housewife," but she was not interested in household chores or motherhood. "She couldn't cook," Alan recalled. "We had pineapple and cottage cheese salad, and tapioca pudding every day. I think the happiest day of my mother's life was when cold cuts became popular. We

Alan playing "dress-up" at an early age.

had platters of cold cuts. My father sold appliances and my mother didn't know how to use them. I thought birthday cakes were supposed to be at a forty-five degree angle so you could write 'Happy Birthday' on them. We ate out a lot. My mother was short and fat. And so was I."

Pete and Alice had wanted a daughter. "I messed it all up," Alan said. "My mother didn't know what to do with me. And I had no interest in sports so my father didn't understand me at all. If he had any feelings, he never expressed them."

In grade school, Alan realized an interest in performing. He volunteered to play a Mexican folk dancer in a school pageant. "Of course, I didn't know what I was doing, and I couldn't dance, but I was a trouper. I just got on that stage and shook my maracas and shimmied in a sombrero."

The Sues family moved from Ross to Palo Alto when Alan was five years old. Pete's business thrived, and a second son, John Murray Sues, was born in September, 1931. "Another son," Alan mused, "but John was a born sportsman and my father finally had the son he *really* wanted."

"We moved fifty-two times," Alan laughed. "My brother and I could pack our room in forty minutes. My father was a brilliant business man, but every time he saw anything start to grow in the yard, it made him nervous. I remember one time my mother had just gotten the living room together, and my father came home saying, 'God's country! This is God's country! I want to live and die here!' And that was always the cue. We knew we were going to move again. My mother ran through the living room screaming, 'God's country! God's country!', while yanking down the draperies. She'd put them up with thumb tacks. My father would have made a good gypsy but he was too straight to wear an earring."

Alan's brother, John Sues added, "Neither one of us learned to spell. We went to fifteen different schools in ten years."

"I think that's how I got into comedy," Alan explained. "I was never a fighter, and with comedy you could sort of get through it. It was hard on a kid moving that much. I was always 'the new kid' at school. I would throw a joke out to see who was on my side. I was always at the point of desperation, being thrown into circumstances where some people would come out swinging and some would come out with jokes. And making people laugh can make the most unappealing person popular."

The constant moving was also tough on Alice Sues. "She never had a chance to make friends, either," Alan said, "and she had absolutely no sense of humor, unfortunately." At that time, cigarettes and alcohol were common props for people in social situations. Both Alice and Pete were heavy drinkers. "My mother said she drank a little. She did. She drank a little every ten minutes. It sounds harsh to call her a drunk, but she was."

In 1934, Pete became Vice President of the Los Angeles division of the Meyberg Company. He contacted numerous real estate agents and carefully reviewed photographs of available houses in the Los Angeles suburb of El Monte, then quickly purchased a modernist, three-bedroom house on ten acres of barren, flat land. "He never consulted my mother," Alan recalled, "he just liked the pictures. He came home and said, 'We're moving!' Long before, my mother had stopped asking where to.

"The walls and floors of the new house were made of cement. It was like living in a tomb, but John and I loved it because we got to roller skate around the house before the furniture was delivered."

Living in a rambling, three-bedroom house with a Cadillac in the driveway presented a problem for young Alan at school. "Not only was I the new kid, now they thought I was the rich kid, too. I was 'pantsed' three times."

Alan remembered his first Christmas in El Monte, which he described as "a truck garden with a quarry." Alan decided he wanted a puppy for Christmas. "I started dropping hints," he said. "I said, Jesus, I've got to get a puppy. A little fox terrier. I started off small but I worked up to a shepherd. Christmas finally came and I bounded out of bed expecting to find a puppy under the tree. Instead, there was an enormous tank filled with tropical fish! Not my idea of a dog. I guess my parents got *puppy* mixed up with *guppy*. Five too many martinis? I was furious. I don't think in my whole life I've ever been quite as mad that I didn't get my way. After presents had been opened and everyone else went into the dining room for Christmas breakfast, I cranked up the heat on the tank and boiled the fish. After we ate cold cuts and pineapple salad, we all came back into the living room. My mother yelled, 'The fish! The fish!' All thirty-five were floating on the top of the steaming water. 'Oh, what could have happened,' I said, while I was strapping on my roller skates. They never figured it out."

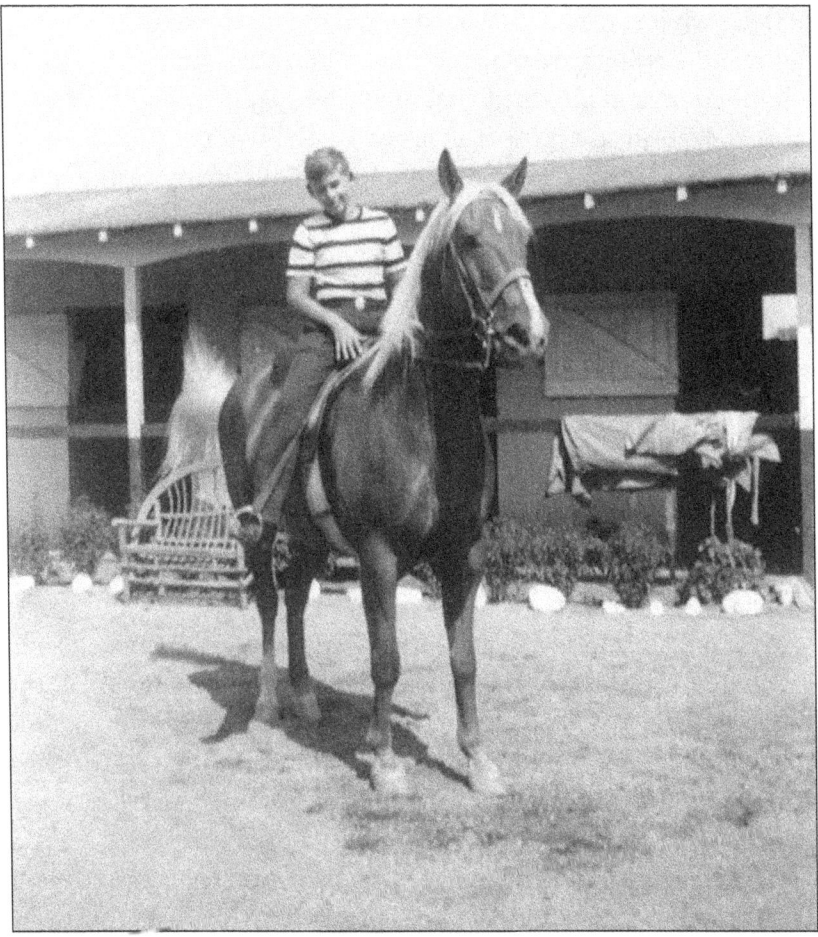

Alan at the horse ranch. 1936

It didn't take long for the Sues family to move again. Pete developed an interest in race horses. He bought an old chicken ranch, built stables, bought horses and became a breeder. "He didn't know the first thing about horses," Alan said, "but I was very interested in horses, and I wanted a pony. I never got one. I never got so much as a rocking horse. My brother was never interested in horses, but my father gave him three ponies over the course of two years. Bucky had zebra-striped legs. Bucky thought he was a dog. He chased balls in the back yard, and when he sat down in the grass, he stretched his front legs out in front of him like a dog does. He even chased the car if we were in it driving around the property.

After a while, my father decided to sell the place. For some reason, John and I brought Bucky into the house. He walked through the dining room and into the living room. Suddenly, a couple with two kids walked in to take a look around. The woman screamed, her kids thought it was a laugh riot, and we couldn't move the horse. We had to move all the furniture out to get him turned around and out of the house. My father sold the house, but he never bought my brother a horse again."

Alan recalled, "While John got a pony, I got a pigeon. My father thought that I should raise carrier pigeons. I thought it was funny to take the bird out of his cage and let him hop on my father's head. My father belonged to a stuffy men's club in downtown Los Angeles called the Jonathan Club. One day he was getting his hair cut there and the barber said, 'Mr. Sues, do you realize you have head lice?' My little birdie had infected him. That was the end of my pigeon."

Pete Sues' financial assets grew as RCA Victor radio sales soared in Southern California in the late 1930s. After a short time, the family moved to Glendale, and concurrently purchased a lakeside lot in Lake Arrowhead, a forested resort in the San Bernardino Mountains east of Los Angeles. "This was perfect," Alan explained, "since my mother was petrified of water."

Alan's father built a large house with a boat slip and a twenty-foot dock, and purchased a motor boat from a catalogue, sight unseen. "He bought himself a ship captain's hat and a white jacket with golden epaulettes on the shoulders. When the boat arrived, we christened it *My Wish*, and we all went down to the dock to take a spin. Because my mother was panicked by water, we had gotten her blind drunk. My father and I sat in the front, and John and mother sat in back. We took off and were out on the lake for some time when I turned around to look at mother. When she got nervous, she would laugh. And she was laughing hysterically.

"I said to my father, 'Listen, we really have to stop. Mom's getting out of hand.' And the man who was so in touch with his family said, 'I always knew Alice would love this.' I said, 'Dad, don't you think we should go to shore?' And he said, 'Alan, I don't know how to tell you this, but I don't know how to park this boat.' So we zipped around in circles until we ran out of gas. As the motor sputtered, we headed to the dock, which my father crashed into. He peeled all the chrome off the front of his new boat. My mother passed out and we carried her up to the house. The next weekend we drove up to the lake house and the boat was gone. It had sunk next to the dock."

The house at Lake Arrowhead was as big as a lodge, and made of logs. Alan and his brother enjoyed swimming and exploring the woods. His parents, however, were lonely and lost in the quietude and remoteness of mountain living. "They were both stiff drunk by noon," Alan said.

The winter was especially challenging. "None of us liked the snow," Alan stated. They spent one Christmas at Lake Arrowhead and Alice's mother and sisters and nieces and nephews descended upon the Sues mountain getaway. "There were cots all over the living room," he explained. "It looked like the battlefield scene in *Gone With the Wind*. Too many people arguing and fighting. It was so festive. My mother wanted a real Christmas tree, so she bought one from a local fellow selling trees. He must have seen her coming. The tree was enormous. The branches were tied up and we had a hell of a time getting the damn thing in the house. When they cut the ropes, the branches opened so wide you couldn't move around the room at all. We had to crawl around under it. It was bigger than the tree at Rockefeller Center. And they had to use a chain saw to cut it up to get it out of the house.

"My mother subscribed to *California Sunset* magazine. That's where she got her recipe for pineapple and cottage cheese salad. She decided an arts and crafts project would fill in the time. There were instructions on how to put Bavarian designs on paper plates, and then lacquer them so you could use them for decoration or hors d'oeuvres. We all sat around and worked diligently on our plates, and my father got swept up in it. When people slugged in from the snow, they would remark about our Bavarian paper plates. 'Oh, Alice, that's marvelous what you've done! Look what you've done, John and Alan!' Mine was the most artistic, naturally. They always said that. Finally, my father jumped up and screamed, 'Look at mine! Look at mine! Nobody's paying any attention to mine!' And he went running around the room shoving his plate in everyone's face like a two-year old kid. Then he made himself a drink and played jacks with my oldest cousin. We warned everyone who came in, 'Look at Pete's plate. Admire Pete's plate, or Big Daddy will have a conniption fit.' It was so much fun up there in the mountains."

Alan with his brother, John. 1937.

Faced with boredom and his woeful lack of boating skills, Pete quickly lost interest in the lake property. "Once my father kicked his nautical phase, he decided he was interested in big game," Alan recalled. "He bought himself a safari outfit and a pith helmet and drove us to Gay's Lion Ranch outside of Los Angeles. There were hundreds of lions running around, and crazy men chasing them. Then we went to an alligator farm nearby. The place was crawling with alligators. My father wanted me to sit on a two-hundred pound man-eater, but there was no way I was climbing on an alligator for a picture. Across the street was an ostrich farm. I never knew Los Angeles was so damn exotic. Kids could sit in little wagons and get pulled around a track by seven-foot tall ostriches. I didn't fall for that one, either."

Pete and Alice did not believe in giving their sons allowances. Alice had fur coats, fine feathered hats and diamond jewelry, but was miserly when it came to the more usual expenses in life. "On the rare occasion my father handed me money," Alan said, "he grumbled, 'Oh, God, he's not *doing* anything.'"

Alan's first job was working in a grocery store. He thought he would be setting up food displays and directing customers to specific food aisles, but instead, he was assigned the chore of cleaning the public restrooms. The job lasted two days.

His second job was working as a waiter at Yosemite National Park. His family vacationed at the Ahwahnee Hotel in Yosemite Valley. "It was the first time I had ever gotten along with a lot of kids," Alan explained, "and they were all working there."

He had to lie about his age to get hired, and his parents allowed him to stay there for the summer. He served meals in a tent in Camp Curry. "We took pats of butter and flipped them up to stick to the canvas overhead. When it got hot, the butter would melt and plop down on people's heads. I thought that was the greatest thing I'd ever seen in my life!"

Serving meals in a tent didn't compare to working as a waiter in the luxurious Ahwahnee Hotel. "But it was all so beautiful there. The deer ate out of your hand and the bears chased you up a tree. It was a natural wonderland. I felt like the forest dwelling beauty in the book *Green Mansions*. Well, not exactly, but I *did* feel like a forest dweller. Of course, when you're a kid, after a day, it all looks the same."

Alan experienced his first crush in the wilds of Yosemite. "I fell in love with a girl who drove a LaSalle convertible and wore real pearls around her swan-like neck. She worked as a life guard at the pool. I tried to impress her by diving backwards into the pool, which wasn't easy because I was so fat. I was very tall for my age, and the pool was only four feet deep. I sprained all ten fingers and wore finger splints for a couple of weeks. No matter what I did, she put me down. When I approached, she'd say, 'Oh, here it comes again, kids. Get in the pool and I'll get rid of it.'"

At the end of the summer, Alan took the train back to Pasadena. "I wasn't anxious to go home," Alan recalled. When he got off the train, Pete was waiting. "My father said, 'My God, you're fat. Get in the car.'"

While Alan was away in Yosemite, the Sues family had moved into a five-thousand-square-foot, five-bedroom mansion on prestigious Earl Drive. "It was a huge house in Flintridge with a long driveway lined with oak trees," Alan said. "My mother gave me the impression we were struggling, but we had a big place, plenty of food, and now she had two employees in the house."

Alice had hired a lady to cook, but would never ask her to serve the family. "Mother said it was too embarrassing to have her serve us like a waitress. But it wasn't too embarrassing to ask me. So I did the serving."

Pete hired a man to care for their horses, who also doubled as a chauffeur. Alan and John never took the bus to school, but were driven in an old Packard, one of the family's several cars. "My brother and I hated it. We'd wedge ourselves way down in the back seat so our friends wouldn't see us being driven to school."

During the next couple of years, the Sues family bought a tiny, rustic cabin near Lake Arrowhead, and a four-hundred-acre alfalfa ranch in the Los Angeles suburb of Saugus. The ranch came with fourteen resident Mexican immigrant workers. "My father didn't speak Spanish, and the poor workers didn't speak English. My father blamed them for anything and everything that went wrong.

Even when he lost control of the tractor and drove it through the side of the barn, he managed to blame those guys."

Pete bought additional acreage to build an adjacent ranch house. "My father worked hard, and he expected us to work hard, too. My mother and I baled alfalfa, which is quite a job. And I dug fence-pole holes for miles.

"My father did a lot of research about farming. He was always trying to increase his harvest. He purchased something called hybrid alfalfa from some shadowy person who told him it would yield seven crops a year instead of four. My father, whose new costume was farmer's overalls and a pitchfork, proudly said, 'Al, everybody will be looking at this ranch!' We didn't know that he had actually purchased marijuana instead of hybrid alfalfa. The ranch was raided by five state troopers with shotguns. They jumped out of their cars and said, 'Is Sues here?' My father said, 'That's right. Pete Sues. Farmer. Here I am. I guess you're here to check out my alfalfa.... See, Al? I told you they'd be coming from all over!' Well, they sure did. My father talked his way of it, but we had to plow it all under."

In 1944 Pete and another business associate formed a company with movie producer/director Clarence Brown to handle the Southern California distribution of Zenith radios, Coolerator refrigerators, Speed Queen washers, Thermadore electric ranges and many other appliance lines. He also moved his family into a spacious mansion on Chevy Chase Drive near Descanso Gardens in Flintridge.

Years earlier, Alan had stopped trying to have a "father-son relationship" with Pete. "The only thing he cared about was business," Alan said. "That's probably why he was so successful at it, but there was nothing left for his family."

One day, Pete took Alan for lunch at the Jonathan Club in Los Angeles. "I thought I was in a Sherlock Holmes movie," Alan recalled, "all these stuffy old men in three-piece suits smoking cigars and pipes, and sitting in stuffy old chairs in cavernous, dark rooms."

At first, Alan thought his father intended to establish some sort of fatherly camaraderie with his son. "He wanted to talk to me all right," Alan said. "He told me he was having an affair with a female business associate who lived in Chicago. I couldn't say a word. I don't know if I was shocked because he was talking to me like an adult, or because he was having an affair, or simply because I never thought the old iceberg was capable of or even interested in sex! He told me not to tell my mother. And, he said, I was now *responsible* for her. He said the living arrangement would remain the same, and he would support her, but I had to take care of her well-being. I was the oldest son, and it was my job. I was seventeen."

When Alan was sixteen, he had jumped the fence at Paramount Studios in Hollywood and wandered onto a cavernous soundstage. The film *Holiday Inn* was in production, and the stage was decorated with a replica of a rustic inn, snow covered trails and trees, and a horse and carriage. Bing Crosby was preparing to film a scene.

"I was amazed," Alan said. "It was sunny and hot outside, and in this building was a complete snow-covered country house. It was a winter wonderland, and I thought, this is magic. This is for me."

Alan stealthily returned to the studio many times to watch movies in progress. When he was occasionally confronted on a soundstage, he said he was working with the wardrobe department. "And I'd duck between racks of costumes to get away," he explained. "I even ate in the commissary and saw lots of movie stars."

His career interest was a problem for his parents, though. "I had no aptitude for business. I just wanted to be an actor. My father was absolutely flummoxed, and my mother was upset, too. They thought show business was frivolous, unimportant and for sissies. My mother told me, 'If I thought you were queer, I'd rather you were dead.'

"Her words stayed with me for the rest of my life. It was awful."

Despite his parent's protestations, Alan enrolled at the UCLA drama school. After three weeks he quit. His professor told him he had a "Jimmy Stewart quality" and he should model himself after the star. "But one Jimmy Stewart was enough," Alan joked. "For me, one was one too many."

World War II was raging in Europe, although the Allied forces were making marked advances during the summer of 1944. On July 18, Alan was drafted into the Army.

Alice berated her son. "My mother said I would never wake up, and I would be court-martialed. She had me so panicked that I bought an alarm clock and set it to all hours for two weeks before I shipped out. I wanted to practice getting up early."

Pete drove the family to Montrose, California, where Alan caught the bus that would take him to basic-training camp. "I got into an argument with my brother," Alan recalled. "And the whole family got into it. My parents took my brother's side, as usual. We were all screaming at each other. When we pulled up to the bus stop, I jumped out of the car and yelled, 'I'm glad I'm out of here! I hope I never see you again!'

"My mother said, 'The Army will do you a lot of good.' My father shouted, 'You never worked a day in your life. They'll march the shit out of you, and then you'll know what's really going on…' I ran past a wall of wailing women in scarves, crying and blowing kisses to their departing sons. Fathers were proudly shaking their kid's hands and slapping them on the back. 'Go to hell,' I screamed at my family.

"As I pushed my way onto the bus, I was yelling out the windows, 'Shove it! Get out of here! Move this bus! Get me out of here!' It didn't occur to any of us that I might get hurt or killed in the war, or worse, captured by the enemy."

Alan's experience in the defense of his country was no less idiosyncratic than life at the Sues home. He arrived at camp late in the evening and was instructed to go immediately to bed. He was assigned to a barracks that was oddly empty. At four o'clock the next morning he awoke. "I thought, *Oh, God, I've missed the boat!* I jumped up and ran to shower. I shaved and got dressed."

As the light of dawn crept through the barracks windows, he noticed that sometime during the night, all the beds were filled. "I'm a sound sleeper, but Jesus." However, as the men awoke, Alan realized he was the only Caucasian in the building. "I thought that was very strange because at that time, the service was segregated. They actually had 'Negro' barracks."

During the next several weeks of training, he had little personal interaction with his barracks mates. "We marched around in circles all day," Alan said, "and went from classroom to classroom, and nobody ever talked to me. I was the only white guy in the bunch. I really looked cute in my Army uniform, though. The neck looked

P.F.C. Alan G. Sues. 1944.

like something Balenciaga had designed. It was six inches away from neck all around. My cap was way down over my ears, and I wore enormous, heavy boots. I carried my manual. I never went anywhere without it because I was sure I was going to do something wrong."

After eight weeks, Alan took a train home for his first leave. He sat next to a uniformed officer who told him he hadn't seen him before in the group. He explained to Alan that he was a doctor and wondered why he hadn't seen Alan pass through his office.

"I said, that's strange, I'm having a perfectly marvelous time in D Battery with all the kids." After a long pause, the officer said, 'I suppose you're told this a lot, but you don't look at all Negro.'

"What?" Alan asked. "This may come as a shock to you, but I'm really not a Negro."

The officer then accused him of being ashamed of his race. "He said, now, listen, that's a wonderful race. And you're going to be very unhappy if you keep putting it down. It's unfortunate that you don't look Negro, but you are a Negro. I said, wait a minute, I'd know if I was Negro for crying out loud!" They argued for a moment, and then the officer instructed Alan to come to his office as soon as he returned from leave.

"That was perfect," Alan said. "I certainly wasn't going to tell my mother that the Army made me a Negro." His time at home was anything but restful. "My parents knew I would be shipped off to Europe, but my father needed work done on his new one hundred acres, so I dug a cesspool during my leave."

Upon his return to camp, Alan went directly to the office of the doctor he'd met on the train. Somehow, someone erroneously stamped "Negro" on Alan's induction papers. "I guess they had two stamps. One was 'White' and one was 'Negro' and somebody picked up the wrong stamp. If I hadn't met that doctor on the train, I might have gone through my whole tour of duty as a Negro, which I probably would have liked." D Battery was designated for African-American servicemen. "They fixed their mistake," Alan said, "and by three o'clock that afternoon I was on a train to Fort Sill in Oklahoma. *I* was their mistake. They warned me, don't tell anybody because *you* will get in a lot of trouble! I had a sinking feeling about this Army business."

Alan followed in his parents' footsteps and had become an accomplished drinker by the age of eighteen. "It was a matter of survival," he said. Oklahoma was a "dry" state, which meant the sale or use of alcohol was prohibited by law. "That was hard to take," Alan explained, "as if the service wasn't hard enough. A friend told me to sign up for kitchen duty at once. I was reluctant until he explained that the vanilla extract the cook used was forty proof. It wasn't as smooth as vodka, but I smelled a lot better."

Alan shared his Quonset hut at Fort Sill with five other fellows. The family of one kid sent him the fixings to make his own moonshine. "They were professional bootleggers from Tennessee," Alan recalled. "I was very fond of him. We mixed it all up, and hid it under the guy's bunk. One night, he woke us all up by running back and forth yelling, 'It's ripe! It's ripe!' We all had a couple of swigs, and it was worse than awful. Suddenly, the guy yelled, 'I made a mistake! Too much lye! Don't drink it! My uncle did this once and it ate the enamel off his teeth!"

In November 1944, Alan began twelve weeks of training as a switchboard operator. Fort Sill, Oklahoma, was buried in snow. For weeks, he practiced constructing a communications tent in the frosty outdoors. "I had to dig through four feet of snow and down four feet into the frozen ground," he explained. "I didn't know how good I had it digging a cesspool in sunny California.

"I had to sit crunched up in this tiny hole talking into the switchboard. My bootlegging buddy from Tennessee leaned over and said, 'Hey, I heard we got a march order. We're going back to camp for Thanksgiving!' I said, 'My God, that's marvelous!' I put in a call to A Battery and B Battery and said, 'March order!' We all started moving out across a hill and all of sudden shells started bursting all around us. We were under attack for Christ sakes! I thought, *Oh my God, what have I done?* The next thing a helicopter landed and the general got out, trudged through the snow, and said to the colonel, 'Who gave the march orders!?' The colonel said, 'I got it from the major, sir.' And the blame went down through the ranks. I thought, *Oh, shit.* The blame had reached down to our lieutenant. I was withering, and tip-toeing backward behind a truck. They found me and dragged me to the general who yelled, 'Who gave you the march order!?' I smiled my prettiest smile, shrugged and said, 'Well, I thought…' The general screamed, 'Thought! Are you out of your mind!? Thought? What are you doing? You don't *think* here! Do you know what this *means?*' And I thought, *Oh, yes, I know what it means. My head off at the shoulders.* The general screamed, 'this means we've lost the *pennant!*'

"*For Christ sakes,* I thought. *What pennant? We could have been blown up!* Tennessee, who smelled like a distillery, which was one of his few redeeming qualities, confessed that he *thought* they were going to give us marching orders. I had taken it as an *order*. More fun in the Army."

During his training, Alan discovered he needed to wear glasses. "I was having terrible headaches," Alan recalled. "I went to see the doctor and said I was having migraine headaches, and he said, 'Oh, sure you are sweetheart.' He prescribed aspirin! I was taking so many I coughed up white smoke."

Finally he was sent to the eye doctor. "I sat in the doctor's office with a bunch of guys and we got the bum's rush with the exam. The doctor was hurrying to have lunch with the colonel that day. I got my new glasses in a week and when I put them on, I could not see a thing. Absolutely nothing. But the round, steel rims were very good looking.

"I wanted to surprise my parents on my next and final leave home before heading out to war. My mother hated surprises, but I rang the buzzer and she opened the door and barked out, 'Jesus Christ! He's cross-eyed!'"

When he was home, Alan went to see the family eye doctor. His Army diagnosis was wrong. "I was a little bit far-sighted, but they had given me glasses for someone who was terribly near-sighted." The new glasses would not be ready before he returned to Oklahoma, so his mother assured him she would take care of it and send him the new glasses.

Alice sent Alan a pair of glasses with dark pink frames. "She was giddy, or drunk," Alan said, "or vindictive. I was afraid to go to the men's room. I never had so many cat-calls in my life!"

Within days, Alan got his orders to sail for Europe. He took a train to Baltimore, and got blind drunk. "I don't remember much except waking up and hearing we had a five hour layover in Chicago. I had a hangover and staggered over to the USO. I was trying to get a cup of coffee, my hand was shaking and a very attractive WAC asked, 'Having a little trouble?' I said, 'You'll never believe it.' She asked me what I was doing. 'Being unattractive, what else?' I said. So we went from the coffee bar to the joy juice bar. I proceeded to get drunk all over again. We had a chummy moment before we got into a cab to go back to the train. As I got on the platform, my Chicago sweetie yelled out, 'Big Al!' and ran over and handed me three dozen bright yellow jonquils. So, I'm staggering through the train car to my seat, dragging my barracks bag on the floor, wearing pink glasses and holding dozens of yellow jonquils. I sat down next to a soldier who took one look at me and asked, 'California?'"

After hours of drinking on the train, Alan arrived in Baltimore. When his name was called, he was passed out on the floor. "I nearly poisoned myself with alcohol," he said. "I was in the dispensary for two days. When I fell, I broke my pink glasses, and I missed my ship going overseas. That was the only bit of luck I had in the service."

On April 16, 1945, Alan set sail for La Havre, France. "We traveled in a convoy of ships that was not protected by gun boats. I was assigned a bunk at the very bottom of the ship along with nine hundred other guys. After about four days at sea, the motors stopped because submarines were detected nearby. The guy next to me, a peach of an optimist, said, 'We're at the bottom, right in the line of torpedoes. If they hit us, we're finished.' For a minute, I thought it was a joke, and then panic set in. I clung to my little crib in complete horror and never went on deck for the rest of the trip."

It was raining when he arrived at La Havre twelve days later. The city had been leveled by Allied air attacks during the Battle of Normandy. "There were piles of rubble smoldering all around," Alan remembered. "Everything was in splinters and blinds were dangling from blown out windows. And I remember seeing all these colorful movie magazines scattered around in the debris and blowing in the breeze. It was the only color in the place. It was cold, and we marched. A lot. The truth is I was petrified.

"We arrived at a camp called Lucky Strike. All the camps were named after cigarette brands. The camp was one big field of boot-deep mud. Chaplains were running around giving Last Rites to wounded guys on gurneys. The sergeant said, 'Men this is going to be pretty rough.' Talk about understatement. It was hell."

The soldiers slept in the mud. "We were shipped around and around in circles. We traveled five days on a burned-out boxcar that obviously caught the wrong end of a bomb. It was snowing and raining, and Jesus, it was terrible. I couldn't sleep. I was afraid I'd roll out of the boxcar in my fart sack onto the tracks."

The next stop was an encampment used to treat soldiers who experienced post-traumatic syndrome. "They were all nuts and ran around the place screaming. They told us how much trouble we were in for on the front. We could hear artillery fire nearby. The guys would laugh at us and say, 'Ha, ha, love is just around the corner!' They woke us up at four o'clock in the morning, made us strip to the waist and do pushups in the snow. We had to run up the hill, down the hill, up the hill, down the hill. Jesus, I wondered what side some of our officers were on."

Alan had been trained in artillery, and had been using a carbine. Suddenly, he and his fellow servicemen were handed Springfield rifles. "I didn't even know what it was," Alan said. "We'd never seen one before. They told us to clean them. We were being moved to infantry. It really scared the shit out of all of us."

One night, the soldiers were called to the mess hall for a rally. "There was a platform where a lieutenant got up and starting talking. He said how tough it was going to be on the front. He got more and more excited, and then just lost his marbles up there in front of us. They dragged him off the stage. It was loony."

Being so far away from his family, and literally in the line of enemy fire, Alan felt emboldened to explore his sexuality. He had felt homosexual urges for several years, but never acted upon his feelings. He was aware of other soldiers stealing intimate moments when the lights went out. It wasn't long before he began a relationship with an officer. "He was very macho, and he told me we couldn't say a word about what we were doing. I don't know if he was sexually attracted to me, or just so desperate being in the middle of nowhere with no women in sight. But I was more afraid than he was. Still, it worked for me. Considering what was going on around us, it was a good distraction."

In a short time, Alan's division was moved closer to the action. They were housed in the ghostly remains of a badly bombed factory. The new recruits were on one side of the wreckage, and the veterans were on the other. Half of the building was open to freezing rain and snow. "We were on the fourth floor," he recalled. "One night, an old guy started running back and forth, waving his arms and screaming for help. He just lost his head and eventually ran off the open edge of the fourth floor. He fell to the ground and died."

The next morning, Alan and his fellow soldiers were called to breakfast. "We marched to breakfast, like everything else. Nobody talked about the jumper. They gave us a scoop of powdered eggs. When I finished, I said to a friend that I was still hungry. He said he was too. We whispered because if you spoke aloud, an officer would jump up and scream at you, and order you to do pushups for the crowd. I went from two hundred and twenty five pounds to one hundred and fifty. My uniform never fit. The boys would laugh at me under their breath. I was always a crowd pleaser. So, we go back to the line to get more breakfast. The lieutenant said, 'Oh, you want more, huh? Well, I'll just fill up your tray then.' A pyramid of powdered eggs. I didn't want *more* eggs, I wanted *real* eggs. Then he made us eat all of it—at gun point! Somehow, I got mine down, but my friend vomited all over the floor. The lieutenant made him clean it up. Then he filled the guy's tray up again and made him eat it. My friend vomited again. They let me go, but I don't know how long my friend had to go through that abuse. The next time we had a meal, though, he ate like a bird."

Alan and his fellow soldiers finally got their marching orders to head for the front. The next day, the war ended. "In the nick of time," Alan said. "Then we transferred from company to company. I never got to really know anyone. One night, four of us were sitting around drinking cognac. We were a little nervous because the Germans were known to poison booze and leave it behind. So we're drinking, and two of the guys started frothing at the mouth. I had just gulped a big glass of it. Nothing happened to me, but one of the guys died. My mother's horrible cooking gave me a cast iron stomach. Maybe her slop had saved my life.

"We were so bored. We just got hammered each night. For fun, we'd strip and chase each other around the trees in the snow. If only we had a deck of cards. Nobody got shot, but a few got pneumonia. We still moved around a lot, and I eventually ended up near Nuremburg."

The buildings in the town had been used by the Germans to imprison Russian soldiers. The Russian prisoners had been freed by the Americans, and were waiting to go home. "They were all shell-shocked," Alan said. "By this time, the place was used as a prison for the Germans. My job was to guard the German prisoners who were forced to dig up the Russian soldiers they had killed and buried in shallow graves, recover any identification on the bodies, and re-bury them properly. You could smell it miles away."

Most of Alan's time was spent watching over the prisoners. "You were on duty for two hours and off for four, but you rarely got any sleep because the Germans were always trying to escape. One of their tricks was to rush out of the barracks and make a run for the fence. The guards just sprayed them with machine guns. Then their comrades had to dig their graves the next day."

One day, Alan was guarding fourteen German prisoners who were cleaning latrines. When they were finished, Alan was horrified to discover that two of the prisoners were missing. "One of the Germans pointed to a nearby tree," Alan recalled. "Two Russian soldiers were standing there, smiling and joking. They had taken my two prisoners, beaten them, and buried them alive."

Alan was then moved to a large villa in the countryside that had been used as a "baby factory" by the Germans. "Blond, blue-eyed studs serviced all the young German girls breeding their super race," Alan recalled. "All the files were still there with the most clinical coupling instructions in the world."

He returned to his duties as a switchboard operator. "I was working for a major who was bucking for colonel. One day he called and told me to call Able Battery. We were in Headquarter's Company. I tried to call, but couldn't get through, and I told him so. Even after the war ended, Germans were cutting the lines so we couldn't communicate. I tried several times, but no answer. All of a sudden the major called and screamed, 'You goddamned son-of-a-bitch! Why can't you get Able Battery?!' I cracked. I said, 'Listen you asshole, I can't get anybody! You've got everyone out marching around in formation like idiots instead of checking the lines. I've had enough of that!' I pulled out his cord, cutting him off, thinking he was in another building. He was in the next room. He burst in and charged at me. 'Oh, you've had enough? Get the fuck off my switchboard!' I said, 'Do you really want it off?' He screamed, 'Yes, I do.' What he meant was that he wanted me off the switchboard at the end of my shift, which was four hours away. There were a series of boosters on the switchboard which allowed us to contact Switzerland or Paris or Brussels. Everything had to be lined up and sometimes it took days to get through. I said, 'You want me off? All right, I'm off!' And I pulled all the switches including the delicate boosters. 'Go to your room,' he screamed, 'and prepare for court martial!'

"I got dressed and suddenly heard a voice, 'Private Sues, report to the office.' I walked in and saluted the major. 'Private Sues,' he said, 'we really haven't had a talk. We haven't gotten to know each other very well. I feel we should have a chance to get with our men and understand them.' I thought, *Okay, what are you doing, sweetheart? Get on with it. Pick it up.* Then he said with a big smile, 'Look who's behind you. It's your cousin.' I had never met my cousin before, but I knew he was a colonel in the First Division. Thank God he happened to come by looking for me. I had a real lunch in the officer's mess that day. And he helped me out of the jam because he outranked the major."

Before being shipped home, Alan was stationed in Biarritz, France, for a short time. The resort city in the south of France had been converted into a transitional campus for American troops preparing to return to North America. "I met a very attractive girl with Veronica Lake bangs. She was wearing a smart red blazer, a white pleated skirt, and flat shoes with spats, which were popular with the French girls. We proceeded to get hammered and we cribbed it. I didn't know many civilians, but I knew an English woman through a friend of mine. She was a dowager, tall and slender with a marvelous straight nose, hair swept up, expensive Chanel suits. She lived in a villa and invited me to dinner. Bring a friend, she said. The mayor would be there. It was all very grand. The salon was beautiful with butlers running around. I walked in with my new date with the Veronica Lake bangs and the entire room gasped. Dinner was unbearable. I had brought the most famous whore in all of Biarritz. Apparently, she was a terrible streetwalker of the tomato throwing variety. 'If you don't pay me, you get it in the mouth.' The sensitive flower turned into Tiger Lily right before my eyes. I dumped her because I thought since she was such a legendary whore, she should have been a much better lay."

After ten months in France, P.F.C. Alan G. Sues left Europe for the United States on June 10, 1946. He arrived at Fort Dix, New Jersey, on June 19. "I had an Eames Medal, a Good Conduct Medal, and a World War II Victory Medal," Alan said, "and all of my war-time earnings of $533.04."

Years later Alan pondered, "It was a funny thing about the war. Everyone looked like they were wearing costumes and over-acting. None of it seemed real to me. I never could get a real sensation of people doing the awful things they were doing. As horrible as it was—my time with the German prisoners—I never had the realization that people are really evil. I never saw the real battle action, of course, but still, the evil of it all never really sunk in with me. I know how terrible it all was, and maybe it was just too much for me to take in. It was hard to find any humor. It was too awful to believe."

Act 1
Scene 2

1946–1954 "I washed my hair in the toilet bowl, and realized I had finally arrived in New York."

Being back in Flintridge with his family was as painful as he had remembered. "I lost so much weight in the service," Alan said, "but I still had my huge, protruding ears. I was home only a couple of days, and when I came down to breakfast, my mother, who was already plastered, said, 'Ah, ha! Jumbo's down for breakfast! Can't let him out on a windy day, huh? Has to go through a door sideways!' *Jesus*, I thought, *haven't I been through enough.*"

Pete's business responsibilities kept him away from the house. His firm had broken national records for RCA television sales. While Alan was away in France, his father had served as president of the Electric Club in Los Angeles, and become a director of the Pacific Coast Electrical Association. "I barely saw him at all," Alan recalled. "If he wasn't at the office, he was out of town."

While Alan was in the service, his younger brother John was left alone to deal with their parents. The care and keeping of Alice had landed in *his* youthful lap. John anxiously shared family battle stories with his brother. Alice had discovered that Pete was carrying on with his female business associate in Chicago. At first, John explained, Alice took responsibility for her husband's indiscretion, blaming his wandering eye on her frumpy, overweight self. But the affair took its toll, and Pete told his wife he wanted a divorce. One night Alice got drunk and pulled a rifle on her husband, intent on killing him. John jumped into the fray and wrestled the gun away from his mother, but not before she got off two thunderous shots that tore through the wall.

"That was a rough time and I think we both took each other into our confidences about really personal things," Alan said, "and it brought us together as brothers."

The G.I. Bill provided newly discharged servicemen with money to attend college. Alan decided to use the money for acting classes at the Pasadena Playhouse. Since opening in 1925, the Playhouse had earned a respectable, national reputation, and many Hollywood stars had studied or performed there including William Holden, Eleanor Parker, Victor Mature, Tyrone Power, Robert Young and Robert Taylor. In 1936, the Playhouse added a two-year College of Theatre Arts program, which provided many different classes such as makeup, voice, speech, stage-movement, dance, theater technique, theater history, and an introduction to Shakespeare. The program cost seven hundred and fifty dollars.

"I'd always been kind of funny," Alan said, "but I thought I could overcome that and really be good in dramatic roles. In class, I got up to do Hamlet's soliloquy and I got entangled in a big black cape. People hollered and laughed as I got more and more wound up with that cape. Finally, I got an ovation, and that was the end of my serious acting."

After years of being teased about his big ears by schoolmates and especially his own mother, Alan had developed a complex about his appearance. "It got so I couldn't act with people because I turned sideways to talk to them," he explained. A friend recommended a plastic surgeon. The doctor performed the painful procedure of cutting and pinning back his ears. While his head was wrapped in bandages, he was told that the play *Anna Lucasta* was being cast at the Coronet Theater in Los Angeles.

While a friend drove him to the theater, Alan hastily removed his bandages. The director gave him a script and instructed him to read. "I've always been a lousy reader," Alan said, "but I started to read and I thought, *My God, I'm killing them!* The few people in the theater were laughing and rolling on the floor. I read for nearly a half hour. So the director said, 'Thank you very much. If we need your type, we'll call you.' I thought that was a strange thing to say until I got into the theater lobby and looked in the mirror. All my head sutures with long black strings were hanging down from my ears, and every time I moved, the strings—and my ears—were swinging back and forth!"

Alan's friends at the Playhouse included George Nader, a fellow student who became a well-known movie star. "George was in a couple of plays at the Playhouse. He was the best looking guy I ever saw," Alan said. "He was very rugged. And homosexual. He was such a mix of opposites, it was confusing. But he was magnetic. What a smile! George met another student named Mark Miller there, the two became lifelong lovers. And somehow, Rock Hudson wormed his way into the mix. *Very* intriguing."

At the time, Alan was having an awkward affair with an older, divorced mother of two small children. "Every time the kids came around," Alan said, "I hid in the closet. At the same time, I was meeting guys and having flings, but it always made me feel so guilty. I was wrestling with being gay, and had a bunch of quickie affairs with women then. It was a tough time and I went to a shrink somebody recommended at school."

The bohemian nature of the school's environment encouraged Alan to explore his sexual feelings, but he was racked with guilt, and feelings of being perverted. "There were lots of sexual shenanigans going on there," Alan recalled. "Teachers and students, students and students. I'd never met so many homosexuals, and they ran the gamut from up-tight football-types to flaming queens. At that time, homosexuality was a crime. I knew I wanted to be with men, but it was frightening. What my mother said about queers haunted me. And you could get arrested for dancing with another man, or even holding hands. But the atmosphere at school was very good, very welcoming, very creative, and everybody was accepted."

Alan met a young man in class named Charles Pierce, and they became fast friends. "I just loved him" Alan said. "Charles was terrific. Very talented and funny. He was bold and unapologetic, everything I wasn't. And he was liberated. He'd dress in a tuxedo and impersonate famous movie actresses. He was wonderful."

Charles, who later became an acclaimed professional female impersonator, spent a lot of time off-campus with Alan, enjoying the blue-plate specials at Albert Sheetz restaurant a few steps from the playhouse. Occasionally, they sprang for a more expensive dinner at Robert's French Restaurant a few blocks away. Nardi's bar, located across the street from Albert Sheetz, was a favorite hangout for playhouse students. They also snuck off to a gay bar called Club La Vie in nearby Alta Dena. "Charles led me astray," Alan said, "but he did it with style. And a sequined turban."

There were many gay and lesbian bars and clubs in Hollywood in the late 1940s. Charles introduced Alan to the Flamingo Club on Cahuenga Boulevard. The club was hosted by a woman named Beverly Shaw who wore a fashionable skirt, nylons and high heels, but dressed as a man from the waist up. The nightspot featured gay and lesbian cabaret performers. Alan was taken with an old drag queen named Lucian. "I loved that place," Alan said. "It was tiny. The bar was off to the left. There were a few tables and chairs around. The stage was in the back and there was a narrow ramp that led out into the audience. I think it was old plywood because it dipped under the weight of anyone walking on it. Lucian would sashay across the stage and pick people in the audience to joke with. He'd say to a guy in the front row, 'I remember you when we were in the Navy together. You were a Rear Admiral.' He was terrific!"

One of the most infamous "pansy clubs" in Los Angeles was located at 1114 Horn Avenue, just above the Sunset Strip. "You had to climb these steep steps up from Sunset," Alan recalled. "The view of the city at night, twinkling lights, so great. They couldn't advertise it as a gay club, but it was." Café Gala played host to an interesting mix of high society, gay men and women, and to many Hollywood celebrities. Christopher Isherwood described the club, "it was so nostalgically reminiscent of all the other times—the baroque decorations and the cozy red velvet corners, the sharp-faced peroxide pianist with tender memories and a tongue like an adder, the grizzled tomcat tenor, the bitch with a heart of gold, the lame celebrity, the bar mimosa, the public lovers, the amazed millionaire tourist, the garland cow, the plumed serpent and the daydream sailor."

Twin baby grand pianos—played by the husband and wife team of Edie and Rack— flanked a small stage in the middle of the intimate, candle-lit room. Bobby Short often played at the club, and Cole Porter and Judy Garland were frequent patrons. Many times, the late night crowd was treated to an impromptu performance by Garland.

A fey entertainer named John Walsh was the performing host of Café Gala. "He was an older guy, but so funny," Alan said. "He was dressed in a tuxedo with a top hat and sang filthy songs while he twirled and flicked a long, pink chiffon scarf. He told wonderful stories and knew how to work a room. He was hilarious. I dated him for a while ... the cradle robber."

Both Lucian from the Flamingo Club and John Walsh from Café Gala would influence and inform Alan's own repertoire of gags, stories and mannerisms. He later admitted to actually stealing some of their jokes for his standup routines.

Though he enjoyed his new bohemian friends, Alan was overwhelmed by classes he felt were insignificant and unrelated to acting. He managed to get himself thrown out of classes several times, and after eight months, he was finally dismissed.

His mother's constantly discouraging words only motivated him. "But it wrecked my self-confidence," he said. "I was fearless with an audition, but if I got called back, or actually got a part, I froze." Alan landed a few small roles in plays in La Jolla and Santa Barbara, California. He petitioned to go back to the Playhouse and was accepted, but in the interim auditioned for the national company of *Happy Birthday*, and got the small role of a sailor in a saloon scene.

Happy Birthday, written by Anita Loos, produced by Rodgers and Hammerstein and directed by Joshua Logan, had played for two years on Broadway. The "cocktail party" comedy was originally written for Helen Hayes. The story concerns a mousy librarian who becomes infatuated with a handsome bank teller. Miriam Hopkins took the leading role in the National Company, supported by veteran actress Enid Markey. Rehearsals began in September 1948. After a three day tryout at the White Theatre in Fresno, the play opened a three-week engagement on November 1 at the Biltmore Theater in downtown Los Angeles.

Edwin Schallert reviewed the play for the *Los Angeles Times* on November 2. He wrote, "*Happy Birthday* for all its deficiencies turns out to be amusing in a robust and whimsical way. Miss Hopkins is resourceful to the last degree through the entire kaleidoscope. Her first venture into a saloon becomes an adventure assisted by pink ladies, straight Scotch, sloe gin, crème de menthe, and more straight Scotch. It isn't long before the other characters literally dance upon the stage."

Enter Alan.

Alan's friends at the Pasadena Playhouse had taught him a few things about "upstaging," which is the practice of drawing attention away from your fellow actors while you are sharing the stage. "I had a scene with Miriam Hopkins," he explained. "I moved downstage—closer to the audience—and away from her, thinking I would be better seen. When we left the stage, the delicate little Miriam called me over. 'Don't you ever do that to me again!' she hissed, and she slapped me across the face! My teeth clattered. I didn't try it twice."

Enid Markey had been a silent film star. "She was tiny," Alan recalled, "and her eyes were as big as lighthouse beacons." In a scene in the play, Alan was supposed to dip Miss Markey in an exaggerated dance step. One night, he dipped her out of audience sight. "Well, she bit my hand so hard, it drew blood," Alan recalled. "And I thought, gee, this show business stuff is really rough."

The tour took Alan to several cities before completing its run in Chicago in 1949. Having tasted life as an actor, Alan had no intention of returning to Pasadena. "I told my parents I was going to New York. They were none too happy. They didn't understand or appreciate show business. They thought I was throwing my life away. They didn't even come to see me in *Happy Birthday*! They had time for my brother's ball games, though."

Pete's company, Sues, Young and Brown, Inc., had expanded its operation into Northern California to distribute more new appliances. More importantly, the company negotiated the exclusive right for the state-wide distribution of MGM records. Pete became a sought-after motivational speaker at retailer conventions throughout California. "My father was great at telling other people what to do," Alan said.

"TV Growth No Flash In Pan, Sues' View" was the headline in the *Los Angeles Mirror* on June 14, 1949. Pete Sues was quoted, "TV is competing more and more for the consumer's dollar, topping by far the comparative expansion of other innovations in the home appliance field over the years." Pete knew the appliance business. With his annual business topping $10 million, he moved his company into a new forty-thousand-square-foot building on Bronson Avenue in Los Angeles.

Alan's father set up a trust fund for his two sons' education. "I asked them for help," Alan recalled, "and they refused. My parents said they wouldn't give me a penny for what I wanted to do. And they didn't. But I went to New York with the little bit of money I had to take some acting courses at the American Theater Wing with Robert Lewis. I couldn't wait to get away."

About his older brother's show business aspirations, John Sues said, "Since he was seven years old he never thought of anything else. He was so funny, I hated him. In those lean years everyone told him to get out of show business. I'm sorry about one thing. I said it to him once, too. Yet he really never minded it. He's really a gutsy guy."

Alan found a room in a drafty old warehouse in Hell's Kitchen in New York City. There was no heat in the building. "I collected newspapers from the trash," he explained, "and slept under them to keep warm." A prostitute who "sounded like Betty Boop, but packed heat" lived in the room next door. A Japanese family of eight lived on the other side. There was one bathroom at the end of the hall. "You had to fight your way in to use the toilet."

With no contacts or referrals, it was hard for Alan to find his way in Manhattan. "I didn't know anybody," he recalled. "I didn't know how to find actors and find out what was going on. I saw actors rehearsing soliloquies on the subway, but I was too shy to ask them about castings. I didn't know enough to go to Actor's Equity for help, so I hung out at the lunch counter of the Astor Hotel because someone told me out-of-work actors hung out there. I didn't know how to ask anyone if they were in show business, so I'd eavesdrop, and I think the guys thought I was trying to pick them up."

The venerable Astor Hotel was a popular meeting place in Times Square. The hotel bar had a reputation as a discreet rendezvous spot for gay patrons. "New Yorkers had a more sophisticated attitude toward gays," Alan said. "The Astor bar actually allotted an entire side to gay men. I didn't find actors but I found the *boys* when I moved from the lunch counter to the drink counter.

"I loved the automats. During the day business people would be in there buying little lunches and coffee, but late at night, the automats were a refuge for the real flamboyant queens in town. For forty cents you could get an egg sandwich and a cup of java and the best damn floor show in town."

In spite of an apparent tolerance for gays, problems existed in New York as they did in California, and most states. Julius's bar in Greenwich Village was the oldest cocktail lounge in Manhattan. By the 1950s it was attracting gay patrons. The New York State Liquor Authority had regulations that governed establishments that sold alcohol. One rule ordered bars not to serve liquor to anyone subjectively perceived as "disorderly." At that time, homosexuals were considered "disorderly." Bartenders often threw out homosexuals, or forbade them from facing other male customers in order to avoid "cruising" in the bar.

"That's why we usually would go out with women," Alan explained. "They were cover. The girls played along and we all had a pretty good time."

There was a bar on West 45th Street that catered to servicemen on leave. "They were gay," Alan recalled, "or drunk and undecided. They were easy marks for action, but it was a dangerous place, too. There was some real rough trade there, but—nothing like a guy in uniform."

One of the more interesting ways to meet fellow homosexuals was at a social gathering called a "progressive dinner." Gay men and some female hangers-on met for drinks at a local bar or someone's home. They then moved to another apartment for more drinks and appetizers, another's apartment for dinner, and finally another apartment for dessert and after-dinner drinks. People would come and go, some joining in for dinner, others arriving for dessert and aperitifs. "We were moving all the time," Alan explained. "It's harder to hit a moving target."

It was at a progressive dinner than Alan met a young singer/dancer named Larry Kert. "Larry was tall and thin and all legs," Alan recalled. "Boy, did he have gams. He was very *limber*. He was dancing in a Broadway show called *Tickets, Please!* He was loud and funny and completely himself. I'd never met anyone quite like that. He didn't give a shit. He worked a lot, too, and eventually starred in the original *West Side Story* on Broadway. We became friends and he introduced me to Fire Island."

Fire Island is a sliver of land off the south shore of Long Island. At that time, accessible only by the Sayville Ferry, Fire Island had no roads and no cars. There were many small cottages, and the beach was accessible by a series of wooden boardwalks. Duffy's, a large bar and dancing hall in Cherry Grove, had the only electricity on the island, and was a favorite hangout for the large gay population.

"I first went there for a weekend with Larry and a couple of other friends," Alan recalled. "We had no place to stay, but most of the guys didn't. We just drank and partied all night and caught the ferry back on Sunday night. I'd never seen anything like it. Just about the only thing anyone wore was a bathing suit. Every time I went there I'd pick sand out of my ass for a week. Since there were no roads, if anyone went out for groceries or beer, they'd wheel the stuff back in a red Radio Flyer kid's wagon. All those big musclemen in little shorts pulling toy wagons was quite a sight. It was like a fairy tale; no traffic, no lights, no pants, and nobody watching."

After a few months, Alan finally landed an audition for the road company of *Mister Roberts*. The night before, he and a friend drank martinis until they passed out. When Alan awoke, he discovered his friend had dyed his hair bright orange during their drunken partying. He hurried to a drugstore and bought hair dye. On the way to his audition, he stopped in the men's room of the subway and worked on his hair. "After twenty-five minutes," he recalled, "I washed my hair in the toilet bowl, and realized I had finally arrived in New York."

An agent named Maynard Morris met him at the theater and told him to take his shirt off for his reading. "He had a voice only a dog could hear," Alan said. "It was freezing in the theater, and I'm completely hung over and trying to focus on the script. All the while I'm reading, I can hear Morris saying to the producer, 'If you don't like *him* I know somebody else *very* good.'

"As I'm leaving, he said, 'I didn't know you had a big scar. It won't work. kid.' I didn't know what the hell he was talking about until I got home and saw the dye had dripped down my back and left a terrible mark."

Alan auditioned for another show called, *Talent '50*. It was an annual revue designed to showcase the talents of young performers for an audience of agents and producers. While Alan was waiting to be called to the stage, a young woman began to flirt with him. "She pointed at me, smiled and winked. I thought she meant it for somebody else. When she was called to the stage, she walked past me and said, 'I've got the hots for you.' I thought, well this girl has lost her touch, but I couldn't wait to see what she was going to do. Her name was Penny Malone.

"She was really funny. She got up there and told the accompanist, 'I've got a little special material.' He said, 'I'm sorry but I can't play special material.' She said, 'Sweetheart, are you kidding? This is nothing. Just a few bars.' She took the end of her sheet music and threw it and it unfolded like an accordion and ran the whole length of the damn stage. The accompanist fell over. She had terrible material. Very crude. In one number she was a female detective called Dickless Tracy. Then she did a number with a black muff just below her navel, singing, 'I've got it under lock and key.' But she was funny in spite of the material. The piano player said, 'What key are you in?' She said, 'Any key. I transpose.'

"When she came off the stage, I told her, 'You're the funniest thing I've ever seen! We should be a team!'

"She wore a man's double-breasted jacket with wide shoulders, and a straight skirt, and regulation Red Cross shoes. Her face was absolutely beautiful. Round, very Irish, with bangs. She said, 'I had to borrow these duds to get here. Let's have dinner.' We went to Eisenberg's, and she blurts out, 'Dutch! You pay your way, baby, I pay mine.' When we finished, she picked up all the dishes and went into the kitchen. In about a half hour she comes back out and said, 'I didn't have enough money.' I thought, *Jesus, this girl's wild. I've got to know her.* I told her, 'Tomorrow, I'm gonna find a rehearsal space and we can work on an act.'"

The next day, Alan secured a rehearsal hall, but Penny did not show up at the appointed hour of one o'clock. "She left me a number and I called and they gave me another number. It took four days to track her down. Each person had a different number for her. Finally I had a tip and called the Belvedere Hotel. I asked for Penny Malone and they rang a room. A husky voice answered, 'Yeah?' I said, 'Is this Penny Malone?' The husky voice said, 'Yeah.' I said, 'Where have you been? I've been looking for you for four days!' She croaked, 'Who the hell is this?' I said, 'It's Alan. Alan Sues. Where have you been?' She said, 'Listen, sweetheart, I'll call you back. I'm banging a drummer.' I never heard from her again, but she starred in an Off-Broadway hit, and she recorded an album of dirty party songs a few years later called, *Penny Malone Sings?* Her big hit was, "Let's Be Neurotic Together."'"

Alan never worked with Penny Malone, but he was chosen to do a sketch in *Talent '50* with Kay Medford. "It was a musical version of *Streetcar Named Desire*," Alan said, "with a line of chorus boys in tights dancing behind us. We killed 'em.

"I wrote the material. Kay was Blanche and I was Stanley. Kay sang, 'Choo-choo train coming down the track. It's a streetcar named desire, now don't look back. I'm thinking about my sister's husband, Stanley. He's strong and handsome and virile and manly. I know it would be a terrible sin, if I would make a play for him. Turn off that light, and sit down boy. I'll tell you my story, it's the real McCoy. First I need a little nippy, then I'll tell you how I became the talk of Mississippi. I had trouble in the family plantation, so I moved to a hotel near the railroad station. In that small hotel, I went straight to hell…'

"Tennessee Williams should have sued me. Kay never talked to me again."

Like all struggling actors, Alan experienced a vast array of unusual jobs. One of the first was working in a funeral home. Dressed in a black suit and wearing white gloves, he directed mourners through the stuffy rooms. "We were all out-of-work actors there, and we tried out different dialects and accents on the grieving public."

A dancer that Alan knew told him about a job he had, and was about to give up. The fellow went to an older man's apartment and "stretched" his neck for $10 a visit. The dancer was leaving town on tour and offered the job to Alan.

"I thought he was kidding," Alan said, "but I took the job. I went to the man's apartment on 58th Street. He lived on the top floor. He told me he got hurt in a car accident and he needed to have his neck "stretched" until it cracked. So I did it once a week for almost a year. He gave me ten dollars cash a week. It was great, but I noticed he began to enjoy it a little too much. While I cracked his neck, he would grunt and moan. Finally, I'd had enough and I handed him over to another struggling actor I'd met."

Whelan's Drugstore chain in Manhattan was looking for a "fill-in" counterman. "They asked me if I knew how to make sandwiches and pull a soda. I learned early on not to say 'yes' or 'no' on a job interview. So I said, 'Do I know how to make sandwiches? Are you kidding?' I got the job, and I had no idea how to make sandwiches or pull sodas." He worked at several Whelan's outlets from Grand

Central Station to Harlem, and finally the Bronx. "It was an awful job, but I was eating pretty good!"

While working at the drugstore counter, Alan moved to the Pickwick Arms. "It was another rat trap, but affordable on my tiny salary." Alan was thrilled when Charles Pierce, his friend from the Pasadena Playhouse, moved into the building in early 1951. "We did the rounds together, visiting casting agents every day looking for work. We probably killed any chance of getting work because every time we walked into one of those offices, we both cracked

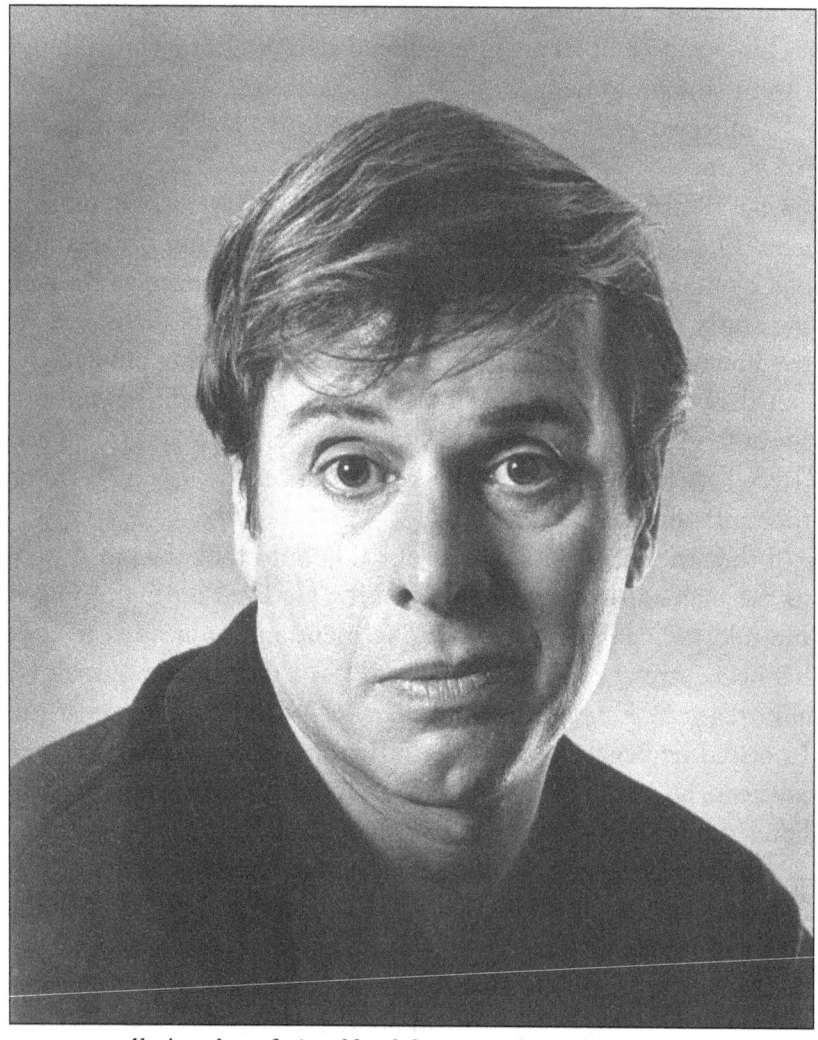

Alan's early professional head shot. 1951. Credit Bert Torchia.

up laughing." Charles was very comfortable with his sexuality and dragged Alan (who was more discrete, and still uncomfortable with his physical urges) to many gay clubs and bars in the Village. "I had a great time with him," Alan said. "I guess you could say he emboldened me. My mother would have said he was a very bad influence."

One of Alan's favorite spots was Bergdorf Goodman's upscale department store on Fifth Avenue in midtown Manhattan. "Charles and I went there all the time," Alan recalled. "They had a fur department, and Charles would hide behind mannequins and try on fur coats. I saw Irving Berlin and Noel Coward in there. And Greta Garbo shopped there! She wore sunglasses and hats so people wouldn't notice her, but she stuck out like a sore thumb. She lived a few blocks away. One day, Charles decided we would follow her home. It was raining, and we only got about a block along, and she turned around and swung her umbrella at Charles. I was embarrassed, but for Charles, it was like he won a jackpot!"

After six months of hearing "No" from agents, Alan got his first film job from the Max Richards Agency by sticking his head in the office door one day to ask for work. He was driven to Long Island and told to stand on a mound of dirt and wave as the camera passed by him. "That's all I did. No lines. I was never so humiliated and irritated." As it turned out, the movie was an educational short film for U.S. servicemen about the prevention of syphilis.

"I never knew if I had it or not in the film, but for the longest time, when soldiers who were on leave in New York seemed to recognize me on the street or in a bar, by their looks, I had it!"

Alan became acquainted with composer Alec Wilder who lived at the Algonquin Hotel. A prolific composer, Wilder wrote many cabaret songs for singer Mabel Mercer, as well as the hit "I'll Be Around," made popular by the Mills Brothers. "He fascinated me because he would sit in the back room with all his music stretched out in front of him and he would be guzzling sherry or port," Alan said. "A very classy guy. This was in the middle of the all the clattering that was going on in the restaurant. He'd be talking to you rapid fire and as he was talking, he would be scoring a musical piece at the same time! Alec knew everything about music, and he knew everybody *in* music."

Wilder referred Alan to a guy who wrote comical musical material. "His name was Frank Hetherton," Alan said. "He was staying at the Belvedere Hotel. I called him and introduced myself. He had a high shrill voice. He told me he'd meet me between shows at the bar in his hotel. It was next to Madison Square Garden.

"At five-thirty, I walked into the bar. It was filled with show girls in feathers and tights, side-show freaks, and a man in a formal red suit and top hat. They were circus folk bellying up to the bar. Ringling Brothers was playing at the Garden. Suddenly, I hear this high, shrill voice screaming, 'There he is! There he is! That's Alan Sues! I've found my true love! He's the one I've always loved!' I froze. He was dressed like a circus clown with a red nose, makeup and big, floppy shoes. A waitress had pointed me out to him. He yells, 'If there isn't any room you can sit on my face!' *Oh, Jesus*, I thought. *How can I get out of here? I'm outnumbered by circus roustabouts.* Then he exclaimed, 'Alec said you wanted material!' He ran over to the piano and pushed away some dame who was playing. He sat down and reeled off some really funny stuff."

A short time later, the guy called Alan and told him the new material was ready. Alan made an appointment to meet him at the Algonquin with Alec Wilder. "The guy was nuts and I didn't want to be alone," Alan said. "So the guy dashes into the restaurant there dressed like a clown again. He screams out, 'There he is! I can't wait till we go to the park and you take me home and tie me to the bed!' Thank God he was thrown out of the hotel.

"Then he came to the Pickwick Arms where I was staying. The front desk called me and said, 'You have a guest. A Mr. Hetherton.' I said, 'My God, don't send him up.' The girl said, 'Well, he's causing a lot of trouble. He's got a pack of dogs and he's dressed like a Zulu Indian.'

"It was just nuts. Finally, I heard he was red-lighted on the circus train, which meant somebody didn't like him and they beat him up and threw him off the moving train. I never got my special material."

One day Alan and Charles Pierce sat for hours in the waiting room of producer Archer King. "We laughed at all the nuts that came through the office, trying to see King," Alan recalled. "A tall, blonde show girl wrapped in white fox tails and wearing a skin-tight black dress walked into the room. "She was chewing gum and she looked at us like we had been shot out of the ass end of a skunk. Just then, Archer King stuck his head out of his door and said, 'I'm sorry there's nothing today.' The blonde said, 'Are you Archer King?' He said, 'Yes'. Then she said, 'I just want to tell you something. I'm not right for anything. So don't call me. And if you do, I won't pick it up.' She turned around and marched out. Charles and I fell on the floor laughing. It was like living in a Damon Runyon novel."

In October 1951, Judy Garland began a nineteen-week concert engagement at the Palace Theatre on Broadway at 47th Street. "I loved Judy Garland," Alan said, "I don't know how many times Charles and I saw her at the Palace. You could sit in the balcony for a dollar, and we'd scratch the money together and go every week. Each time, Charles would go into the theatre as Charles Pierce and come out impersonating Judy Garland—singing, yanking his hair, and staggering down the stairs, through the lobby and onto the street."

After doing his television commercial – for Swift's Ice Cream – Alan got a job in summer stock in Hamilton, New Jersey. "I packed everything I had in a couple of cardboard boxes and bought a bottle of booze with my last buck. I should have bought some food."

Alan's first experience in summer stock was terrible. He and his fellow actors lived in a barn and performed repertory throughout the stifling hot summer months. The theater was filled with bats, and was located next to an old mill with a water wheel. The actors couldn't hear each other on the stage. "We did Noel Coward's *Tonight at 8:30*. Every night at 8:30. All summer."

Tonight at 8:30 is comprised of ten, short one-act plays. "We did three of them, and I was in all three," Alan recalled. "And so was an adorable darling named Sally Dozier. I wanted to hit her with a lead pipe. The rest of the company was marginally better. Sally and I played Lily and George Pepper in a one-act called "Red Peppers." We wore matching tuxedos, and sang two songs, "Has Anybody Seen Our Ship?" and "Men About Town." Noel Coward and Gertrude Lawrence originally played the parts. They had nothing on us. Sally couldn't sing, couldn't dance, and had no rhythm.

"The producer's idea of producing was to change the running order of the three acts without telling the cast. One night I went down the steps, across the patio, down the hall, up the steps, and down the hall and got into my "Red Peppers" tuxedo, then down the hall, down the steps, down the hall across the patio up the steps and onto the stage wing and heard, 'But Lavinia!'—a cue from another one act. I made a bee line down the steps, across the patio, down the hall ripping my clothes off, up the steps into the hall and in the dressing room—which doubled as my bedroom—changed, ran down the hall, down the steps, across the patio, up the steps and onto the stage. I didn't miss my cue, but I could hardly speak."

The company of actors had to walk through the woods to a dining hall to eat. "We found out that if it was someone's birthday, they'd give us all a chicken dinner and a cake. So each week we made up a birthday for someone in the company. To make it look real, we gift wrapped a few empty boxes and reused them each week. It was the only good meal we got."

When he returned to Manhattan, Alan found a room in a place known as "The Morgue." Alan explained, "It *had* been a morgue, but the room was $5.50 a week. The place was filled with actors, singers, dancers, musicians and artists, or, as the landlord said, hookers, pimps and faggots."

Alan took a depressingly small room that was three and half feet wide and nine feet deep with one tiny window at the end. "With my artistic hands and wild imagination, I promptly decorated it to look like a Laundromat. I drew washing machines on one wall and had a rope across the top where I hung my clothes because there was no closet. It was kind of a nice looking Laundromat and made me wake up in the day thinking I was more productive than I actually was."

There was one shared kitchen for all the tenants. "Everybody wrote their name on a hard-boiled egg in the refrigerator. That's all we had to eat. One day I saw a girl crying hysterically because someone had stolen her egg."

To earn tips from some of the girls who lived in the building, Alan sat on the front steps and directed their "johns" to the respective ladies' apartments.

"The guys in the building were better off than the girls," Alan explained, "because there was no hot water on any of the floors. You had to boil water in the kitchen over a big open fire, which made me wonder if that's where they used to cremate dead bodies. The guys who boiled the water and carried it up to the working girls on the second and third floors were paid a quarter. If you were really down and out, you'd boil a lot of water that week."

"It was easy to get discouraged," Alan said, "but I was determined to make it. I even spent some nights in the subway because I had no place else to go. If I went back to California, I'd be a failure and I'd be lost. And, I'd have to deal with my father."

Many odd jobs followed, among them, serving ice cream at Howard Johnson's, nude modeling for art classes ("that paid a buck and a quarter, which was good money"), and working the service counter and Christmas gift-wrapping at Mark Cross, a luxury leather goods store in Manhattan.

"I did pretty well at Mark Cross until Kay Thompson came in one day. She had quite a stride, like a coach who marches back and forth in front of the bench during a football game. She was a movie star, but she had a great act with the Williams Brothers, then, and little Andy Williams. They played the Persian Room at the Plaza Hotel. She was very boisterous and a high kicker. When she walked in, I yelled out, 'Hi!', and gave a tremendous high kick. She was not amused. She reported me to the manager.

"Mr. Churny, the manager, asked me to meet him for lunch across the street. I thought I was getting sacked. Fortunately, he was an aspiring actor and fall down drunk. We both got hammered and he forgot about the whole thing."

Alan even sold his blood for extra money. "I'd sell two pints at a time," he explained. "I'd offer one arm then the other so they didn't know I got tapped twice that day. Then I'd stagger away so weak, I spent all the money eating at the automat."

For a winter holiday, Pete and Alice flew to New York and stayed at the Plaza Hotel. "I used to sit in the Plaza and *watch* people eat," Alan said. "I had to remind my parents I was *living* in the city. I was freezing my ass off and conned them out of five hundred dollars to help with my expenses. But it came with a price.

"My father was resentful. He lectured me about how successful my brother was since he started working for him. My father believed acting was meaningless. And in his head, if he thought someone did something meaningless with his life, then he was meaningless, too. That's what he thought of me, and he told me so. He talked me down so much I felt like I was an inch tall. My mother just sat there pounding martinis like they were shots. When my parents left, I was so fucking mad, I bought a camel hair coat with the money. Of course, before long I hocked it for eleven dollars so I could eat."

One of Alan's favorite jobs was working as a window-dresser for Saks Fifth Avenue. While the store was closed, he and another fellow worked throughout the night arranging displays on the floor and in the windows. "He was a crazy guy. He'd dress up in couture gowns and fur coats and high heels and hats, and parade around the store. I loved him. He'd even get in the store windows in drag. Cops would drive by and slow down when they saw him sashaying in the window. He'd wave and blow kisses!"

Once, Alan's drinking nearly got him arrested for grand theft. "I lied my way into a good job at Kenyon and Eckart, one of the biggest advertising agencies on Madison Avenue," he recalled. "It was hard to get a job there, because you needed a college degree. I told them I went to school in Switzerland and Paris so they couldn't check up on me. I got hired, and bought a grey flannel suit. I really looked like a Madison Avenue type of guy.

"Of course, my job was to deliver the mail to each office from floor to floor. I was the best dressed mail boy in town. I got to know everyone who worked there – 'Hello Grace, Good morning Ethel, How are you George?' I was very popular. But I got bored, and when I got my first paycheck, I decided I could advance my career if I dated the red-headed number who was one of the secretaries for the president of the firm. I took her to a chic restaurant and bar called Tony's. We never made it to dinner. We both got soused on martinis and got thrown out for groping each other under the table. I poured her into a cab and gave the driver ten bucks to take her home. Of course, from that day on, she wouldn't talk to me. I was stuck delivering the mail in my grey flannel suit.

"One of my other chores was to take the office petty cash to the bank each day, and deposit it. I liked that because it meant I was out of the office for a while. One day I met a couple of friends for lunch before I went to the bank. I was acting like a big shot in my grey flannel suit, and we all got hammered. I was spouting off, 'Yes, men, I really think that Madison Avenue should be moved to Lexington. It's closer to the East River.' I didn't know what the hell I was talking about.

"When I staggered back to the mailroom, the manager asked, 'Did you deposit the petty cash in the bank?' I thought, *Oh, Jesus! Petty cash! What did I do with that fucking bag of petty cash?!*

"'Oh, sure,' I mumbled. 'Of course.'

"He said, 'I'm sure glad you did! I bet you were surprised when you found out how much money you were carrying. I didn't want to tell you because I thought you'd be scared.'

"I said, 'What?'

"He said, 'Well, it's not every day that I put thirty-two thousand dollars in the petty cash bag.'

"I said, 'Oh, right,' turned and ran all the way back to the restaurant. I couldn't find the bag and no one had turned it into the management. I thought, *Oh, my God, I'm going to prison! I can't' go to prison, I'm too pretty!* Finally, we were picking through the garbage in the kitchen and found the bag at the bottom of the swill pail. The money was still there. I shot through the revolving doors at the bank about a minute before closing. I handed the bag over to the teller and while she was counting it out she said, 'Say, this money smells like roast beef.'"

Alan was still working in the mail room when he was cast as a comical sailor in a production of *Panama Hattie* starring singer Betty Reilly at St. John Terrell's Music Circus in Lambertville, New Jersey.

The 1,800 seat theater in the round was actually an enormous, seasonal canvas tent. "I thought we all joined Ringling Brothers," Alan explained. "We had an amazing time and all got drunk on opening night. Betty fell into the band pit in her sequined gown, and me, and another actor playing a sailor fell in, too, when we tried to pull her out.

"There was a girl in the company named Mary Miles. She swore like a sailor, and her voice sounded like Minnie Mouse on halcion. She was dumber than a five pound bag of stupid. I never stopped laughing. She had just gotten back from performing in a Paris clip joint, where she bombed. She'd pour French dressing on her salad, and sigh, "Ah . . . the memories . . ." We were all staying at the Lambertville House, which also functioned as a retirement home for the locals. We tore the place apart. Running naked around the halls, drunk every night. I loved show business.

"The show did very well and we were extended, but a hurricane blew the tent down and we were all sent packing back to New York. I'd never had so much fun in my life."

The most colorful and artistically satisfying job Alan found was working as a photo assistant for fashion photographer Clifford Coffin. Coffin was a *Vogue* magazine photographer and his elegant portraits were featured on multiple covers of the popular and trendsetting periodical. He nurtured the careers of many of the leading models of the day, including Suzy Parker and Jean Patchett. He discovered Elsa Martinelli and Audrey Hepburn, both of whom modeled before turning to acting.

"Coffin was a terrific photographer," Alan recalled, "but he was nuts. He was a screamer. He managed to misplace everything he worked with, and he never *asked* for anything, he just *screamed* for it. Jean Patchett was spectacular. She was so beautiful and refined. She was the "calm" in Coffin's storm. I don't know how she stayed so relaxed while he ran around yelling and waving his arms around. He'd be having a breakdown and she'd be polishing her fingernails and cooing, 'Oh, Cliff . . . Oh, Cliff.'"

The fashion world introduced Alan to new and interesting characters. "I loved working with the models. We shot Patty Eng who later became a famous art dealer in California. Patty was striking and had a shocking little baby voice. She was married to Phil Peyton, a drummer who worked with the jazz saxophonist Charlie Parker at the Open Door in Greenwich Village. We'd hang out there a lot. Everyone wore French berets then. When I showed up wearing one, Patty laughed and said I looked like some guy in the alley selling watches out of a suitcase.

"Patty and I used to toss a few at the Cedar Tavern, too" Alan said. "She was so smart and cute. And she loved art. We used to drink with Jackson Pollock and Mark Rothko. The bar was in a poor area, but close to the Village and a lot of artists had studios there. Pollock was a manly-man. He would come in covered in paint, and pound the hooch.

"One day I got an audition for a part in new show. I always looked younger than I was and the part was a teenage boy. I didn't know what to do so I called Patty. She knew all the model makeup tricks and I thought she could help me. She told me to put raw egg whites on my face. When it dried, she said it would tighten my skin and make me look younger. So I did that and grabbed a cab to the theater where the audition was. When I hurried through the lobby, some guy saw me and mumbled, 'Oh, no. You're all wrong for the part.' The egg whites had dried and my skin was so tight I could barely open my mouth to speak. The casting guy asked, 'Do you have a speech impediment?' That didn't go well. When I was leaving I looked at myself in the mirror and was horrified. The skin on my face was so tight I looked like a six-foot tall Spanky McFarland! When I got home I called Patty and said, 'What the hell did you do to me? My skin is so tight I can't move my face.' She said, 'Oh honey, I told you to let it dry and then wash it off.' I said, 'Jesus Christ, you never told me to wash it off!' She laughed and said, 'Oh honey, that's so funny.'

"Patty had a couple of model girlfriends we called the two Carols," Alan recalled.

"Carole Eastman was a stunningly beautiful blonde with a hysterical sense of humor." Eastman later became a screenwriter and wrote four feature films for Jack Nicholson. She was nominated for an Oscar in 1970 for the classic "rebel" film *Five Easy Pieces*. The second Carol, Carol McCallison, was also a successful print model. She married Francesco Scavullo, an iconic fashion photographer who shot covers for *Harper's Bazaar* and *Town & Country* magazines.

"Scavullo was great," Alan said. "He was short and always wore a little pilot hat with rhinestones. I also assisted him on a lot of fashion magazine layouts. He was a master stylist with the sets, props, clothes, everything. He was meticulous and spent all this time styling the shot. Then—pop—a couple of quick snaps and it was over."

Alan discovered another way to earn a little extra money on the photo sets. "I told the models I could teach them to dance. I had taken some dancing lessons with Rudi Gernriech in Los Angeles before I moved to New York. Before he became a fashion designer, Rudi danced with a choreographer named Lester Horton. Well, the models were beautiful, but they had no rhythm. Between shots we'd be tap dancing away, but we never got past a basic time step. They were a lot of fun, though, and I earned a couple of extra bucks. In spite of my abject poverty, those were exciting days."

When he could save a few dollars, Alan enrolled in acting classes. "I studied at the Herbert Berghof Studio, but I didn't have enough money to pay for lessons with Berghof's wife, Uta Hagen, so I was stuck with him. He was the poor man's Uta Hagen. I didn't see much point in it because people who knew less about acting than I did sat around and criticized me. I thought the best thing to do was just get a damn job and learn as you go."

Alan met another young actor named Ronny Graham, and they began to make rounds together. Ronny was a clever comic and introduced Alan to little clubs in Manhattan that were looking to book short-term stand-up comics and specialty acts. Ronny also told Alan about auditions for a new Broadway show called *New Faces of 1952*. Alan blew his audition. "I fell over a couch and forgot while I was there." Ronny was more successful. He was cast in the production, and also hired as a sketch writer.

Other than some extra work on the television programs *Omnibus*, *Kraft Television Theatre*, and *Studio One*, acting roles were all but non-existent. Determined to find work as a performer, Alan followed Ronny Graham's lead and pulled together a nightclub act for himself.

"I just could not work without props," Alan explained. "I introduced myself as that bright-faced boy from California and I came out with a helmet on and said, 'I can't go on. My mother's paid all this money to clear up my skin and look at me.' I also did an imitation of Bette Davis and Ronald Colman, and I played the tuba. I played the "Third Man Theme" on the tuba which was a funny idea to me. Then I had a Mona Lisa prop, which I made. I put a plaster head in her likeness on top of a broom stick. Then I draped it with a lot of chiffon that flowed to the floor. I held her and sang, 'Gee but it's great to be staying out late, walking my baby back home.' Then we did a little tap dance together and I would say to the head—Quit smiling at him! Then Mona Lisa and I would get into a terrible fight and I would walk off and fire a blank gun at her. The audience didn't know what the hell I was doing."

Alan got an audition at Number One Fifth Avenue, a popular nightclub in Manhattan at the time. "I'm always nervous about auditioning," Alan said. "I always think I'm incompetent." The audition was rough and further complicated when people mistook the blast of his blank gun to be a real gunshot and ran screaming. Nevertheless, Alan landed a spot at Number One Fifth Avenue in early 1953.

Singer and comedienne Pat Bright was on the bill. "She was a snappy girl," Alan recalled. "She'd been on the *Paul Winchell Show* and sang on *Ed Sullivan*. I'd start to go out and I'd say to Pat, 'How are they?' She'd say, 'Well, they're great for me, sweetheart!' I'd go out there and absolutely bomb. I had a following of four. The rest of audience had come in from Yonkers and didn't know what was going on. I'd get out a few bars and there was a mad dash for the bathrooms. You had to work in front of a big pillar that was mirrored. It was almost like playing in the round with yourself."

Alan scraped some money together and hired a fellow to write a number for him. "It was called, "I Understand." Gripping lyrics – 'My father was an understander. You've seen those men in the circus, the guys on the bottom. Well that was my father. You've seen the guys in the circus. Thirty-five guys on one man's shoulders. Well, that was my father, the one on the bottom.'

"It was the worst number. He must have taken it out of a trunk. You couldn't make up something like that under water.

"The only line that struck my fancy was, 'My mother used to stand on my father's head and so he went through life with athlete's head and my mother had bald feet.' But I had to plow through five pages to get to that one good line. I was playing to an audience of one—my accompanist, Milton. Everyone else was talking and drinking and snapping their fingers for the waiter."

Alan decided that if he came out on the stage in a woman's bright red wig and picture hat, and wore dangling earrings with enormous prisms, it would make the song funny. He thought he should open

Alan's head shot in 1953. Credit Marcus Blechman.

his act with the newly retooled number. "Well, I walked on the stage and said, 'I'd like to sing that old favorite "I Understand." I shook my head and one of the dangling prisms hit my tooth and cracked it to the gum and I nearly blacked out. I staggered off the stage screaming in pain. Of course, the audience thought *that* was fucking hilarious! I played there for months."

Oliver Wakefield was a British comic, schooled in music hall humor, who also appeared at the club. He billed himself as The Voice of Inexperience. "He did monologues and said the most arcane, idiosyncratic things," Alan said. "I just loved him. He was the funniest thing I'd ever seen. 'Alan, what you do is indescribable,' he said one night when we were both drunk backstage. 'You've begged and clawed your way from nowhere, and here you are on the brink of obscurity'."

While Alan was appearing at Number One Fifth Avenue, he auditioned for a role in a new, dramatic play called *Tea and Sympathy*, written by Robert Anderson. The story concerns a young student in a male private school who is more interested in the arts than sports. His classmates, house-master, and even his father torment him for his "effeminate" interests. The house-master's wife sympathizes with the young man and pursues him to prove that he is, indeed, a "man." Everett Evans later wrote in the *Houston Chronicle* that the play was "one of the first plays to tackle the then taboo topic of sexual orientation and related prejudice."

Alan was called back over a period of three months and eventually read for the director, Elia Kazan.

"He scared me to death," Alan said.

Kazan was one of the most accomplished, and controversial directors in motion pictures and the theater. He had won an Oscar for his direction of the classic film *Gentleman's Agreement* and two Tony Awards for directing the plays *All My Sons* in 1947 and *Death of a Salesman* in 1949.

After his reading, Kazan asked Alan, "What do you do?"

Alan answered, "I do an act where I imitate Bette Davis and Ronald Colman, and play the tuba."

"Would you bring your tuba on the road?"

"Of course. If I could get Bette Davis, I'd bring her, too."

Kazan said, "Well, you've got the part."

An unusual problem presented itself, however. Alan had been living hand to mouth for so long in New York that he had lost a lot of weight. At six foot two, he looked very thin weighing in at 170 pounds. "They actually wanted me to put on weight," Alan explained. "All the other guys in the show were slim and attractive, but I was cast as the bully and they wanted me to be mean and fat. I had to put on another 40 pounds because they wanted me to have a *cruel* look. It was the only time in my life I liked being fat because it got me on Broadway."

Rehearsals began on August 16, 1953. Alan's fellow actors warned him that his equity contract allowed the producers to replace him within the first five days of rehearsal. "I panicked and did every self-destructive thing I could possibly do to myself," he recalled. "I stayed up all night, every night, plastered." He arrived for rehearsals at the Ethel Barrymore Theater hung over. He'd check in with the stage manager and then hide under the stage. Once the five days had passed, Alan began to feel a little more secure, but someone had told Kazan what he had done. The director decided to play a joke on Alan.

During a rehearsal, Kazan sternly called out from his seat in the theater, "Alan, when you're finished on the stage doing what you're doing, would you come and see me?"

Alan thought he was about to be fired. "I ran up the aisle expecting him to say that I was through. But he said, 'Uh . . . say Alan, would you get me an ice cream bar?' Everyone there fell on the floor laughing."

The theme of *Tea and Sympathy* was provocative for the time, and many thought, scandalous. When approaching a dramatic play, most directors will identify and work on the "heavies." Kazan wrote in his autobiography, "We had two of them: the father of the boy who was suspected of homosexual tendencies in a prep school, and the husband of the woman who, at last, chooses to perform the act of sympathy that saves the boy. The father had been so insensitive to his son's problem and pain that the young man had grown to be self-doubting and isolated. The husband was so insensitive to what his wife needed from him—he was so macho, so conventional, so doggedly old-fashioned—that his wife was starved for human warmth. The result? She could be deeply aroused by the need of the boy and respond to it totally."

Alan said, "It sounded like my parents."

The supporting cast included Dick York, Leif Erickson, and John McGovern. Alan played the role of a school bully named Ralph. He recalled, "Dick was a great guy and his wife, Joey, was cute as a pixie. Leif Erickson was a movie star. I'm tall, but he towered over me. He was humorless. When he smiled, it meant he wanted you to scram. I just wanted to ask him about his ex-wife, Frances Farmer, but that wasn't the way to go."

Newcomer John Kerr played the conflicted young man. "John was the blandest handsome man I ever met. He was married. He wasn't exactly the life of the party. Years later, he become a lawyer, which explained a lot."

Oscar-nominated actress Deborah Kerr made her Broadway debut in the starring role of the housemaster's wife. Kerr had starred in numerous films including *Julius Caesar* and *The Prisoner of Zenda*. Her most recent film, *From Here to Eternity*, was still playing in movie theaters when *Tea and Sympathy* premiered. "She was very beautiful with copper-red hair," Alan recalled, "and she had the most beautiful hands I'd ever seen. And her voice. And she was very, very funny. I was never really star-struck, but she was wonderful to work with. That she'd knock down a beer after the show was a plus, too."

Alan explained, "The material was touchy. Kazan was a terrific director, but he practiced method acting, which was new to me. He was a master at manipulating your feelings. He was very encouraging. You really had to *become* the part. But everything was about sex for him. He talked about the sexual motivation of each and every character and scene. He could squeeze sex out of a rock. In the case of John Kerr, he did. John was a little meek in rehearsals, so to help him really *feel* the part, Kazan took Deborah aside and told her she needed to fuck John so he could really play the part of the confused boy. So she did. And it really helped."

The playwright, Robert Anderson, sat in for most of the rehearsals. "He was not temperamental at all," Alan said. "He looked like a Harvard professor. He was a communications officer in the Navy during World War II. That gave us something to talk about."

The play opened at the Shubert Theatre in New Haven, Connecticut, in September 1953. "We were there only four days. The reviews were great, but I thought they couldn't wait to get us out of there. One of my lines was, 'I saw them bare-assed in the dunes'," Alan explained. "That line kept us out of Boston. Those were the times."

After a two-week engagement at the National Theatre in Washington, D.C., *Tea and Sympathy* opened to great acclaim at the Ethel Barrymore Theater in New York on September 30. On October 1, Brooks Atkinson wrote in the *New York Times*: "Since Robert Anderson is a sensitive writer, it is fortunate that some sensitive actors are playing his drama. Under the direction of Elia Kazan, it restores our theater to an art again with a fine play put on the stage with great skill and beauty. *Tea and Sympathy* is a play that catches a group of characters in a complicated web of hostilities and sympathies and looks deep into the hearts of its principal people. It is an extraordinarily illuminating piece of work full of moods and subtleties of insight."

Seven leading New York critics praised the show. For most of its long run, *Tea and Sympathy* was sold out weeks in advance.

"I had a good-paying job at last," Alan said. "I felt like I had finally made it. People would say to me, 'Oh, I saw you in the play,' and it felt good. I had a few bucks in my pocket and I could finally afford to go to Sardi's once in while.

"It was always such a struggle for me to keep my weight. I thought I had a free pass to eat, but I ballooned. My costume would actually get tight and I'd go on crazy crash diets. Deborah called me Suesburger because I talked about eating all the time. But she was wonderful. She gave imported, delicate bone china teapots to everybody in the cast for Christmas."

Deborah Kerr and John Kerr left the show in May 1954. Oscar-winning actress Joan Fontaine and a twenty-two year old actor named Tony Perkins assumed their roles. The dynamic changed markedly with the two new leads. "There was a vulnerable, tender interaction that Deborah and John had," Alan recalled. "Joan was great, but a little brittle, and Tony was no wall-flower. Instead of vulnerable, he was almost predatory in the role. He moved like a cat in heat. He was much more sexy than John. Every gay guy wanted to jump on Tony, and most of them did. He had more stage door Johnnies than any actress in the show.

"Tony was the most ambitious and calculating actor I'd ever met," Alan continued. "He was bookish, and looked like a fraternity boy. I liked watching him. He was so anxious and high-strung he made me feel as calm as a cucumber. He charmed people, but had no interest in women at all beyond using them to get something he wanted."

Tea and Sympathy playbill. 1953

One day word got to the actors that Fontaine's sister, actress Olivia de Havilland, was in the audience and wanted to come backstage following the show. The cast assembled in Fontaine's dressing room to greet their Oscar-winning visitor.

"There was a knock at the door," Alan recalled. "Olivia de Havilland was standing there with her gloved hands folded primly in front of her. She smiled and gently rocked her head and said, 'Joan, Joan, Joan . . . what can I say?' And Joan answered, 'You can say goodbye.'

"You could have cut the air with a knife."

At Christmas in 1954, Fontaine called the actors into her dressing room following a performance. "She was sitting at her vanity, assiduously knitting," Alan said. "There were two cases of booze on the floor at her feet. She uncrossed her legs and as she kicked each box she said, 'Bourbon and Scotch. Take one. Merry Christmas.' She was a genuine broad."

Tea and Sympathy was one of the longest running plays on Broadway. Alan stayed with the play for 712 performances until it closed on June 18, 1955. His parents never came to New York to see their son in his first Broadway show.

Act 1
Scene 3

1954–1962 "I'm a better sketch artist than a stand-up."

In 1953, before *Tea and Sympathy* had opened, and while he was appearing at Number One Fifth Avenue, Alan met a beautiful dancer named Phyllis Gehrig at a friend's party. Phyllis had appeared in several Broadway shows including *Brigadoon, Bloomer Girl* and *Oklahoma!* A few months later, he saw her walking on 7th Avenue at 58th Street. He chased her down in the rain to get her phone number. "I was getting on the bus when I noticed her. I bummed a pencil off the bus driver. When I got back on the bus, I got a round of applause."

They dated for a couple of months, and decided to get married. "All my friends were gay," Phyllis Sues remembered. "I was a dancer and all my friends were involved in dance. Alan had some of the same friends. Stanley Simmons danced with me in *Brigadoon*. He became a costume designer for ballets. His partner was another designer named Frank Thompson who worked for Marlene Dietrich. They had a great place at 53rd and 8th and we spent a lot of time there. Bob Talman and Bob Magnus lived together in a beautiful brownstone at 62nd and 3rd. We called them the Two Bobs. Talman was a writer. We were a tightly knit little group. We laughed together, ate together and danced together."

While Phyllis was appearing in a show in Chicago, Alan found a floor-through apartment on 47th Street near the Ethel Barrymore Theater. "Phyllis was out of town, so I had to move all her things. She was the original packrat. She saved everything. I'd open little tiny boxes and there would be two beads and a button and a bone in them. I moved practically her whole apartment on the bus, including ice cream chairs."

Not surprisingly, Alan had cold feet as the date approached. "I couldn't sleep at my apartment alone, so I'd go over and sleep with other people. That was my excuse anyway. I didn't know what was happening to me. *Why was I doing this*, I wondered. *Why was I getting married?* Most of my friends in the play said, '*Married?* You're not getting *married* are you?' That certainly helped."

The wedding service was scheduled on Washington's Birthday in 1954, the day Phyllis returned from dancing in Montreal. "She told me to pick out something from her trunk for her to wear since there would be no time," Alan recalled. "So I called Stanley to ask for help. He said, 'Well, she's no spring chicken. I say black.'

"I found a chapel in the Presbyterian Church on Park and 64th. I had to pull this all together myself." Alan called his mother to tell her he was getting married. "My mother said, 'Oh, yeah?', and I said, 'Yeah! Are you happy now? Finally? What are you going to give us?' And my mother said, 'How rude!' and hung up on me." Alan met Phyllis at the airport. "She came off the plane and I said, 'Hi, Phyllis!' And she walked right past me! I ran after her and yelled, 'Phyllis! It's me, Alan!'

"She said, 'Oh, hi.' I said, 'Don't you still want to get married?' She said, 'Oh, yeah. Sure. But my feet are aching and I'm tired and I haven't slept for thirty hours.'

"We got in a cab and had nothing to say. How have you been? What have you been doing? We were like complete strangers.

"We got crocked on Bloody Marys at our new apartment and staggered to the church. We were in the minister's office before the service and he asked, 'Do you realize what a serious thing this is?' Phyllis started giggling, and then she became hysterical laughing. I mumbled some excuse to the minister and dragged her out to the altar. Stanley and Frank and the Two Bobs stood up for us, and a bunch of our male dancer friends wearing cowboy hats, a little rouge, and tap shoes were there in the chapel. It looked like an audition for *Oklahoma!* And my little bride all dressed in black. I can't imagine what the minister was thinking."

"The ceremony," Phyllis said, "was insane."

After the service, Alan and Phyllis took a cab to a small reception that had been planned by their friends. "Phyllis was the only woman in the room," Alan said. "I was drinking cheap champagne and eating chicken a la king when I realized I had a matinee performance. I grabbed a piece of the wedding cake and ran to the theatre."

Soon after their marriage, Phyllis became a replacement dancer in the musical *Kismet*. "For a while, it was pretty good," Alan explained. "We were both earning money, but I began to get tired of doing *Tea and Sympathy* every day."

"We had a great time in New York," Phyllis remembered. "It was like a fairy tale. We both worked in big hits, so doors were always open. After the shows, we'd rush home, get all dressed up and hit all the clubs. There were great night clubs in that town. Sophisticated and glamorous. Fascinating people. It was great. We did have a physical relationship then, but I knew Alan was gay. I don't know if he had any boyfriends at the time, though. He was more cautious about that, and he was concerned with what his family thought, although he never really admitted that. His relationships with other men were mostly casual encounters, I think."

Alan in 1955.

With the encouragement of their friends, Alan and Phyllis decided it would be a good idea to work on an act together. "We worked like dogs in a rehearsal hall whenever we had a minute. Phyllis was very funny naturally, but the moment she tried, it was a disaster. We pulled together all sorts of props, and Stanley and Frank helped us with costumes and accessories. I still had my tuba, and we did a circus number and some song and dance stuff."

Phyllis's friends, composer Dean Fuller who wrote *Once Upon a Mattress*, and dancer Dick Beard, helped them with the act. In July 1955, Alan and Phyllis were booked in a few clubs in New England. They packed their steamer trunks, Alan's tuba, and Phyllis's ill-tempered schnauzer named Foggy Dew in a tiny Nash Rambler they christened Ogden Nash, and drove to Falmouth, Massachusetts.

"Every night we bombed," Alan recalled. "We worked with Ellis Larkins, a great jazz pianist who played for Ella Fitzgerald. When he heard he had to play for a comedy act, he was humiliated. Half way through the act, he got so bored he took off his colored glasses and swung them around in his hand. He was the type who played the piano with one finger . . . dink, dink, dink, dink. We wanted a big opening with a lot of pizzazz. His playing was fine for Ella, where she sang nine notes for every *one* he played. I needed a lot of good things behind me when I performed. Like a tune. Plus I had a tin ear. Phyllis was very musical. If someone dropped a pot, she would break into a rousing tap number.

"One night, Donald Cook stumbled into the club. He was appearing at the Falmouth Theatre next door in *Champagne Complex* with John Dall."

Cook was an accomplished film and stage actor. Dall was a handsome young leading man who played the calculating killer in Hitchcock's 1948 film *Rope* and the trigger-happy murderer in the 1950 classic *Gun Crazy*. Both actors had starred in *Champagne Complex* on Broadway several months earlier. The comedy was a colossal bomb and closed after several performances. A young actress named Monica Lovett also starred in the summer stock production.

"Well, Donald Cook thought Phyllis and I were the funniest things he'd ever seen. We became fast friends. Donald and John were terrific. Donald was chasing after all the young girls, and John was chasing after all the young boys. I told Phyllis, 'Now, *that's* an act!'"

Alan was intrigued by Dall. "All that killing made him very attractive," he recalled. Alan had a fling with Dall beneath the fragrant evergreen trees. "Monica Lovett was a Catholic virgin, and was hung up on Donald Cook. He was always trying to get into her knickers. He'd just look at her, and she would sigh and faint. Their play was advertised as a light-headed comedy. The only thing light-headed about it was Monica Lovett, the delicate little wildflower."

As it turned out, Alan and Phyllis were booked into the same towns in which Donald was scheduled to appear. "He said, 'We'll all go together like a troup! Like a band of gypsies!' I liked his style.

"Monica and John traveled in Donald's spacious station wagon. Phyllis, Foggy Dew and I were jammed into the little Nash. Between my fat ass and all our trunks and props, our Nash weighed more than Donald's station wagon. It was hard to keep up with him, and we hit every piece of fucking loose granite on the road in New Hampshire. When we finally got there, it was comfortable at least. We stayed in a nice little room over the nightclub."

One night Shelley Winters came to the club. She had seen Alan and Phyllis's act a few days earlier. "She sat there with a big sandwich filled with mayonnaise spilling all over her fingers. She'd bark out, 'They're wonderful aren't they? Aren't they just wonderful? You know what they're going to do next?' And then she told all my jokes before I had a chance to. Every time I said something, it had already been said by her fat ass. She was the worst heckler I'd ever seen. But Donald Cook thought we had somehow added her to our act, and he was rolling on the floor."

After a few weeks in the pine tree wilderness of New England, Alan and Phyllis returned to New York. They were offered a one-week engagement at Le Ruban Bleu, a well-known supper club on East 56th Street. Alan recalled, "Julius Monk was the manager. He said, 'If you make it, and you probably won't because it's a tough room, but if you do, we'll extend you.' We stayed three months.

"Monk was quite a guy," Alan said. "He had real panache. He wore beautiful three-piece suits and white gloves. He had the strangest accent and it sounded like he had marbles in his mouth.

Alan and Phyllis Sues, 1955. Credit Bruno of Hollywood.

He would sort of roll his eyes and tug at his white gloves when he spoke. He had an amazing vocabulary and half the time I didn't know what the hell he was saying. He introduced the acts. 'Ladies and gentlemen, and friends of style, may I direct your attention and applause … now we present the scintillating rhythms of a charming and disarming couple.' After being at Ruban Bleu for years, he got fired right after we appeared there. I hope we didn't have anything to do with it."

Alan and Phyllis's act evolved and during their engagement they dropped certain bits and added some new material. "We did a number called "The Japanese Legend." It was a take-off of *Little Red Riding Hood*. Phyllis wore a red wig and a bright red geisha girl costume that Stanley created, and we called her Little Red Riding Kimono. I played the Big Bad Wolf." They shared the stage with Dorothy Loudon and Professor Irwin Corey.

"Dorothy was dynamite. She was a smash," Alan recalled. "And Irwin Corey was something else again. He always looked like he just rolled out of bed. One night before the show, he came up to me backstage and said, 'Alan, I've got a couple of real beauties tonight. Beauty queens! I got one for you.' Well, he introduced these two dames who looked like they were dragged there behind a truck through the dirt."

With a few good notices under their belt, Alan's booking agent mistakenly thought they were ready for the road. "Our first club date was in Pittsburgh. We arrived at this dump and Phyllis took one look and burst into tears. So did I. The place was filled with hookers working the drunks at the bar. The manager of the joint, some gangster-type guy with a broken nose, asked for our music. I told him I had music for a piano, a trio, or up to sixteen pieces. But he had something better in mind. I said, 'Oh, Jesus, what is it, sweetheart?' He said, 'It's an organist.'

"Have you ever tried to do a comedy act accompanied by an organ? Nothing like it. We were fired after our first show. We were lucky to get out alive. There were no dressing rooms. Phyllis had to change costumes in a banquet hall at the far end of the bar. On our first and only night, she hurried in there to change and walked into a wake."

While they were in Pittsburgh, they sought out a female impersonator named T.C. Jones. A friend of Phyllis's said they would enjoy meeting him. Jones had become famous on the club circuit with his spot-on impersonation of Tallulah Bankhead. He was appearing at a bar in town, and they sent a note to him backstage. "While we were waiting," Alan said, "a big girl kept flirting with me. I said, Phyllis, look at that. She keeps winking at me. And I'm not that cute."

Phyllis and Alan, 1955.

Finally she came to their table and said, "Hi, I'm T.C. Jones."

"He was a big, blousy broad with a round pie face," Alan described. "He was with his wife named Connie, who looked like a librarian, and owned a bunch of beauty parlors. That seemed appropriate. T.C. kept going through Connie's purse, and using her lipstick and hair brush. I think her primary wifely duty was taking care of his wigs."

The next day, Alan and Phyllis had lunch with Jones and his wife at their apartment. "There was a big picture of him in drag on a table in the living room," Alan explained. "It was signed, 'To my lovely wife Connie.' I couldn't wrap my head around *that* one. T.C. was on a diet because he was getting ready to go to New York to open in *New Faces of 1956*. There was some controversy when the producer Leonard Stillman hired him because that type of act was usually only booked into certain nightclubs. This was a big step up. Paul Lynde was going to direct the show. We had nuts and berries for lunch, but I thought he was terrific. He had a great act. He wasn't doing drag. He was really a convincing woman on stage."

Alan and Phyllis decided to cancel their next booking and drive directly to St. Louis to prepare for their engagement at the Crystal Palace. They were just outside of Indianapolis on a long, desolate stretch of snowy road when Alan lost control of the car in a freak wind. The car rolled down a fifteen-foot embankment, and smashed into a culvert. When Alan came to his senses, he found Phyllis unconscious and buried under their trunks and props. She had a large gash in the back of her head. Alan crawled up the steep, snowy hillside and flagged down a truck. They were taken to a nearby hospital. Phyllis needed twenty-four stitches in the back of her head, and she'd broken her shoulder. Alan suffered from pulled ligaments in his chest and neck, and required traction.

"The only hotel in town was called the Newcastle Plaza, which was decorated in early dirt," Alan recalled. "I got an enormous room with double beds, but the room had no closet." Until Phyllis was discharged, Alan slept in one bed and Foggy Dew slept in the other.

Phyllis was released after a week. "They wanted her out of there as soon as possible, because she was causing a lot of trouble with her big mouth. We were running out of money for doctor bills. Phyllis was calling everyone she knew for a handout, and called our agent to blame him for the accident. I was still in so much pain and the doctor told me to soak in Epsom salt.

"I told Phyllis I was going out to buy Epsom salt and she said she wanted more aspirin. There was no drug store open in the whole town. I didn't know what to do. The only thing left was a liquor store. I bought the best and biggest bottle of scotch I could find. When I got back to our room, I said, 'The drug store is closed.

There is no medication, so I bought a gallon of booze.' Phyllis said, 'Oh, Jesus. Thank God!' We got plastered."

The car had been demolished. They sold it for scrap metal for twenty dollars, and called a friend in St. Louis when their money was about to run out. "He was marvelous," Alan said. "It was a three hundred and fifty mile round trip, but he came to rescue us. We couldn't go back to New York because we had sublet our apartment."

After spending a week in St. Louis with painful injuries, no funds, and no work, Alan reluctantly called his parents who were now living on a horse ranch in the Los Angeles suburb of Chatsworth, California.

Alan and Phyllis flew to Los Angeles at the end of January 1956, and moved in with Pete and Alice Sues. The move, though necessary, strained to the limit Alan's tenuous relationship with his parents.

"His parents were drunks and very controlling," Phyllis recalled, "especially his father. Alan didn't seem to know how to act around them. He was very unhappy with himself. After we were married, Alan's drinking increased and became unmanageable. It was vodka or gin, and bitters. He always battled his weight, and always thought he was fat. He never thought he was any good in show business. Furthermore, his parents had no interest in that part of his life at all. They had no interest in him.

"His mother would get drunk and belittle him to his face and in front of me. It was awful. I think being homosexual was also a big problem for him. In a way, he was ashamed of himself, and he was also on the defensive at the same time. He was very conflicted. It's a shame because he was so talented. So creative and artistic. He was incredibly funny. That's what I fell for, his sense of humor. He was a fabulous story-teller, and could take over a room. And no matter how much people laughed, he never thought he was good enough. All that came from his mother."

There was no work for the couple in Los Angeles. As soon as they recovered from their injuries, they got a booking at the revered Purple Onion nightclub in San Francisco. Pete gave Alan an old Cadillac, and he and Phyllis packed their props and costumes and drove north. Their original engagement of one week was extended to last throughout the summer of 1956. They shared the bill with comedienne Phyllis Diller, in her first big professional gig. "Reviews were good," Alan recalled, "crowds were good, and we really had a great time. Phyllis Diller was sensational. She made fun of herself, but not in a bad way. She wasn't afraid to look like a clown. She was so self-assured. I liked that. I learned from her."

Phyllis Diller said, "Alan was inventive, not a standup comic, but a funny *performer*. A clown in the classic sense. He could make me laugh, but his eyes were always sad. His eyes didn't laugh."

Alan's friend, impressionist Charles Pierce, was performing at Ann's 440 Club in North Beach at the same time. The club, owned by a singer named Ann Dee, also featured T.C. Jones, and introduced audiences to singer Johnny Mathis. Alan introduced his wife to Charles, and they barhopped into the early morning hours after their respective shows.

Phyllis and Alan also befriended comic Mort Sahl who appeared at the Hungry i, located across the street from the Purple Onion. "Mort was so sharp and funny," Alan recalled. "He'd come on the stage with that day's newspaper and use the headlines to launch his monologue. He was very political, and very liberal, and I was always amazed at his ease on stage. He sort of laughed along with the audience. I asked him once how he did it, and he said he had no plan and no routine. Sometimes he didn't even look at the paper before he hit the stage. I was very envious of his talent."

"We met up with Mort sometimes after the show for drinks," Phyllis recalled. "Alan was on an endless bender while we were in San Francisco. He was miserable. He drank heavily all the time, and that bothered me more than anything. It would be time to go onstage, and he'd be nowhere to be found. He'd be drunk at the bar and it drove me *crazy*. I always wondered how he could do a show drunk, but he did. He never missed a line, never missed a cue, but it drove me nuts."

When they returned to Los Angeles, the couple reluctantly stayed with Pete and Alice until they found a place of their own.

"Thanksgiving was the last straw," Alan said. "My brother and his wife and kids came to dinner. My mother insisted on cooking. We waited so long, a few of us began to play Bridge. I threw a bad card and my father screamed at me, called me names, and left the table.

Alan and Phyllis in Los Angeles, 1956.

When we finally sat down to eat, my mother staggered out of the kitchen carrying the turkey. She was dead drunk. She fell to the floor and so did the cooked bird. My father jumped up and shouted, 'Well, that's a Norman Rockwell scene if I've ever seen one!'

"I wouldn't say that living with my family was perfect Hell, but the only way I could get any sleep at all was to finish off a bottle of booze every night to drown out my mother's noise. But I learned something important. It wasn't fear of failure that motivated me—it was fear of living with my parents a minute more."

Alan and Phyllis rented a little house on San Vicente Boulevard near Cynthia Street in Los Angeles. "It was actually a shack on a dirt road," Phyllis recalled. "We called it Tortilla Flats. Alan decorated it on a shoestring and made little chintz curtains for all the windows. We didn't have anything to put on the walls, so Alan painted reproductions of famous paintings all around."

Phyllis began to work with some regularity as a dancer on television. In early 1957, she landed a recurring role on *The Jack Benny Show*. Alan booked a small guest role in the television series *December Bride* and was cast in his first feature film at Warner Brothers, *The Helen Morgan Story*, starring Paul Newman and Ann Blyth.

"I was reading my lines too loud," Alan recalled. "The director, Michael Curtiz, was upset. He told me it wasn't legitimate theater we were doing. I didn't have to yell. When I came back from lunch, somebody was standing in my place on the set. I thought I had been fired. I called my agent who told me to stay in my dressing room and he'd come right over to see what was going on. When he got there, he came to my door and said, 'Listen, you dope, that's your stand-in out there.'"

As Phyllis became busier with work, Alan's performing career floundered. "It's strange," Alan said, "if a woman is working and her husband isn't, she rarely feels bad about it. It didn't seem to bother Phyllis, but it bothered me a lot."

In a short time, Phyllis and Alan rented a large, two-bedroom house on Horn Street in the hills north of Sunset Boulevard that belonged to their New York friends, Bob Talman and Bob Magnus. As far as Phyllis was concerned, her relationship with Alan had all but ended. "Our marriage was over by then," Phyllis said. "We had separate rooms. We had no physical relations anymore. My room was stark, but Alan decorated his room to look like a Moroccan palace. It was amazing what he could make out of nothing."

One night, Alan picked up a fellow. "I stopped at a liquor store and bought a bottle of bourbon. I drove to the Sunset Motel which was about the most rundown tacky dump I had ever seen in my life. The room had on old iron bed with a threadbare chenille bedspread, a bare light bulb hanging overhead and two dirty tumblers. We had a few belts. It was so romantic we were kind of like machinery bumping into each other. We decided to take our clothes off and I went off into the corner and turned my back at the same time grabbing for the light cord. We got into this ice cold bed and all of a sudden, a woman in the next room screamed, 'You dirty son of a bitch!' And then, "BANG! BANG! BANG!'

"We jumped out of bed, threw our clothes on and shot down the alley to the car. We didn't say a word, we just stared straight ahead. *Oh, my God, what happened*, I thought. *We've been exposed!* I dropped him off where I found him and never saw him again.

"For four or five days afterward, Phyllis kept saying, 'I don't understand you. You keep reading the papers. You've never read the newspapers!' I was looking frantically for who was shot in the motel."

In a moment of despair, Alan decided to see a psychiatrist. His drinking was getting the best of him, and his feelings about his sexuality often led him into compromising and dangerous situations with men he casually encountered.

Although Los Angeles had become a seeming paradise for post World War II gay men and women, who relocated from all around the country, it was nevertheless a dangerous place. Until 1975, oral and anal sex acts were felonies in California. Anyone convicted of engaging in oral sex could be sentenced to up to fifteen years in prison, and an anal sex conviction could earn the hapless offender a life behind bars. At that time, the most common charge was something euphoniously called "lewd and lascivious conduct." A certain California Penal Code under anti-vagrancy statutes prohibited soliciting or engaging in lewd or dissolute conduct (specifically homosexual relations), and prohibited loitering in or around a public toilet for the presumed same purpose. Although those offenses were treated as misdemeanors, anyone convicted was required to register as a sex offender for the rest of his life.

Not only was homosexuality essentially against the law, it wasn't until 1973 that the American Psychiatric Association declassified homosexuality as a mental illness. Until then, some gay men and women were forcibly treated with drugs and electro-shock treatment to "cure" their "illness" as a condition of their sentence if convicted of a sexual offense.

Such a sexual offense conviction was devastating not only on a personal level, but on a professional level as well. Job loss was a distinct fear. Actors' contracts included "morals clauses" which allowed the contracting movie studio or producer the right to fire anyone arrested for "lewd" conduct.

"You had to be very careful," Alan said. "I was thinking about my work, and I was thinking about my parents. It was tricky who you could trust. Johnny Ray was a big time singer then. He was arrested for trying to pick up a guy in a public restroom, and it almost wrecked him."

The Los Angeles Police Department hired young, good-looking Vice Squad officers who entrapped patrons in gay bars on a regular basis. The LAPD also hired handsome, out-of-work actors to pose as "gay bait" in public bathrooms and public parks where men sometimes met for sex.

Santa Monica Beach was an easy mark for the Vice Squad. Undercover officers lurked in the public bathrooms and waited for guys to solicit them. "They could blend in," Alan recalled. "They wore bathing suits and suntan lotion and nothing else. Don't ask me where they kept their badge or gun.

"I'd be laying around the beach and if I saw a gay guy heading for the bathroom, I'd warn him the cops were in there. That sort of shit happened all the time."

The Crown Jewel, an "upscale" gay bar "for suits" on 8th Street and Olive in Los Angeles, was owned by a defense attorney named Harry Weiss. Interestingly, Weiss was a flamboyant homosexual who owned a couple of other gay bars and made his living defending gay men who were arrested on morals charges—often men entrapped in one of his own establishments. He knew people in high places and got his clients off, but for a price. His fee could run in the thousands of dollars.

"The problem was," Alan explained, "he set the guys up himself. This happened to a couple of my friends. Weiss would be in the bar when the police came in and he pointed out who to arrest. As the guys were hauled out the door, he would hand them his business card. It was quite a racket.

"We were hassled all the time. There was a bar in Hollywood that would play the *Star Spangled Banner* when the Vice was at the door. Everyone would separate. I'd salute."

In the spring of 1957, Alan met a young ensign named Jack Gilbert at the Mocambo nightclub in Los Angeles. Ella Fitzgerald was performing, and the men met at the bar. They went back to Gilbert's motel room that night.

Years later, Gilbert recalled their affair in a letter to Alan. "Next day you took me by your place, talking all the way. You said you and your wife Phyllis were doing show-cases. We did the L.A. motel thing a lot. Later you drove me to your father's spread in the Valley. No one home that day. You told me that your father was a self-made man and that he was on your case to be like him. After we were through in the house, we parked at the end of the road and you poured your heart out to me. You said your analyst told you our friendship was good for you, but you were having a problem trying to figure out how things would go with me being in the Navy. Those were warm, sharing times. Neither of us had our guard up."

Jack loved Alan's sense of humor. "His laughter was infectious," he said. He recalled a couple of jokes that Alan delighted in telling. "Two gold prospectors on a hot train headed west to strike it rich—one guy asks the other if he has a squaw. No, the guy says, couldn't afford one. So the first guy calls his squaw over and tells her to go get water since they are thirsty, and it's hot and dusty. The squaw goes out and returns with water which the two guys gulp down. So the guy sends her out again for more water. They wait and wait, and finally the squaw returns with an empty bucket. The guy asks, 'Why is it empty?' She replies, 'White man sitting on well.'

"The other one was—how can you tell if a dog's owner is gay? When the dog barks, he goes 'bowsie wowsie.'

"I told him a little Navy limerick that cracked him up good. 'Cabin boy, cabin boy, he really was a nipper. He lined his ass with broken glass, and circumcised the skipper.'"

Gilbert was stationed in Long Beach and spent many weekends visiting Alan in Los Angeles. The men continued their affair until the young officer moved to Florida a few months later for training.

Alan met Jack at a particularly difficult time in his life. His marriage to Phyllis had unraveled. His show business aspirations seemed stymied. His uncontrollable drinking and despair had driven him to seek psychiatric help. For the first time in his life, he felt compelled to pursue a romantic relationship with a man. Still, his fear and guilt overwhelmed him.

"Neither of us said, 'I love you,' but we felt it," Jack recalled. "The fact that he seriously wanted to leave California and go with me to Florida told me he cared and, of course, Phyllis weighed on his mind. It was not to be. Our mutually closeted situations demanded otherwise. I convinced him two closeted guys just would not work out."

Jack left the Navy after several years and traveled around the world. Nearly twenty-five years after first meeting, Jack reconnected with Alan. They spoke on the phone and exchanged letters. They considered picking up where they had left off so many years before. "Still so many issues for him," Jack said, "fears. His shrink advised him against our getting together so that faded. He was loveable, smart, hilarious, loopy, warm, and a true friend. I still grin when I remember his writing 'Fuck You' on the bottoms of his tennis shoes to distract his opponent. Strangely, I can still smell the sage cologne he used when we met."

With acting jobs seemingly out of reach, Alan decided to pursue another business. With his wife's earnings, he leased a commercial space on Santa Monica Boulevard in Los Angeles in the summer of 1957, and opened a retail shop called Gazebo.

"I thought it would do him good. We had the store for a little more than a year," Phyllis explained. "We both worked in it, but mostly I did. Alan was out shopping for little things to sell in the store. He went to a five and dime store that sold cheap, imported things from Japan. He picked out ashtrays and planters and common things like that, and marked them up and sold them to people who would never step foot in a five and dime.

One of Alan's original, hand-made hats. Photo by Jerry Jackson.

"I designed a couple of things, and Alan designed a beautiful, feminine organdy jacket, which I sewed. Bob Magnus's mother was a seamstress and she sewed a few things for us, too. One day I told Alan beach hats were the latest thing for women. I told him he should design hats.

"He could paint, and design furniture and clothes. He could do needlepoint, and he made me a beautiful faux zebra bag. He was all over the place, and that was the problem. He couldn't fully commit. To anything. Probably he should have been a designer. He may have had a better life. He wasn't working in show business, just couldn't get a job. He wasn't very aggressive about it, and I don't think he really liked it."

Alan designed several hats, and was surprised when customers snatched them up. "I went downtown to Olvera Street, and behind it was a wholesale store for hat makers," he explained. "I bought a lot of hat frames and went back and made hats which were crazy looking beach hats." One day, a woman came into the shop and suggested that Alan go into the wholesale business with his de-

Alan and Phyllis in The Holiday Show, 1957.

signs. He put together a collection and took them to a distributor the woman had recommended.

After several weeks, he received a wholesale order for three hundred hats. "I was in over my head," Alan said. "I didn't have anyone to make hats except me and Phyllis." Alan borrowed some money from his father, and hired some actor and dancer friends. They worked in the house on Horn. In a short time, Alan was selling to Macy's, Gimble's, Lord & Taylor, Bergdorf and Henri Bendel, and Bullock's and Robinson's department stores in Los Angeles.

"We sold to every state, but I wasn't a good businessman. I spent more money buying materials and paying the workers than we could sell the hats for."

Alan called his brother for help. 'I went over," John explained, "and I went in the back, and around a table were all these men and women singing and playing the bongo drums. I told him, 'I think I've found your problem.' All his employees were out-of-work show business friends and they did virtually nothing."

In late November 1957, Alan and Phyllis gave their act another try and opened in a production called *The Holiday Show*, produced by Don Sheffy at the Cabaret Concert Theater in Los Angeles. Accessible by a long flight of stairs that descended from Sunset Boulevard, the Spanish Mission style building was dark and moody. Two eccentric women owned the theater and sought out and encouraged young performers. Many people got their start at Cabaret Concert Theater including writer Billy Barnes and his wife, actress

Joyce Jameson, Jackie Joseph and Ken Berry, singers Ruth Olay and Ketty Lester, and comedienne Jo Anne Worley.

The Holiday Show (later renamed *The Don Sheffy Show*) included dancers, singers, impressionists and comics, and featured Kathleen Freeman and a rotund comic named Wayne Tucker. The production was favorably reviewed in the *Los Angeles Times* on January 3, 1958, "Its wit is sharp and it is fresh and stimulating, a very cleverly put together show. It is a recounting of the old glorious days of vaudeville, and is chock full of fun and memories. Alan and Phyllis Sues brought bounce and humor to their unique purveyal. Their tongue-in-cheek delivery and deft showmanship stamp them as high class entertainers." The show ran for three months.

Running a retail business during the day and performing every night for months had strained Alan's tenuous relationship with Phyllis to the breaking point. "One night," Phyllis recalled, "we were invited to dinner at a friend's house. Alan was drunk and surly, and said he didn't want to go. I went without him and I met a producer named Norman Pincus, and we hit it off. That night when I got back, I told Alan I wanted a divorce. We were leading completely separate lives, and there was just no reason for us to be married. He seemed surprised. He didn't think I meant it. I got a job with Liberace in Las Vegas and I left. I never went back to Alan. I actually had the marriage annulled."

Alan explained, "Norman came to help her move out. He was not the prettiest face I've ever seen, but he had an immaculate new car. He walked in, smiled and said, 'Phyllis has told me how artistic you are. A real *decorator*. And you really pulled this place together.' I don't know what ever held me back from just hauling off and giving him a haymaker right there."

Norman Pincus produced the hit television comedy series *The Real McCoys*, which premiered in 1957. "Never one to miss a chance to take a swipe at me," Alan recalled, "my mother said, 'Well, she left you for the real McCoy'. She thought that was very funny. Until the day she died, whenever the subject of my divorce came up, she'd toss that bon mot into the fire."

Alan took the divorce very hard. "It was another failure and I decided to solve my problems by drinking. A lot. And I did for weeks. And weeks. I drank till I blacked out."

"Alan called Norman and told him I was a bitch," Phyllis said. "I didn't see him very often until after Norman died."

One day in 1958, a young man named Jerry Jackson walked into the Gazebo. He was a professional photographer, and a dancer and choreographer. "That's where I met Alan," he explained. "The shop was really beautiful, and he had decorated it himself. He faux-painted lattice work on the windows and walls, and it was stunning. Alan was very animated. Very bombastic. We made each other laugh immediately, and became good friends."

Tony Duquette, a well-known artist and decorator, had also taken notice of Alan's artistic skills. Walking past the shop one day, he noticed the elaborate front doors. Alan had pressed flowers between the glass panels in the doors because stained or beveled glass was too expensive at the time. Duquette invited Alan to visit his studio nearby on Robertson Boulevard. The cavernous building had once been a silent movie studio that belonged to Norma Talmadge. Alan was overcome.

"I'd never seen anything like it," he recalled. "It was spectacular and filled with tapestries, centuries-old Asian antiques and porcelains, Moroccan decorations, wood carvings, stained glass windows, baroque mirrors, and animal-skin rugs. He could make magic out of trash. It was amazing." Alan became friends with Duquette and his wife, Elizabeth. "He called her Beagle for some reason, "Alan explained. "They worked together on art commissions. At that time, they worked on elaborate interior designs."

Impressed with Alan's painting skills, Duquette hired him to assist on a job decorating a new restaurant on Sunset Strip called Cyrano's. Alan had to stencil the letter "C" on the director-style canvas chairs in the restaurant.

Jerry Jackson recalled, "They were running really late, working right up until the opening. The stencil paint was not completely dry and when people sat, and later got up, they had the letter "C" painted on the back of their clothes."

In the summer of 1958, Pete Sues was stricken with a serious bout of throat cancer. He survived a delicate operation and recovered. He decided to give shares of his business to his son John, sell the remainder, and retire. "He didn't give me a nickel," Alan said. Pete and Alice bought a small ranch in Solvang, and moved to the little community to raise horses.

"My father never did anything small," Alan explained. "He wore cowboy boots and a huge Stetson and strutted around the ranch like he knew what he was doing. He didn't really know what he was doing, but he knew how to hire people who did. And he bred winners. The house was filled with Breeding Cups and trophies. He even became President of the California Thoroughbred Breeders Association."

John had worked for his father for several years. He was originally an advertising manager, and soon became Vice President of Marketing. With his father's guidance, and assistance from Pete's business partner, film director Clarence Brown, John developed what would become a very lucrative business of product placement in motion pictures.

"John was the perfect son for my father," Alan explained. "He followed my father in his business. I sure didn't. John got the gold mine, and I got the shaft. I got nothing."

Without Phyllis's income, it was impossible for Alan to operate the Gazebo. He closed the store in mid-1958, but continued to make hats at home for his wholesale buyers. To supplement his meager earnings, he began to work with a young commercial photographer named Joyce Rainbolt, who had photographed his hats for several magazine advertisements. "Joyce was a brilliant photographer who understood light and color," Alan said, "but she didn't have an original idea in her pretty little head."

Throughout the fall, Alan worked on many commercial assignments with Joyce including several Chanel and Max Factor advertising campaigns and numerous editorial features for *Vogue* magazine. "I used to style all the shots and set them up. She would say, 'Well, dear, I'm thinking of something in beige.' And I'd come up with an elaborate idea for the shoot, and she'd say, 'Yes, dear, that's *just* what I was thinking of.'"

In spite of being busy and enjoying the work, Alan fell into a depression that was exacerbated by his dependence on alcohol. "I would go out at night and get so crocked I didn't remember where I parked my car," Alan recalled. The psychiatric sessions didn't seem to help him find any peace.

In February 1959, Joyce accepted an assignment to photograph teenage Rock 'n Roll star Ricky Nelson on a concert trip to Phoenix, Arizona. "Neither one of us knew who he was," Alan said. "I said to Joyce, 'What the hell does Ricky Nelson look like?' And she said, 'I haven't the vaguest idea.' We ran over to the airport newsstand and thumbed through movie magazines until we found a picture of him."

Alan and Joyce met Nelson at the Los Angeles airport, and flew with him to Phoenix, snapping pictures on the plane. "He wore a white leather jacket and he had one expression," Alan said, "a sneer. But it worked for him. He was the horniest kid I ever met. He nailed every female in his path that moved."

Before the actual concert, Joyce and Alan shot Ricky getting off the plane, being swamped by thousands of screaming teenage girls, eating in his hotel room, plucking his guitar, laying around the swimming pool, riding a horse, and performing an outdoor concert. Alan got so inebriated on the free-flowing alcohol that he became unruly. He was put on a plane and sent home.

"I didn't have the money to pay the cab driver when I got back," Alan said. "I was ashamed of myself and I never worked with Joyce again."

With help from his brother, Alan opened a hat shop in a tiny storefront on Melrose Avenue. Jerry Jackson was Alan's production manager. "He actually made the hats in my apartment," Jerry said. "He'd be sitting at the sewing machine working away and wearing a Cleopatra wig with a plastic snake wrapped around his head. He was very creative but had a hard time focusing his attention on any one thing."

It wasn't long before show business lured Alan back into the spotlight. He met a girl named Joan Amateau who was a "male impersonator." Alan said, "Never met one of those before, at least one who got paid for it. I thought she was sort of funny and she helped me with some material. One of her jokes was, 'Hello there, buddy. I just came back from a wonderful place that we could make into the next American resort city. You know what it is? Bang-cock! It's got everything Vegas had twenty years ago. Absolutely nothing.'"

Joan Amateau had been recently divorced from television producer Rod Amateau, who was responsible for several successful comedy series including *The George Burns and Gracie Allen Show* and *The Many Lives of Dobie Gillis*. "Joan came out of it with a big, fat bankroll and a bratty kid named Chloe," Alan said. "She was helping me write an act. We would talk into tapes and she did very funny things because she did nothing but impersonations of men. It's hard to find a comedy writer who knows about men. Most comedy writers lean toward writing funny women."

Alan tried out his new standup routine at the Mont Vista Lodge in Upton, California. The resort, located at the foot of the San Gabriel Mountains, included rental cabins, a hotel, tennis and volley ball courts. Comics Buddy Lester, Leo Fuchs, and Mickey Katz frequently headlined at the hotel. Most of the patrons were Jewish. "It was called The Catskills of California," Alan recalled. "The only thing they had in common with the Catskills in New York was the mosquitoes. We drove for hours to get there and Joan never stopped talking for a minute about how marvelous it was going to be.

"The only person in the audience who got the jokes was Joan," Alan explained. "And she *wrote* them. Her laugh was so maniacal nobody paid attention to me. They were all watching her throw back her head and cackle. Even I did."

Before his next booking at the Ice House in Pasadena, Alan ditched his act and wrote a couple of sketches for himself. "I'm a better sketch artist than standup," Alan said. "And I needed props!" The centerpiece of the act was a sketch about a knight in King Arthur's court who's looking for work and goes to see his agent. "I wore a knight's costume I made, and clunked around the stage waving a rubber sword. A stage hand rattled a bucket of chains while I paced around. I was accompanied by an accordionist who played "La Golondrina," which I thought was hilarious. No one else did though, except Joan."

Alan's friends packed the Ice House that night. Joan had notified the show business trade papers, which was a mistake. "I wasn't

Alan as The Outlandish Knight.

ready," Alan said. "No matter how much we rehearsed, Joan was the kind of gal who would give you four minutes of rewrites as you were about to step on the stage.

"I had devised a new prop. I got a very large umbrella and sewed black fabric all around it so when I opened the umbrella, the fabric was unfurled and it made sort of a tent under the umbrella. I was going to get into the tent and take off my clothes and change into my clunky knight's outfit while my accompanist played his accordion. I didn't rehearse this. It was so black in the umbrella that I couldn't see a thing. I just couldn't manage the change, so after about ten minutes in the dark, I shuffled off the stage while my accompanist played, 'You know that I know that you know that I know.' It was perfect.

"When I saw my brother sitting up front and realized I knew almost everyone in the audience, I panicked and lost all my lines. I bombed. John got stinking drunk and heckled me more than anyone else in the audience!"

Doug Weston had opened the Troubadour nightclub in Los Angeles in 1957. Originally a coffee shop, the club evolved into one of the preeminent venues for new talent on the West Coast. Alan auditioned for Doug, and secured a two-week booking. "He must have been sleep deprived or stoned that day," Alan joked. "The place showcased folk singers and beatniks. I really didn't fit in at all.

"He thought I was hysterical, but the audience thought I stunk. I'd tank every night and stand there struggling to get through and be sweating like a pig. They all just sat on their hands, but Doug was off to the side rolling on the floor. I couldn't understand it. He kept me on for eight weeks and I thought I would go nuts. My shrink was able to buy a new car off me during that run. It was the most expensive job I ever had."

One of the biggest rounds of applause he ever got at the Troubadour happened by mistake. "One night I was leaving the stage after flopping," Alan explained. "A folk singer was coming on after me. 'How's the audience?' he asked. I said they're a bunch of fucking jerks. But I spoke into an open microphone. It was the first night I got an ovation."

On June 6, 1959, *TV Guide* printed a three-page color pictorial featuring Alan and several females modeling his hats. "The beach hats on these pages were created (if that's the word) by Alan Sues," the article read, "a tall, gangling Hollywood actor with a penchant for doing things *way out*."

The article quoted Alan, "I can remember staying up all night turning out 80 hats to fill one order, now we're selling to a line of what the ads call 'better stores everywhere.' I guess I'm in, man."

He was successful for a time with consistent retail sales and strong wholesale orders. "But like most things," Jerry recalled, "Alan grew tired of it. He was not a businessman and he was not organized."

In the summer, Alan pulled together a more ambitious revue. *Tantrums at Nine* was described by its director Jason Lindsey as "a satire on the modes, manners and morals of the day". Jerry Jackson choreographed the show. Everett Sloane, a veteran actor, wrote several songs.

"Alan always tried to do too many things at one time," Jerry recalled. "He wrote a lot of the material and acted in the show, and he designed the sets and decorated the theater. Alan dipped fabric and masks in quick drying white plaster. He tacked the wet material to the walls to look like drapes – a trick he learned from Tony Duquette. The fabric quickly hardened, and he then hung the ghostly white masks all around.

"It looked great, but it was hard to direct him. He just didn't focus at all. Rehearsals ended up with him tossing a ball around to everybody, and production meetings for the hat business turned into joke sessions with him performing. The show went on, but the hat shop closed."

Tantrums at Nine opened at Cabaret Concert Theater on July 7, 1959. Alan's first foray as a producer was well-received by the *Los Angeles Times*. Katherine Von Blon wrote, "*Tantrums at Nine* turned out to be rather tantalizing tantrums, filled with joie de vivre and youthful exuberance as presented by Alan Sues and Jason Lindsey. These young producers have put on a show which has freshness and zest, also certain sophisticated wit and occasionally an ironic twist, along with some clever topical illusions. What with pretty girls and dashing blades, the thing seemed to be strutting high, wide and handsome."

The cast included Diane Honodel, Treva Frazee, Kenneth Eichhorn, Christine Nelson and Wayne Tucker. Some of Alan's comic song compositions included, "Won't You Give Up the Dowry, Dad," "Anything's Legal, If They Don't Catch You," "The Citizens of Dry Prong, Nevada," "Togetherness" and the revealing "The Family Who Drinks Together, Stays Together."

Von Blon wrote, "Alan Sues and Diane Honodel pleased the audience mightily with "Love Those Pale Hands." The Outlandish Knight as purveyed by Mr. Sues and the beauteous Miss Nelson was an amusing satire on knighthood, accomplished with skill and ironic gestures by the two performers."

Months later, the *Los Angeles Times* listed *Tantrums at Nine* as one of the theatrical highlights of 1959. Such an acknowledgment was a great honor. At that time, Spike Jones was performing at the Moulin Rouge, Pearl Bailey entertained at the Cocoanut Grove, The Frankie Ortega Trio headlined at the Crescendo, and Anita O'Day and Buddy Lester performed at The Cloister. "But it wasn't enough," Jerry said. "Alan always second-guessed himself. Despite the sold-out crowds and reviews, he thought he wasn't any good."

Alan gave up the house on Horn and moved into Jerry Jackson's small, one-bedroom apartment in Beverly Hills. He set up a narrow military cot in the living room. "Alan suffered from depression a lot," Jerry recalled. "Sometimes he took to his bed and didn't get up for days. He told me he just wanted to pull the covers over his head and hide. He had low self-esteem issues, and 'completion' problems. He over-analyzed everything. And he had sexual identity issues."

Jerry tried to discourage Alan's drinking, and often questioned whether or not there was any benefit to his psychiatric counseling. Alan had a cat that caught birds and rodents, and brought them into the house. One day she dropped a small lizard at Alan's feet. He screamed and jumped onto a chair. A few days later, following a visit to his psychiatrist, Alan anxiously telephoned Jerry.

"He told me the doctor said, 'What were you afraid of? You don't have a vagina. The lizard wasn't going to crawl up inside you'," Jerry recalled. "Alan didn't know what the doctor was talking about, but he twisted it to mean he was implying that Alan had another personality—a female personality—that he struggled with. I thought the *doctor* sounded nuts."

Despite being broke most of the time, Alan and Jerry managed to have fun together. When they had a few extra dollars, they'd treat themselves to dinner at Alan's favorite Mexican restaurant, El Coyote. "He loved the fat waitresses in the frilly dresses," Jerry said.

Alan photographed by Jerry Jackson.

"One night we were there and he saw a guy he liked. He was always more bold when he had a few drinks in him. He wrote his phone number on a tortilla and asked the waitress to give it to the guy."

One day, Jerry's mother came to visit him at the apartment he shared with Alan. "She was a teetotaler," Jerry explained. "Somehow Alan got her to drink with him and they knocked off a bottle of wine. She and Alan took off and while they were gone, Alan stole the French flag from the French consulate's office, and potted flowers from in front of the Beverly Hills Police Station. The next morning, I found him passed out on his little cot with the flag tacked like a drape across the living room window and potted begonias all round him on the floor!"

Alan moved to a small house on north Fairfax Avenue in early 1960 and began to put together an act with Sally Marr. The diminutive Marr was a former burlesque dancer and comedienne. Although she was credited with discovering comics Pat Morita, Cheech Marin, Tommy Chong, and Sam Kinison, she was best known as the mother of the groundbreaking stand-up comic Lenny Bruce.

"Lenny changed stand-up completely," Alan said. A few years earlier, he'd seen Bruce perform at a club in Hollywood called Peacock Lane. "Then he moved to some strip clubs in the Valley. He was so funny, the audience wanted to see him and not the strippers! He told zany stories, and he was very influential to me. But for my taste, he got unfunny as he went along. The more political he became, the more combative he was on stage."

Alan and Sally worked for months to pull together an act. "It all began to go wrong when Sally told me exactly how comedy should be done," Alan said. "It took her five months to explain it. That and the fact she never wanted to rehearse."

Sally couldn't remember her lines and didn't seem to know how to handle a prop. "Listen, comics have to feel the audience," she told Alan. "We're just going to keep a bare skeleton and once we go out there we will just feel the audience and we'll know where to go."

"It was then I realized why she wasn't sharing a stage with her son," Alan remarked.

"I tried to direct them," Jerry recalled. "But there was no directing Sally."

Jerry worked with them in the afternoon, and Sally had a friend who directed them in the evening. "Sally wanted to direct herself. She barely tolerated Jerry and even her own friend. She referred to them as 'our monitors.' I thought that was clever. This went on for months," Alan said, "until I put my foot down and said the show goes on now, or never."

Sally booked them into a small nightspot in the San Fernando Valley called the Quail Club. "We got there," Alan recalled, "and this four-foot tall guy with a foot-long cigar waddled over and said,

'Sally, baby! How ah ya sweetheart! Give me a couple of jokes, will ya?' His name was Benny. He ran the joint and was the emcee. He also sold Cuban cigars from the coat check room. When I saw the audience looked like a teamsters' meeting, I knew we were in trouble. I was frantically nervous. And the props! We had added about ten props because every time I get nervous, I always add another prop. Sally carried them."

The show opened with a stripper. "She was a gorgeous blond of undetermined age. They had a big spotlight which changed colors! Only if you *wanted* a little living color, of course. I mean, you didn't have to go into the blues and the magentas, which plays well with pancake makeup, but they were there by God, and an enormous big-muscled person was running the lights. That turned out to be Marge, who had a crew cut. The stripper sang, 'Now I'm glad I've got you . . . I've got fever.' Of course the spotlight turned red, and she forgot the rest of the lyrics. I thought the place had caught fire."

The next act on the program featured a tall, slender boy. "He wore a Western-style bolo tie, the kind that came down in big ribbons, and a red vest and white pants and white sneakers. He twirled a flaming baton until the room filled with blue smoke. Then Benny came out, and while the smoke cleared, he told some slam-bang jokes. He put his hand over his eyes and said, 'This is *Hawaiian Eye*.' Then he put his hand over his chest and said, 'This is *The Untouchables*.' Then he put his hand over his crotch and said, 'This is *The Price is Right*.' He closed with, 'I should be on television. Don't cha think? Don't cha think?' They loved him."

The premise of Alan and Sally's act was simple, and not very original. Alan was supposed to be doing a solo standup routine. He came onto the stage and before he could say anything, Sally would yell from the back of the room, "Hey, hey, hey, dear! You forgot your lunch!" Playing the role of his mother, and dressed like a former chorine, she walked through the audience, got onto the stage and started talking about chicken soup. Then she told the audience how great her son was, and she urged him to tell a story. Before he could get through the story, she'd interrupt him and say, "No, dear. That's not right." Then she'd finish the joke.

Alan Sues, 1961. Photo by Jerry Jackson.

"It was a great idea," Jerry said, "but it didn't work because she went off book all the time. She'd start doing her old burlesque bit when she got on the stage, which had nothing to do with Alan, or what we had rehearsed."

"The only thing the audience laughed at was anything a little off-color, so Sally decided to really let them have it," Alan recalled. "I realized where Lenny got his dirty mouth. She had one charming stage habit. If the audience didn't like her, she just flipped them off.

"We got in the car to leave and it was like everything had changed. That was the end of it. I was stunned. It was like our whole relationship had completely changed. She was on to someone else. A couple of days later, she called and said something about how she thought it would be very good if we played different types of mothers and sons, and we could play college tours. I said, 'Well, you've got to have an actress for that.'"

In spite of the travails, Alan liked Sally Marr. "She was a real broad. We'd be walking down the street and she'd ask strangers for twenty dollars, and then she'd give it to me. 'Take it, sweetheart,' she'd say, 'you need it more than I do.' She always had a satchel full of stolen things like watches, cutlery and silverware. She sold me a great silver money clip."

Alan enrolled in night school at Hollywood High and took a few art classes. Though he had a good eye for color and a flair for design, his limited resources made it impossible to collect genuine antiques and imported furnishings. Using design books and magazines as reference, he taught himself how to refinish furniture. He bought odds and ends at yard sales and junk shops to furnish his little house on Fairfax.

Tony Duquette provided Alan with some decorating work now and then. Alan painted murals in several of Duquette's home commissions, including Alan's old friend from New York, choreographer Tony Charmoli. "I painted murals of a tropical jungle on the walls of Tony's home bar," Alan explained. "I even painted the floor and ceiling."

"We barely had money to eat at times," Jerry recalled. Alan refinished used furniture he found at yard sales and occasionally sold the restored pieces.

In March 1961, Alan was finally cast—in a tiny role—in *The Honeymoon Machine*. The MGM comedy was written by Lorenzo Semple, Jr. The story concerns Navy personnel on a spree in Venice, Italy, who chase a couple of pretty girls and try to break into the bank of the local casino using the ship's computer. The film stars Steve McQueen, Jim Hutton, and Paula Prentiss. *The Honeymoon*

Machine was released in August. Alan's part in the film was not memorable, but for the rest of his life he proudly told anyone who would listen, "I did a film with a Steve McQueen!"

Diane Honodel, an actress who worked with Alan in *Tantrums at Nine*, gave him a sweater for his birthday. She had purchased the expensive cashmere at the Broadway Department Store at the corner of Hollywood and Vine. "We were broke," Jerry explained. "Alan decided to exchange the sweater for food, so I drove us to the Broadway. He had no idea what he was doing, and he never understood money very well. He picked out cans of smoked oysters, and the clerk told him he had more credit. He said we'll take it in beer. They told us to pull the car around to the back, which we thought was strange, and then they loaded us with cases and cases of beer. That was the trade-in. So we lived on smoked oysters and beer for days."

The Golden Carp was a gay bar on Beverly Boulevard near the 24-hour Hollywood Ranch Market on Vine Street. "That was great," Alan recalled. "You could pick up a trick at the Carp and a bucket of chicken wings at the Ranch Market. A real night on the town!"

Another well-known gay bar called The Carousel was located in Venice, a small beach community south of Santa Monica. "We used to go dancing there," Jerry recalled. "It was against the law for men to dance together, and when we heard the cops were coming, they'd turn up the lights and we all stopped moving and stood still when the police walked through slapping billy clubs in the palms of their hands."

The Carousel was also popular with beatniks, bohemians, artists, and the Hollywood crowd, and attracted many celebrities. The hostess of the bar was a towering black drag queen named Exotic. She dressed like a man in a formal suit, but wore a woman's makeup and wig. "At the end of the evening," Jerry remembered, "she'd yell out, 'Get a six pack and a trick, we're closing!'"

"Leslie Caron would be there, dancing around," Alan said, "and I loved it. Before the night was over, Jerry and I would be dancing on the bar." Actor Jack Larson, who was famous for playing the role of Jimmy Olson in the television series *The Adventures of Superman*, was often there with his young boyfriend, an aspiring writer/director named James Bridges. Bridges would later write box-office hits including *The Paper Chase*, *The China Syndrome* and *Urban Cowboy*.

Alan and Jerry befriended Bridges and Larson, and they decided to work on a project together. Bridges wrote a play based on their experiences at The Carousel. Titled *The Days of the Dancing*, the work was directed by Dennis Deegan and choreographed by Jerry. Alan played a character named Pistol, based on the drag queen, Exotic. The cast included Jan Sterling, Stephen Joyce, Henry Brandon, Bob Ennis, and Jack Larson.

On April 25, 1961, the *Los Angeles Times* reported, "A new play with music, *The Days of the Dancing*, will open soon and run weekends at the Beverly Hills Playhouse at 254 South Robertson. The work deals with the question of whether this generation is or is not lost. Or perhaps whether it ought to be found."

Jack Larson recalled, "Jim wrote a play about the goings-on in a notorious and very popular gay bar in Venice, California. It was in the style of Tennessee Williams with multi-layered characters. The papers barely covered the show, and never referred to the gay sub-plots. The gay characters were dismissed as oddballs then. At that time, there were a lot of code words that were used to mean homosexual. It was funny, and complicated. A great cast. Alan was wonderful, and very believable. He was a little like a downed power line snapping and uncontrollably twisting on the pavement."

Frank Mulcahy reviewed the play on May 17 for the *Los Angeles Times*. "James Bridges' new play, *The Days of the Dancing*, which opened at the Beverly Hills Playhouse last week, is an entertaining and slightly offbeat variation of a theme that has captivated playwrights for a long time. Essentially—it sums up the old truism that the past is of no real consequence. Today is all that matters. Fortunately for Bridges, producers Denis Deegan and Edgar Lansbury have assembled a splendid cast, headed by Jan Sterling, which not only gives the stamp of authenticity to the various characters—and with this weird crew that's no easy task—but has an enjoyable time doing it."

Alan said, "I was a little star-struck with Jan. She had an Oscar nomination, and she made a career playing hard-boiled floozies, which I thought was terrific because she really as quite a lady. She

Point of View *playbill, 1961.*

had one of the best lines in a movie I ever heard in my life. 'I don't go to church, kneeling bags my nylons.' I just loved that and I told her I used it all the time. We shared a makeup table. She gave me some great makeup tips, too."

Encouraged by the positive reception of *The Days of the Dancing*, Alan stepped into another musical revue called *Point of View* that opened on October 19 at the Vine Street Playhouse in Hollywood. With music by Hal Borne, lyrics by Oscar-winners Paul Francis

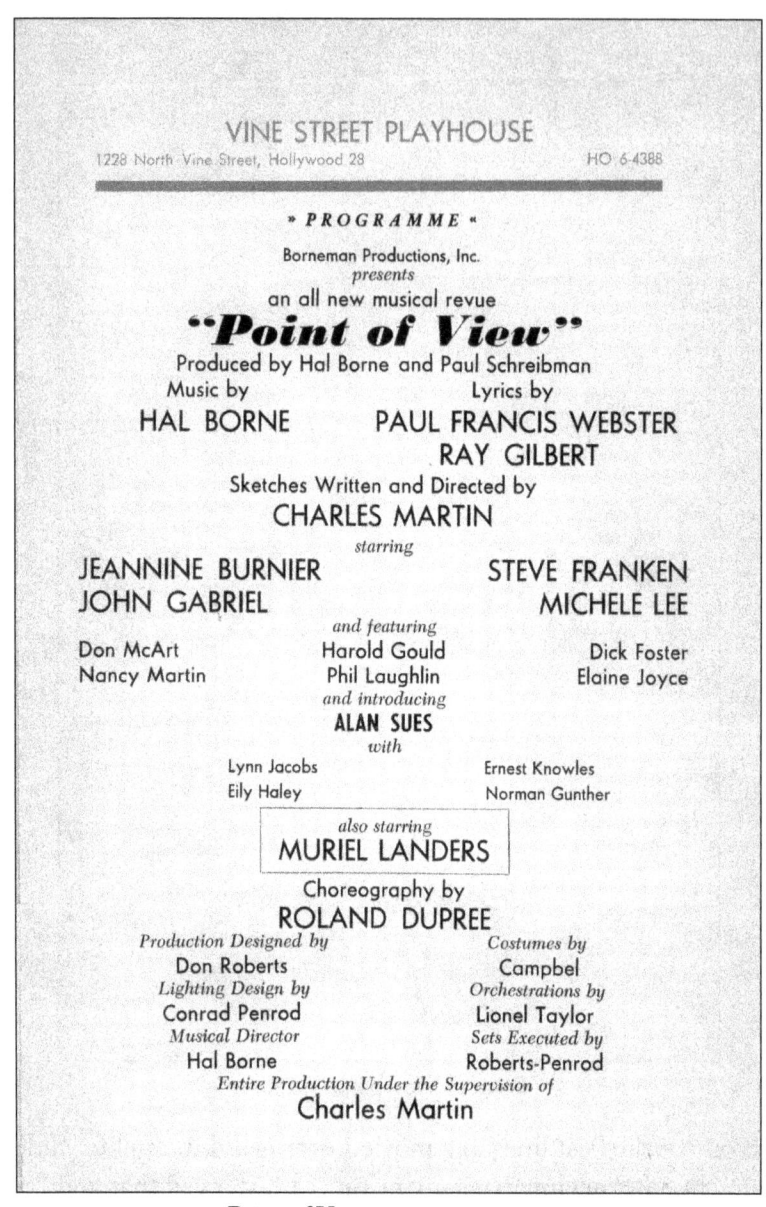

Point of View *programme*, 1961.

Webster and Ray Gilbert, and choreography by Roland Dupree, the cast included Jeannine Burnier, Michelle Lee, John Gabriel, Harold Gould, Elaine Joyce, Phil Laughlin, and Steve Franken.

Alan was featured in several production numbers in the show including, "The Genius," "A Crisis in Hollywood," "At the Movies Revisited," "Effie's Night," "Off Guard," "At Home with the Borgias," and "A Night With Tennessee Williams," all written by Charles Martin. Alan's solo number was called, "Man's Best Friend."

John L. Scott reviewed the show for the *Los Angeles Times* on October 23, 1961. He wrote, "Fine individual and ensemble dancing, a couple of songs with commercial possibilities, so-so singing, and comedy sketches that range from excellent to expendable… that's the story on *Point of View*. After some pruning and tightening, the production should click. Charles Martin's comedy sketches brought mixed reaction from the opening night crowd. Best is "Effie's Night," a hilarious take-off on *This is Your Life* in which funny Jeannine Burnier and Alan Sues costar. There are some fine individual performances in *Point of View*. Steve Franken, a fey comic, scores, and Alan Sues amuses in "Man's Best Friend.""

Alan was happy with the success of the show, and inspired by some of the young, creative performers he worked with. He edited some of his sketches from *Point of View* into a stand-up act, and appeared with his co-star Jeannine Burnier at Ye Little Club in Beverly Hills. The experience gave him a new sense of confidence. "We had a tight, slick act," Alan said. "Jeannine had done a lot of standup and later wrote for *The Sonny & Cher Show*. We stayed at the club for weeks.

"Intimate spots like Ye Little Club were great to try out material. That place was narrow as a bowling alley and the stage was at the far end. The bathroom was behind the stage, so if someone had to go, they'd walk through our spotlight and walk to the back. We could hear them flush the toilet, and then they'd walk back through our spotlight back to their seat. If it was a big beer crowd, they'd be up and down so much I'd get dizzy with the choppy spotlight. Classy joint."

Act 2
Scene 1

1962–1968 "What's a Laugh-In*?"*

In January 1962, Alan was cast in a prestigious production of Shakespeare's *Measure for Measure* directed by John Houseman for the UCLA Theater Group. At that time, the Theater Group was the only professional theater company in the country performing regularly within a university structure. "I got the part because Houseman's wife, Joan, was an actress and she was in *The Days of the Dancing*, and he came to see our show," Alan recalled.

In its third year, the Theater Group decided to produce an Elizabethan classic. "The board chose *Measure*," John Houseman wrote in his book *Final Dress*, "which I presented in a reduced version. I found this dark Shakespearean comedy more difficult to cast among Hollywood actors than our previous, more realistic productions. But, I managed to assemble an interesting cast. I used Virgil Thompson's beguiling score. Our setting was designed and painted by a young California artist, Paul Mathison."

The rarely performed comedy opened on January 15 at UCLA's Schoenberg Hall and ran for twenty-four performances. The large cast included Mariette Hartley, Geoffrey Horne, Marty Ingels, Dan O'Herlihy, Alan Napier, and newlyweds Paula Prentiss and Richard Benjamin.

When he was first cast in the play, Alan met another married couple on the verge of a different kind of stardom. Fashion photographer William Claxton appeared as an extra playing the role of a pimp. His wife, model Peggy Moffitt, played the part of a gum-chewing prostitute. "I was drawn to Peggy like a magnet," Alan said. "She was beautiful and stylish and had a sharp tongue, and she became a super model."

James Bridges, Alan's friend from the Carousel Bar and the author of *The Days of the Dancing*, was Houseman's assistant stage manager, and also played a small role in the production.

Alan found Houseman to be intelligent, codgy and humorless. "But up until then, he was the best director I ever worked with. He had no secret agenda. He was patient. His instincts were razor sharp. Whenever he met anyone, he twitched his nose like he was sniffing them out."

Philip K. Scheuer reviewed the play for the *Los Angeles Times* on January 19, 1962. "Shakespeareans as well as Theater Group regulars should be wending their way happily to Schoenberg Hall between now and February 7, for this university-extension company and director John Houseman have now afforded them the opportunity to see and hear the Bard's seldom-performed *Measure for Measure*. The Theater Group has updated it to the 19th century, Wiener-schnitzeled and Arthur Schnitzlered it all over and given it a suggestion of *The Threepenny Opera*. At UCLA *Measure for Measure* has style, élan and sparkle, and its players—more than 20 principals—are as good as it deserves . . . scoring as buffoons are Jacques Aubuchon, Arthur Malet and Alan Sues."

After *Measure for Measure* closed on February 7, months passed before Alan found work again. As was often the case, when left with little to do creatively, Alan withdrew and fought feelings of depression. "Whenever things were lousy and I was feeling depressed, I'd eat. I used food as a solace. I always took professional rejection personally, and I'd let things people had said to me hurt my feelings. I guess many people do that. Anyway, I was out of work in Hollywood, and getting fatter by the minute."

"Alan was always on a diet," Jerry recalled. "One day we wrestled over a quart of ice cream that actually flew out my kitchen window. He was so outraged, he left in a huff."

His weight was just one more aspect of his self image that tormented him. "Whenever I got a job, I had to go on a diet. I think dieting is the cruelest thing. Unless I'm down to a grape a day, I blow up. I hate being fat. I would give up getting banged in a minute if I could really eat all the time. There is nothing in my life that is pleasant about eating. I've been on all kinds of diets. The long, slow, painful ones and crash diets where I've had to hang on to things I've been so dizzy.

"When I'm fat, I'm guilty. When I'm dieting, I'm miserable. You can really get sick. You put your finger down your throat a lot. They tell you if you go on a diet, it is to prepare yourself for a life-long diet. But there is no such thing as a life-long diet. You don't have a diet as a way of life. How could you walk by a bakery? Your whole life changes. And a rum cake can do it.

"I think one of the greatest tragedies in life is when you've slowly but steadily let yourself go. And that's the time you meet someone

Measure for Measure, *1962*.

that you think is really great. You decide to go whole hog and you get out your smart black suit and tie. You get all showered and shaved, but you avoid the mirror in the bathroom completely—doing all sorts of tricks like just looking at yourself from your neck up. You never let your eyes wander to that big gut hanging there swaying. And all of sudden, you go to put on your black pants and they just go a little above your knees."

To make matters worse, Alan suffered from insomnia, and developed a sleep disorder that caused him to fall asleep while he was driving the car. Even though he regularly visited his psychiatrist, he struggled to maintain a sense of balance in his life. Jerry tried to get him out of his apartment to socialize as often as he could. Keith Rockwell, who owned the Purple Onion in San Francisco, opened a club in Hollywood called The Capri. Charles Pierce enjoyed a long engagement at The Capri, and Alan frequently spent evenings with Charles after the show. "No one could make me laugh like Charles," Alan said.

"Alan was very private with his feelings and emotions," Jerry recalled. "Sometimes I thought he was seeing the psychiatrist just to have someone listen to him who didn't judge him. He didn't open up to me very much.

"He was funny and loved to laugh," Jerry explained, "but there was always an undercurrent of something being slightly off. His happiness was only on the surface. At the same time, he was so uncomfortable in his own skin. He was lonely, too. He never had a boyfriend that I recall in all those years. He dated some guy for a couple of weeks at the most. Then he would decide there was something wrong with each one.

"He didn't talk much about his parents, but he was close to his brother. And his brother accepted his sexuality. He was the only person in his family who knew Alan was homosexual. Even though Alan was in his thirties, he seemed afraid of his parents. He was always seeking their love and acceptance. They never helped him, and he never understood why they treated him like that."

Other than appearing as a bit player in a couple of episodes of the situation comedy *Dennis the Menace*, and doing a few television commercials, Alan's acting opportunities were few until he was cast in a comedic revue in late summer that would recharge his show business career.

Wild Wicked World was conceived by Paul Mazursky and his writing partner, three-hundred-pound funny-man Larry Tucker. Originally asked to take over the Los Angeles production of Chicago's

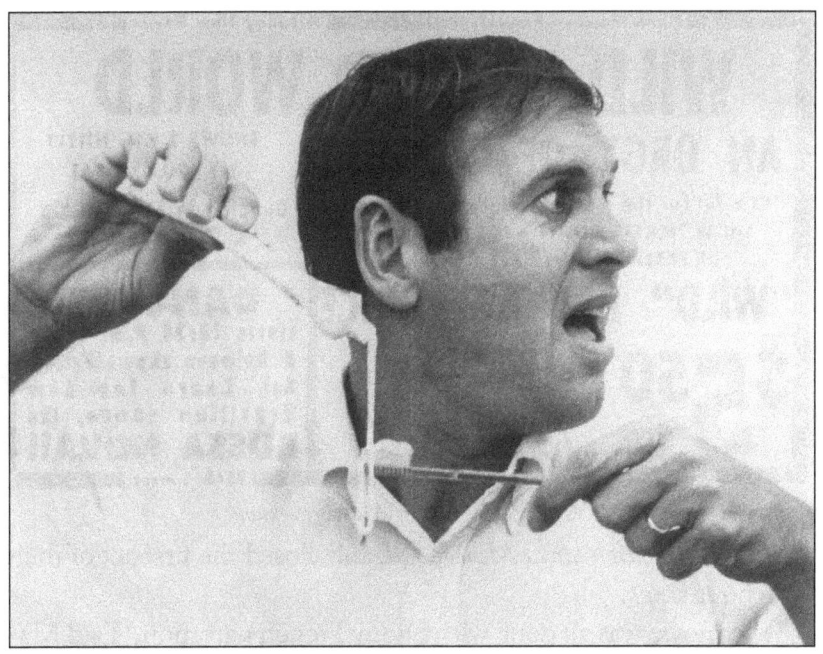
One of Alan's print commercials.

Second City, they turned it into a less successful revue called *Third City*. Mazursky and Tucker wanted to add fresh material to the new show and began to utilize improvisational sketches. "We wanted more laughs, less brain," Mazursky recalled. "Alan was funny in a zany, frantic sort of way. He had good ideas even though they didn't usually have anything to do with what we were doing. He *could* make me laugh. Part of his delivery was this look of complete panic on his face. But it wasn't an act, I think he was having panic attacks all the time. And he always thought he sucked."

"I met Alan when I was cast in *Wild Wicked World*," Joyce Van Patten recalled. "The first section of the show was a collection of sketches we all wrote. I had a great bit set in a prison with Alan. Ellsworth Millburn was our pianist and composer, and he played us off between skits. The second half of the show was all improv. We took suggestions and ideas from the audience and improvised a sketch or song. That type of show was very popular then."

Last Year at Malibu was a short comedic film directed and photographed by actor Vic Morrow. Written by and starring the cast of *Wild Wicked World*, the film was a take-off of the then-popular

Wild Wicked World *advertisement.*

French film *Last Year at Marienbad*, and closed the first act of their two-hour show.

"The movie was all done with phony French narration," Paul Mazursky recalled in an interview. "There was a little bit of piano behind it. And then you see people in tuxedos standing on the beach next to the water. A beautiful looking woman is trying to light her cigarette, but the wind keeps blowing it out. As she's doing it, a three hundred and fifty pound guy in a bathing suit is coming out of the water. It's Larry. He's got seaweed all over his body. He crawls up to them and goes under her legs and out of the sand comes two dummy puppets. Then you see me coming down a hill holding a cross."

Wild Wicked World opened on October 28, 1962, at Gene Norman's Interlude Club at 8568 Sunset Boulevard. Norman, a record producer, impresario, and the founder of GNP Crescendo Records, also owned the Crescendo, a larger venue that featured artists including Louis Armstrong, Count Basie, Lenny Bruce, Don Rickles and Bob Newhart. Most recording and cabaret stars appeared at Norman's clubs in the 1950s and 1960s.

Wild Wicked World was a smash. On November 1, Frank Mulcahy wrote in the *Los Angeles Times*, "It's a pity that the phrase 'milestone in entertainment history' along with the word 'genius' has been so loosely used in the past that when an occasion arises in which the phrase or the word can be aptly applied, it has lost some of the luster. Nevertheless, it must be said that *Wild Wicked World*, a brilliant new revue being presented twice nightly at the Interlude Theater Restaurant, is indeed a real milestone in the art of sophisticated entertainment. The resounding success of the show is, of course, due to the artistry of five young and extremely talented performers: Alan Sues, Joyce Van Patten, Larry Tucker, Elizabeth Shaw and Paul Mazursky.

"The show itself is a little difficult to describe as every performance differs in many ways from the preceding one. This holds true not only for each day but for the two nightly performances. For the main part of the show is improvised to suit the events of the day—always brilliantly, it might be added. The inventiveness and spontaneity of these performers is almost unbelievable."

Daily Variety reviewed the show on October 30, 1962. "Directed and essentially packaged by Paul Mazursky and Larry Tucker of *Third City*, it has the satirical spark and freshness as well as spontaneous informality that lends itself to such presentations. Performers including the directors, Alan Sues, Elizabeth Shaw and Joyce Van Patten, are bright actor-comedians. Sues, Tucker and Miss Van Patten get the greater share of material and deliver well."

Alan recalled, "The only thing we talked about backstage was where to get our suits cleaned, who had the worst body odor, and where and what we were going to eat. Were we going to eat downstairs at the Crescendo or upstairs in the Interlude? Who was going to have salad, and who would sit with who? Are we having hamburgers? Medium or rare? It was the dullest dialogue I've ever heard in my life. I guess we were saving it all for the stage."

The spontaneity and quick-thinking required by improvisational performance gave Alan a perfect opportunity to exercise a skill he thought he possessed but rarely had the chance to explore. "I was always nervous," Alan explained, "but I liked the freedom to express my own sense of humor without being weighed down by a script. Instead of trying to remember funny lines and when and how to deliver them, I could just *let go*, and it was terrific. The audience was involved, too, and that could be interesting."

Alan was so enthused by the positive reviews and standing-room-only crowds that he decided to hire a publicist named Helen Kauffman. "She was a go-getter," he recalled. "She planted fake stories about me in every trade paper in town. I had to stop reading it because I got depressed that I didn't have enough time to get all those things done. She was a good publicist. She did everything, except post wanted posters of me on telephone poles. She got me a good piece in the *Los Angeles Times*."

"A good solid acting background is the healthiest basis for any aspect of theater," Alan told the *Times*. He said he purposely wrote his own material, got involved in directorial activities, as well as set and costume designing. "A comedian must have the sensitivity to respond to the audience and know how to please them—an actor knows what body movement, facial expressions and voice projection is best to get a characterization across."

Alan was elated when he was offered the leading role in an English film comedy. The *Los Angeles Times* reported the news on November 21, "Alan Sues will make his film debut this spring in *The Glass Heart*, an original screenplay by F. L. Abouret. Gordon, Ltd., will produce for Associated British in London."

John Sues married his second wife, Yvonne, in January 1963. Pete and Alice arranged the ceremony and reception at the legendary Alisal Ranch in Santa Maria, just a few miles from their own home in Solvang. The Ranch had a storied past that included being the site of Clark Gable's marriage to Lady Sylvia Ashley in 1949. The ten-thousand acre resort provided a lake, a golf course, tennis courts, a winery, a dude ranch, and hundreds of riding trails for its guests. The accommodations often drew Hollywood celebrities and politicos.

"It was John's *second* wedding," Alan recalled, "and compared to my one and only wedding to Phyllis, which got us *nothing* from my parents, John got the first-class treatment. No doubt about it. We were flown to Santa Barbara for the party, and it was caviar and champagne from morning till night. For some reason, my father seemed to be in a hurry, though. After the ceremony, he said, 'Okay, let's get this show on the road.' Before the luncheon, there was a cocktail hour and my father rushed us through that. He complained about the service and the food all during lunch, and then, in the middle of cutting the cake, he said, 'Well, I guess that wraps it up. We've got to get going.' Finally, I said, 'Do you have another appointment to go to?' My father said, 'Is that supposed to be funny? Do you think you're onstage? This is your brother's day. It's all about him!' I said to John, 'Jesus, thank God he's not going on your honeymoon with you.'"

Wild Wicked World closed on January 22, 1963. Ten days later, Alan was appearing with Edie Adams in Las Vegas. Edie was a Tony Award-winning chanteuse and comedienne who had been professionally partnered on television with her husband, comic genius Ernie Kovacs. With a wink and a wiggle, she also famously impersonated Marilyn Monroe and Mae West. Edie's engagement at the Riviera Hotel was a professional comeback of sorts following her husband's tragic death in a car accident a year earlier.

Edie had seen *Wild Wicked World* and found the performers to be as zany as Kovacs. They all auditioned for her in her Beverly Hills home, with Edie stepping into Joyce Van Patten's roles.

On February 5, *Daily Variety* reported, "Edie Adams' new romp will develop into one of the Strip's most pleasant attractions. An avant garde comedy trio billed as The Munchkins (Alan Sues, Paul Mazursky, and Larry Tucker) is woven into the act, and at times is joined by Miss Adams. Some of the humor will go over the heads of all but the hippies, but basically the ideas and presentation are very funny."

Edie Adams loved Alan. "She told me I reminded her of Kovacs," Alan said, "and that was great. I told her she reminded me of Edie Adams." When Alan took the stage, he looked out at the audience and said, "It's like being in Alaska—so much white fox!" The show ran for three, sold-out weeks, but The Munchkins did not.

"I met George Schlatter when he was producing Edie's act," Alan said. "He hated Paul and Larry and me. We got fired before the end of the run, and George brought in a comedy team called Rowan and Martin to replace us on the bill."

Schlatter concurred. "They stunk," he said. "They were awful. But there was something about Alan, a nervous sort of franticness that was funny. He stayed in my head."

1963 was a busy year of hits and misses for Alan. Plans to produce the previously announced film *The Glass Heart* were scuttled, as were plans by Doubleday to publish Alan's memoirs, *Dial M for Mother*, and an "off-color book about juvenile delinquents" which was a collection of some of his nightclub jokes.

But on March 16, Alan reported to work at MGM Studios to film a role in the comedy *The Wheeler Dealers*. Arthur Hiller directed the feature, which starred Lee Remick and James Garner. Alan had a small role and worked for several days.

While Alan was working on *The Wheeler Dealers*, the entertainment trade papers reported that he had formed his own production company. The first project was a film he had written called *For Laughs*. Initially, Millie Perkins and Scott Marlowe were tapped for the film. Alan's friend, Frank Bunetta, was set to direct the low budget comedy. Bunetta had directed Jackie Gleason, Red Skelton and Sid Caesar on television, and seemed well suited to work with Alan. The project was eventually scrapped when financing could not be arranged.

Alan then hired Ellsworth Millburn, the pianist from *Wild Wicked World*, to arrange special material for his new nightclub act. He also worked with comic actor Larry Hovis on a few skits. Hovis, who soon found success as one of the stars of *Hogan's Heroes* and later worked on the pilot episode of *Laugh-In*, had worked standup on the college circuit. Alan wanted to inject some topical material into his act. "I still had my props," Alan said, "but I was trying for something more contemporary."

Standup comedy was evolving, and catering to the tastes of a more edgy, politically charged audience. At that time, many comics introduced political commentary and satire into their routines. Alan had never been a politically savvy person, and he was feeling pressure to rework the material he was most comfortable performing.

"In early 1963, I saw Lenny Bruce at a little place on Sunset that was very popular called The Unicorn," Alan recalled. "He threw a couple of verbal *cocksuckers* from the stage and the next thing we knew he was arrested. How do you follow that up?"

In late spring, Alan fulfilled engagements at The Shoreham in Washington, D.C., Amato's Supper Club in Portland, Oregon, the

Olympic Hotel in Seattle, the Hungry i in San Francisco, and the Hacienda Motel in Fresno. Jennifer West, a Theater World Award-winning shapely young actress and perfect comic foil, joined Alan for his engagement at the Thunderbird Hotel in Las Vegas in the early summer. "Every good nightclub had a dumb blonde in the show," Alan said. "That's what *I* was to Jennifer."

After returning to Los Angeles, Alan shot a pilot for CBS-TV called *Witch Doctor*, which never sold. In keeping with the "black magic" theme, in early August he was cast in an episode of *The New Phil Silvers Show* called "Who Do Voo-Doo? Harry Do!" Phil Silvers starred as a hapless factory worker constantly looking for "get-rich-quick" schemes. Alan guest-starred in an episode set in Trinidad that featured Silvers and veteran comic actors Stafford Repp and Burt Mustin, who practiced voo-doo to charm a pretty society girl. "Phil was professionally combative," Alan recalled. "He challenged you to be funny, and he "one-upped" you. He was very self-aware on camera, and had what we called 'look-at-me star turns' when he was working. He had a flash in his eye and a self-satisfied look. He was funny, but you got in trouble if you got in his way."

Later in the summer, Alan played a small role in the film *Move Over, Darling* at 20th Century-Fox. Written by Hal Kanter, and starring Doris Day, Polly Bergen and James Garner, the film was a remake of the 1940s comedy *My Favorite Wife*. The story concerns a man who accidentally finds himself married to two women. The cast had the best comic supporting actors in the business including Thelma Ritter, Don Knotts, Pat Harrington, Jr. and Edgar Buchanan.

"The first day I was on the set," Alan recalled, "a blond girl came over to me and said, 'What's your name?' I said, 'Alan. What's yours?' She smiled and said, 'Doris!' That was the most relaxed set I'd ever been on."

On December 5, 1963, *The Hollywood Reporter* favorably reviewed the film and wrote, "John Astin and Alan Sues are memorable in comedy bits." *Move Over, Darling* premiered on December 25, 1963, and became the sixth biggest moneymaking film of the year.

Jay Ward produced and created cartoons, many of which became television classics, including *Rocky & Bullwinkle*, *Dudley Do-Right* and *George of the Jungle*. Along with his creative partner Bill Scott, Ward wanted to transition into live-action television comedy. In October 1963, they filmed a one-hour pilot for CBS-TV called *The Nut House*. If sold to the network, the series was intended as a Saturday morning presentation.

Ward engaged many of his cartoon comedy writers including Bob Arbogast, Allan Burns, Jim Critchfield, Lloyd Turner and Emmy winner Chris Hayward, and created a program of short skits, blackout gags, slapstick comedy and funny monologues. Marty Charnin & Mary Rogers and Jim Rusk wrote special musical material. With a definite knack for goofball comedy, Ward cast Alan and some terrific supporting comedy actors including Jane Connell, Jack Fletcher, Fay De Witt, and Jack Sheldon.

The pilot was performed and recorded in Studio 33 at CBS Television City in Los Angeles. Ward worked with a minuscule budget. The single camera was fixed, so the performers scurried in and out of camera range. There were no sound and light effects. At the end of the show, the cast members waved placards bearing their names.

All of the actors appeared in the sketches, which included, "Drop a Bag of Water on a Friend," "Hollywood Marriages," and "Barge on the Nile." Alan played a frenzied pianist in the final sketch called, "Hello Mom! This is Your Son, Alvin," which ended with an out-of-control musical production number.

"There was a script," Alan recalled, "but once we all got rolling the script sort of went out the window. It was shot on a dime in black and white. It was a great cast and there were high hopes for the pilot. It's interesting because that type of show, with the sketches and blackouts and one-liners came along later in the form of *Laugh-In*. They were similar, but *Laugh-In* was more political."

Jane Connell said, "I'm a character actor. I wasn't a classic beauty or a lead. Alan was a character actor, too. Less pressure and more freedom that way. He was a physical comic, manic really, and facially—very expressive. I thought he was a young man with the soul of an old vaudevillian. We had a lot in common. He could really make me laugh. We all had fun, and *Nut House* was the appropriate title! It looked freewheeling, but it was rehearsed. The concept of the show – the format especially – was so ahead of its time. I made some lifelong friends on that show. And Alan was a very sweet man."

The Twilight Zone was a critically acclaimed anthology series hosted by author Rod Serling. Alan was cast as Wilfred Harper, Jr. in an episode titled, "The Masks." "Odd casting," Alan said, "since the character was a college age guy and I was thirty-eight at the time." The thirty-minute teleplay, written by Serling, concerns a wealthy dying man who invites his greedy, unpleasant heirs to a Mardi Gras party where they must wear specially prepared "Cajun" masks that reveal their "true" selves, or be cut from his will. *The Twilight Zone* was filmed at MGM Studios in Culver City for CBS network broadcast. Milton Selzer, Virginia Gregg and Brooke Hayward completed the cast.

The episode was directed by veteran film actress Ida Lupino, who had established herself as one of the few female directors in Hollywood.

"'Call me mother,' she said, in this deep, gravelly voice," Alan recalled. "And I thought, *Oh, I'm in for it now*. She made everyone jump on the set. She had an assistant beside her all the time and she'd snap her fingers and say, 'Cigarette!' and the guy would scramble and put a cigarette between her fingers. Then she'd snap and say, 'Light!' and the guy would hurry to light it. Then she'd snap and say, 'Drink!' and the guy would actually pour her a drink and hand it to her. She was a tough broad.

"She had a funny way of directing. She said, 'If you feel it—just go ahead and do it. I can edit it out later.' Not a lot of security there. So I got started and she yelled out, 'Oh, my God! You're not going to do it like *that* are you?' It was quite a week."

"The Masks" aired several months later on March 20, 1964, and was one of the highest rated episodes of *The Twilight Zone*.

Alan moved to a small apartment at 8262 Norton Avenue in West Hollywood in 1964. "After all those years of living in cheap apartments with white walls—a new coat every so often to cover the dirt and the cracks—the first thing I did was paint my walls a lovely shade of chocolate brown. Of course, it just made me hungry."

Alan as Wilfred Harper Jr. in the classic TV series The Twilight Zone.

His friend, Jerry Jackson, had moved into the adjacent building the year before. It took Alan some time getting used to the peaceful quietude compared to living on very busy Fairfax Avenue across the street from Fairfax High School.

"In the morning," Jerry recalled, "Alan would throw open his window and scream out, 'Hello, Los Angeles! What the fuck do you have for me today!' One day we were walking on the street in front of his place and a woman walking her dog came up and asked, 'Are you the nut that yells out the window?'"

Alan was guarded with his personal friendships. He had a few close friends with whom he remained loyal and considerate, but he did his best to keep them at arm's length.

Jerry said, "I think it was all about fear. He was afraid of being vulnerable, but he really was a nice guy at heart."

"I used to live near Alan on Fairfax," Joyce Van Patten recalled. "I got sick and for a time they thought it might be cancer. While I was in the hospital, Alan came over to my house and talked with my son Casey, and assured him everything would be all right, and then he took it upon himself to redecorate my bedroom while I was away. He painted the room a bright yellow and made a yellow gingham canopy for my bed and matching pillow covers. And yellow flowers on the nightstand. It was so cheery when I got home. I never forgot his thoughtfulness."

It was important for an actor to be ambitious to remain in the game. Alan relied on his agent for casting calls, and was never comfortable networking with others in the business. "I was not a professional socializer," he explained. "I wasn't comfortable with that, and I didn't get it. Some people I knew could be on the phone asking for work all day with producers and casting agents. I could never do that."

As it happened, many of Alan's friends and associates ended up working on *The Danny Kaye Show*. The hour-long variety show aired on CBS. Jerry Jackson danced with the Tony Charmoli Dancers on the popular variety series. Both Paul Mazursky and Larry Tucker worked as occasional writers for Kaye, and Joyce Van Patten was hired as a regular performer on the program.

"They auditioned actors to work with Danny Kaye for the second season," Alan explained. "But he was too much for me. He was hateful, and conniving. He took an instant dislike to me. I'd never experienced that sort of problem before. He could smile but he could turn on a dime. He was paranoid, and I thought he felt very threatened. He couldn't stand anyone else getting a laugh, and he'd cut you off in mid-sentence. I'm sure the frustration he felt, the denial, overpowered him. He was gay and it was one of the worst kept secrets in town. He was toxic, and I didn't want to be around him. I didn't completely understand it at the time, but later when I thought about it, I took another look at myself. Maybe we saw something in each other that we didn't like, but no one should ever make you feel ashamed of who you are, and that's what I came away with from him."

Larry Gelbart was a production consultant for the show, and was involved in the selection of talent. "I reluctantly auditioned for a spot on the show because I needed the job," Alan said, "but it showed. Everyone encouraged me, but I wasn't any good. Harvey Korman got the job."

Alan didn't want to work with Paul Mazursky or Larry Tucker, either. "They had their own little *boys* club," Alan said. "And Paul reminded me of my father. A pompous ass."

"I think Alan was intimidated by Paul and Larry," Joyce explained. "They were funny, but pretty cold in their approach to work. Alan played around a lot. Paul and Larry wrote and produced *Bob and Carol and Ted and Alice*, and *I Love You, Alice B. Toklas!* They were insiders and worked their connections, but Alan didn't really operate that way."

Alan got an audition to work with Lucille Ball on her hit series *The Lucy Show*, and reported to the Desilu Studios for his appointment. "I got there and was sitting in the office waiting to see Lucy," Alan said. "I was supposed to audition for her in her private office. I was sitting with her secretary there, and we could hear Lucy screaming and swearing on the telephone. It was unbelievable. I hadn't heard that type of language since I was in the service. 'Fuck you, and fuck that . . .' It was deafening and pretty damn intimidating, too. So I was finally called in to see the Queen of Television Comedy.

"By the time I got in there, I was shaking like a leaf. I sat in front of her giant desk. There were Emmy Awards and other awards lined up in a row on the desk and you had to look through them to see her. She was so intense, she could stare a hole through you. She was smoking, waving the cigarette around, and said in a gravelly voice, 'Well, I hear you're funny. Say something funny.' Believe me, funny was the last thing on my mind. Harvey Korman got that job, too."

The Americanization of Emily, written by Paddy Chayefsky and directed by Arthur Hiller, was a feature film comedy about World War II antics in England and France. The black and white film starred Julie Andrews, James Garner, Melvyn Douglas and James Coburn. Alan, his old friend Steve Franken, and Keenan Wynn were cast as sailors.

Garner played an officer who is assigned to the front on D-Day to film the Naval engineers disabling mines in the water at Normandy Beach. The scene was filmed at Mandalay Beach in Oxnard, California, in January 1964. "It was my first time on location," Alan recalled. "We were there for two weeks and it rained every goddamn day. They tried to film the scene in Esther Williams's swimming pool set at MGM, but it didn't work. My character was carrying a heavy movie camera and I was standing in the freezing cold water. My teeth were chattering and I could hardly speak. James Garner asked me what was wrong. He was wearing a wet suit under his costume, but wardrobe had run out and I was just wearing my underwear under the uniform. Garner stopped everything and said, 'I'm not working till he gets a wet suit'. And I got a wet suit.

"Arthur Hiller shot the scene of us coming ashore several different ways. The water was rough and I watched other boats with extras turn over and dump them in the water. I was worried and I stood up to see what was going on and the director yelled out, 'Alan, what are you doing?' I said, 'If I'm going, I'm going out with a song,' and I started to sing *Ave Maria*. Hiller didn't get it."

On March 19, Alan guest-starred on the television series, *Here's Edie*. The highlight of the program was the re-worked "prison sketch" that Alan had written earlier and performed with Joyce Van Patten in *Wild Wicked World*. Playing an inmate dressed in prison stripes, Alan is visited by his sexy wife, played by Edie. She tells him she's working on getting him sprung, but he objects and throws a fit because he doesn't want to leave the clink. He's just been cast as the lead in the prison musical.

"I loved to make Edie laugh," Alan said. "I improvised most of it, and I was so animated and exasperated, Edie kept breaking up. She couldn't stop laughing, and I'd just push it to the limit. She had

Soupy, Edie and Alan on Here's Edie.

tears in her eyes and she'd look around for help from the director, who just let me run with it. We had fun."

In a nod to The Beatles, a newly-popular singing group, Edie, Soupy Sales and Alan wore mop-top wigs and matching suits with peg-leg pants and appeared as The Roaches. In the skit, they were interviewed during a recording session while they chanted, "You ain't gonna step on me!"

Alan then appeared in an unsold pilot for a game show called *Pop the Question*, which was based on the popular radio game show. For several months, he worked on a comedic screenplay he had titled *Fan Male*, about a crazy fan who stalks his favorite star. "We got close with that with a few independent producers," Alan recalled, "but we couldn't make it work. The material was funny, though, and I used bits of it later in clubs. I'd come on the stage carrying flowers, and candy and presents for my favorite star. I had a stack of fan letters I wrote, and I read them onstage."

In the summer, he was cast as a guest star on *Many Happy Returns* in an episode called, "The Shoplifter." Filmed at MGM, the situation comedy was created and written by the talented humorist Parke Levy. *Many Happy Returns* concerned the goings-on in the complaint department of Krockmeyer's Department Store. Alan played the part of a shoplifter who returns stolen merchandise to the store because the items he stole didn't fit. His scenes with the series star, veteran comic actor John McGiver, were hilarious. "It was impossible to crack him up," Alan said. "I tried, but he just pinched his lips, sucked his cheeks in and squinted at me, and I broke up. I loved working with him."

An interesting and potentially lucrative opportunity presented itself to Alan that summer. Los Angeles disc jockey Jimmy O'Neill created a show about rock 'n roll music geared toward teenagers. The original pilot was rejected by ABC. Intrigued by the concept, executive producer David Sontag redeveloped the show. A new pilot starring singer Sam Cooke, and including Alan who provided comic relief, was shot in July. On September 16, 1964, this new pilot aired as the premiere episode of *Shindig*. Along with Cooke, the Everly Brothers and the Righteous Brothers sang on the show. Alan did a comedy bit imitating Liberace.

Singing sensations Johnny Rivers, Jody Miller and the Righteous Brothers appeared on the second episode which aired on September 23. Alan performed a comedy routine, and sang a duet of "Ain't She Sweet?" with singer Jerry Cole.

Although *Shindig* was a quick hit with ratings, Alan's material appeared old fashioned and decidedly out of step with the teenage zeitgeist of the show. What he had hoped would develop into a long-term engagement ended after his second appearance.

"I called myself the king of pilots," Alan said. "I made so many unsold pilots. Some never even got seen." In January 1965, he shot a pilot called *Legal Eagle* for Goodson-Todman Productions at CBS in Hollywood. Alan and Will Hutchins played young lawyers in a firm presided over by veteran character actors Charles Lane and Cecil Kellaway. "*I* never even saw that one."

He filmed a small role in the Doris Day feature, *Do Not Disturb*, and he was cast in an episode of Anne Francis's popular series *Honey West*. Produced by Aaron Spelling, *Honey West* concerned the adventures of a beautiful female detective with 007-style gadgets.

"She had a radio in her lipstick, wore leopard-print body stockings and had a pet ocelot," Alan recalled. "I had to get on *that* show!" Anne Francis's distinct beauty was punctuated by a prominent beauty mark near her mouth. "I had the makeup man put the same beauty mark on my face," Alan said. "We didn't tell anyone and I just walked on the set, and they loved it. Anne fell on the floor laughing. And they kept it in the show."

Alan appeared on *Art Linkletter's Hollywood Talent Scouts*, a summer variety series on CBS, and then signed on for a situation comedy pilot about war. "I had high hopes for that," he said, "so many good people behind it." *Off We Go* was written by Emmy and Oscar nominee Bob Kaufman. Directors Guild of America Award-winner Don Weis was at the helm. The pilot never sold, but aired as an episode of *Vacation Playhouse* a year later on September 5, 1966.

In the fall, Alan was cast in a new Western series, *The Wild, Wild West*. Within weeks, the series about a special agent working for President Grant in the untamed American West became a ratings bonanza for CBS. Alan played the part of one of the murderous Dawson Brothers in "The Night of the Fatal Trap" which aired on December 24, 1965.

In one scene, Alan and his on-screen brothers dash out of a bank and are supposed to jump on horses to make their escape. "One of the actors had never been on a horse in his life," Alan recalled. "I wasn't that good myself, which was embarrassing since my father bred horses. But I was most concerned about my Stetson hat. It didn't fit and I was sure it would fly off my head when we dashed out the door. So the scene begins and I put my hand on my hat as I run out and I yell, 'Taxi!'

"There wasn't one laugh on the set. Then the director boomed out, 'When you're finished with what you're doing, will you go back inside and wait for my direction.'"

Casting Alan in dramatic roles became increasingly problematic. His over-the-top delivery and quick-witted improvisational skills didn't play well in a tightly scripted environment. He was more suited for live performance. His broad, comic style was the result of more than a decade performing on stage to a live audience. He

The Mad Show *in Los Angeles, 1966.*

was much less interested in playing to a camera. It got him into professional hot water time and again.

"I really wanted to do dramatic roles," Alan said, "but I guess the comedy was a more natural fit. It's hard not to get pigeon-holed by casting agents."

More than a decade earlier, *Mad Magazine* had introduced a new kind of "adult" humor in the form of a periodical that ridiculed the absurd aspects of American culture and politics. In late 1965, Larry

Siegel and Stan Hart, regular contributors to the magazine, created a stage revue based on *Mad*. Mary Rodgers, best known as the composer of the hit musical *Once Upon A Mattress*, wrote the music for Siegel's and Hart's lyrics. *The Mad Show* opened off-Broadway on January 9, 1966, and was an unexpected hit.

A West Coast version of the show opened on April 21, 1966, at P.J.'s Theater, a small, cabaret-style room that adjoined P.J.'s night club in West Hollywood. Alan was cast in the musical comedy, and joined original cast members Jo Anne Worley, Paul Sand and Carol Morley. On April 23, Cecil Smith wrote in the *Los Angeles Times*, "From the howling laughter and prolonged applause that greeted its opening, *The Mad Show* may be as big a hit here as it is in New York. It is completely without pretensions. It is neither camp, pop, op, mod or belonging to any other abbreviated craze. It is simply straightforward fun played by five refreshing young performers at a furious pace like a sea-wind blowing through the smog. Fidgety Paul Sand and brassy Jo Anne Worley are joined by rubber-faced Alan Sues, all of whom seemed to be having as much fun with the show as the audience."

"I first met Alan during rehearsals for *The Mad Show* in Los Angeles," Jo Anne Worley recalled. "While Alan was rehearsing and learning lines, I'd sit nearby and tease him and say, 'Bo-ring…This is bo-ring…' That's when I started using that line.

"It's hard to explain what *funny* is," Jo Anne said, "but Alan made me laugh, it's as simple as that. It's about being true to yourself, true to the moment, and trusting the moment. You have to be fearless and spontaneous. Alan had good instincts and timing, and he was always true to himself."

Paul Sand recalled, "We sat next to each other at the makeup table. We played games and pretended an incredible innocence about things. He had an amazing wit energy. He didn't have the compulsive qualities of a standup comic, and he didn't tell jokes, but he had a wonderful and wise way of looking at things. It's funny but preview audiences hated the show. We thought we were finished, but the critics loved it, and then the audiences did, too."

"*The Mad Show* is probably the freshest, funniest, wildest, nuttiest, wittiest, most delightful revue to splash itself onto a Los Angeles

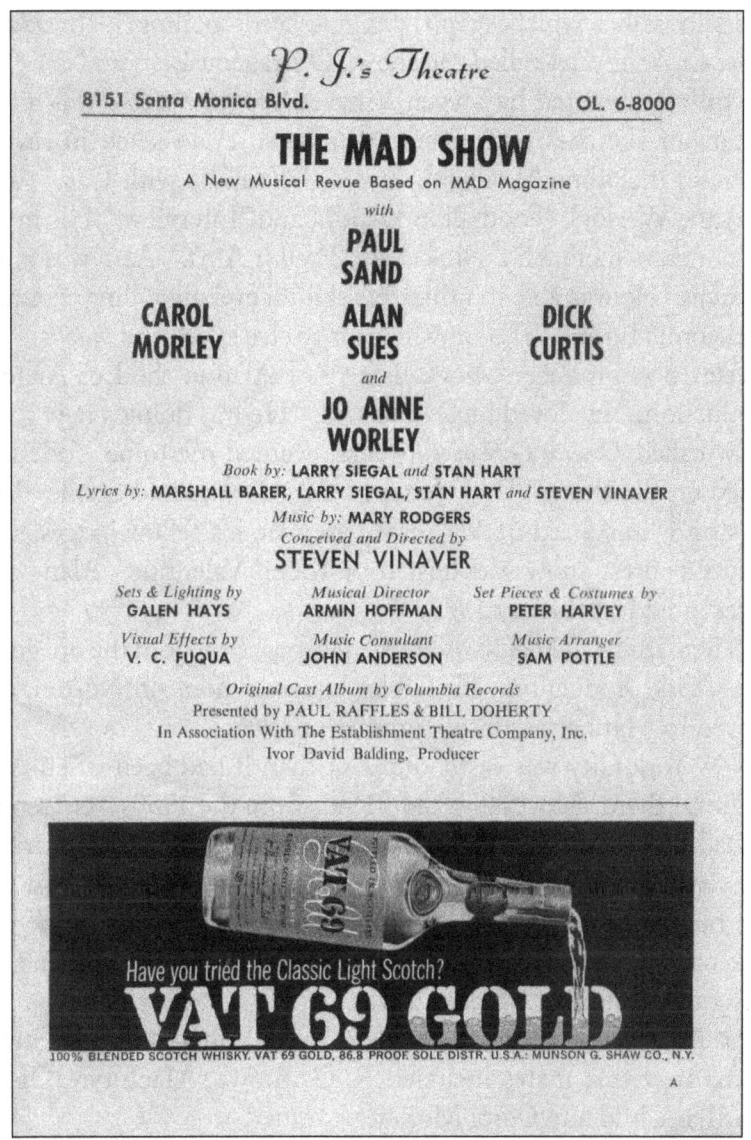

The Mad Show, *Los Angeles cast, 1966.*

stage. You shouldn't miss it!" wrote the *Los Angeles Herald-Examiner*. *Daily Variety* reported, "*The Mad Show* is one of the funniest spreads of nonsensical buffoonery since the cat got caught on the fly paper." The *Hollywood Reporter* wrote, "The dilliest dumplins ever concocted for the way-ins and way-outs. Crisp, clever and contagious, this merry mix-up is studded with flippancies, spoofs and silly sallies which keep the giggle kettle boiling." The *Hollywood Citizen News* called the show, "Outrageously funny."

Skillfully directed by Steven Vinaver, *The Mad Show* was a collection of sketches and musical numbers. Alan acted in several sketches including "Academy Awards," "Handle with Care" (with Jo Anne Worley), "Football in Depth," and "Interview." His musical numbers included a solo called, "Well it Ain't." Alan was in his element. He was able to utilize his skillful eyeball-rolling, exasperated comic timing. The show ran for twelve successful weeks.

Television producer Chuck Barris saw Alan in the Los Angeles production. "He loved me," Alan said. "He was doing a new game show called *Dream Girl of 1967*. He wanted me to be a celebrity judge on the show." Davy Jones of *The Monkees* and Stanley Livingston who starred in *My Three Sons* were his fellow judges. The beauty contest show was hosted by Karen Valentine. Alan's episodes aired in February 1967.

When *The Mad Show* closed, Alan was asked to join the on-going New York production. He sublet his apartment on Norton, and moved to Manhattan in the summer of 1966.

New York City was vastly different than it had been when Alan last lived there. Most of his old friends from the 1950s were retired or had moved away. Still, he loved the vibrant, theatrical spirit of the city. "I was walking down the street," Alan recalled, "and this guy bumped into me and said in a low voice, 'Now, go home and jack off.' I turned around and he was bumping into other guys along the sidewalk. I thought, *Oh, it's great to be back home*."

The Mad Show played at the New Theater on 154 E. 54th Street. Alan's new cast mates included R. G. Brown, MacIntyre Dixon, Marilyn Child and Carol Morley.

"I enjoyed him a lot," MacIntyre Dixon said. "He was a lot of fun, a big tease. He had a very funny mind. He thought differently and had his own perspective. He was very intense, not a relaxed comic. My wife loved him. I bought her a set of Amelia Earhart luggage and he really ran with that. He questioned my motives and warned my wife. Very funny. She thought he was a deeply funny man."

Alan stayed with the New York production of *The Mad Show* until it closed after 861 performances in September 1967. He returned to play a dozen special holiday matinees between December 22 and December 31.

A few months later, Alan accompanied his friend and *Mad Show* co-star R. G. Brown to an audition for Oscar nominee Elaine May who was preparing a new play. "He read, and I was sitting waiting for him, and Elaine May came over and asked me what I did. I told her I was in *The Mad Show* with my friend who just read. She said, 'Why don't you read for this?' I said I wasn't there to read, just support my friend. But I read and when I got home I got a call that I got the part. And my friend never talked to me again."

Directed by Arthur Penn, who was riding a wave of adulation for his film *Bonnie and Clyde*, *A Matter of Position* was the opening offering at the Berkshire Theatre Festival in Stockbridge, Massachusetts. The play, written by and starring May, was about the ups and downs of a troubled marriage. May and Russell Horton starred as the harried married couple.

Alan co-starred with Obie Award-winning comic actor James Coco, Graham Jarvis and Doris Roberts. "Elaine was no walk in the park," Alan said, "but she had a great sense of comedy. It wasn't just about the lines, or timing which is instinctual but technical, it was about *attitude*. And she had *attitude*. She smoked cigars. That says it all."

Alan played the role of a telephone repairman. "We did these improvs, but how much can you improv on a telephone repairman? The only one of mine they really liked was, 'Oh, have I had a day today! I mean, I *really* had a day. I just installed twenty-two princess phones in the YMCA.'"

James Coco and Alan developed a close friendship. To save money, they shared a small house near the theater and enjoyed their time together eating and drinking. "Jimmy was a great cook," Alan recalled, "and I had become a pretty good cook myself. He was terrific. I loved him and loved working with him. He was bumbling and had the best sense of timing. He knew which words were funny *sounding* and hit them right on the head. His whole body shook when he laughed. And he was generous to his fellow actors, which is rare. He let you get laughs and actually helped you get laughs by his reactions. He was just great."

Plans to bring *A Matter of Position* to Broadway were abandoned when the critics trounced the production, calling it "leaden and unfocused." However, the supporting actors were glowingly reviewed. On July 6, 1968, the *Monitor* in Boston wrote, "The best in the play are the three supporting characters, including Alan Sues as a slack-mouthed, awed telephone repairman who turns out to be a religious fanatic. Just standing there watching the chaos swirling about him, he is funnier than the play itself."

After a month in Massachusetts, Alan returned to Manhattan. He was disappointed with the failure of *A Matter of Position*, and pondered his next move. Elaine May was quite impressed with Alan's humor. She wrote a show for Mort Sahl called "An Evening with Mort Sahl." Alan said, "She wrote a great part for me. It was the best chance I'd ever had. Elaine's a great writer and the part was geared to show me off. Well, we started rehearsing and every day Sahl failed to show up. Elaine would say, 'Don't worry, kids. He'll be around sometime soon!' Well, the night of the show we were all set to go on and Elaine came in and said, 'I'm sorry. It looks like there won't be an evening with Mort Sahl because we can't find him.' There went the show. You can't have an evening with Mort Sahl without Mort Sahl."

James Coco's positive perspective buoyed Alan's blues. "Jimmy was very supportive," Alan recalled. "He was a great listener. We were both out of a job, and I was discouraged, but he wasn't concerned at all. If anyone could find the silver lining, he could. He had a knack for finding something funny in anything tragic."

Along with comic talent, Coco had many things in common with Alan. They both suffered from depression. They were both lonely and found solace in food and drink. "We both loved to eat. I could eat a lot, but I never saw anyone in my life who could eat more than Jimmy. He'd order multiple entrees at a restaurant, and eat them all!

"We laughed about our struggles, and he was the most encouraging person I'd ever worked with. He told me, 'Don't worry. Everything will work out. You'll *make* it work out.' He was a very thoughtful guy."

Coco's optimism would soon prove correct. "With no work, there was more time to eat," Alan said. "It was so bleak that I probably would have gotten big enough to play left tackle for the Los Angeles Rams—but I got a shot." One day Alan ran into George Schlatter walking on Madison Avenue, and they had lunch at the Regency Hotel. "George told me about a television show he was doing called *Laugh-In*," Alan recalled. "I'd been working and had never heard of it. I asked him, 'What's a *Laugh-In*?'

"We sat in front of the piano player who was playing "The Whiffenpoof Song" and I couldn't hear everything George was saying, so I kept saying 'yes, yes,' and I guess I said I'd do the show. A couple of days later, my agent called me and said, 'Gee, you're getting pretty good money for this and I didn't even know you knew George Schlatter!'"

Act 2
Scene 2

1968–1972 "Camp is great, but I don't think it's necessary to lay very heavy on the homo jokes."

Laugh-In originally aired as a one-time NBC television special on September 9, 1967. The show was such a success that the network brought it back as a series which premiered on January 22, 1968. The one-hour sketch-comedy program, created by Digby Wolfe and George Schlatter, was influenced by vaudeville and burlesque humor and especially the free-wheeling anything-goes comedy style of Olsen and Johnson, whose blackout gags and "drum-roll corny" jokes inspired many comic acts. The innovative comedy of Ernie Kovacs and the topical satire of the British program *That Was the Week That Was* (written for the BBC by Digby Wolfe), were also strong influences.

Wolfe explained, "*Laugh-In* was basically a joke show and the first of the as-fast-as-that shows. The laughter was very timely, and people were ready by that time to dispense with the long sketches and variety format that had evolved over the years with a singer, guest acrobat and so on. It was the 1960s, the show was irreverent and the time was right for it."

Many years later, George Schlatter explained *Laugh-In* for Susan King of the *Los Angeles Times*. "There was a bubbling kind of political unrest into which the Beatles, Lenny Bruce and *Laugh-In* came and kind of focused the attention on how crazy it all was. What we put into the mainstream was a new kind of brevity and the recognition of the shrinking attention span of the television viewer who had never before been challenged. Into that came Dan Rowan and Dick Martin, who had a very well-known, very successful nightclub act, and this group of performers who were not comics. They were young character actors, really."

Dan Rowan and Dick Martin were tapped by NBC to host the show. Rowan played the straight man to Dick Martin's comic foil. The title of the program was a play on words that described the hippie culture of the 1960s; "love-in," "be-in," and "sit-in." The original cast of "crazies" included Ruth Buzzi, Judy Carne, Henry Gibson, Goldie Hawn, Arte Johnson, Gary Owens, and Jo Anne Worley. Alan joined the *Laugh-In* cast in the second season, which premiered on September 16, 1968.

"I had my own parking space at the studio," Alan said. "There was a big sign that read LAUGH-IN: ALAN SUES. I was driving an old truck, surrounded by Corvettes and Porsches, but I had my own space! The NBC studio was a mass of long, wide corridors. *Laugh-In* production took up a lot of space....makeup rooms, rehearsal rooms and the room where we got together for our first table read each week. The only small things were the dressing rooms. Mine was tiny with a brown couch. It looked like an outhouse. Of course, Dick and Dan had an enormous dressing room with a masseur and a bar.

"NBC was busy then. *Laugh-In*, the local news, *The Tonight Show* when it was taping in Los Angeles, game shows and situation comedies that came and went. The place wasn't too big for George's voice, though. You could hear him bellow no matter where you were in the building. He was invisible while we worked. He sat in a booth upstairs and watched everything, and every now and then you'd hear his voice out of nowhere. I think he was deliberately hiding from us. If he was in the studio with us, and driving us crazy, we'd team up against him and chase him out. It was a little game. I think he enjoyed the chase a little too much.

"I liked rehearsing. One rehearsal room had a piano. We'd all stand around and sing and laugh. Billy Barnes was the musical director. He wrote special musical material. Billy was really brilliant. We had new songs every week. And the cue card guys were the cutest. They'd write the most vulgar words on the cue cards and we'd be reading along and say the words before we realized what we were saying. They thought that was hilarious. It's the simple things that get you at the end of a fourteen-hour day."

"The first thing I did on the show was a scene shot on location at the beach," Alan recalled. "Goldie and Judy were talking when I arrived for the shot, and they looked at me like I was chopped liver. I had to wear a bathing suit. I was obese. I watched the dailies and when I saw my stomach go across the screen—and it went on and on and on—all I could think of was, 'Oh, please make it stop'. But they were all laughing. Everyone but me."

The cast worked with an inspired group of comedy writers including George Schlatter, Jack Mendelsohn, Phil Hahn, Chris Bearde, Digby Wolfe and Paul Keyes. Within weeks of the show's second season premiere, the Monday night comedy became the

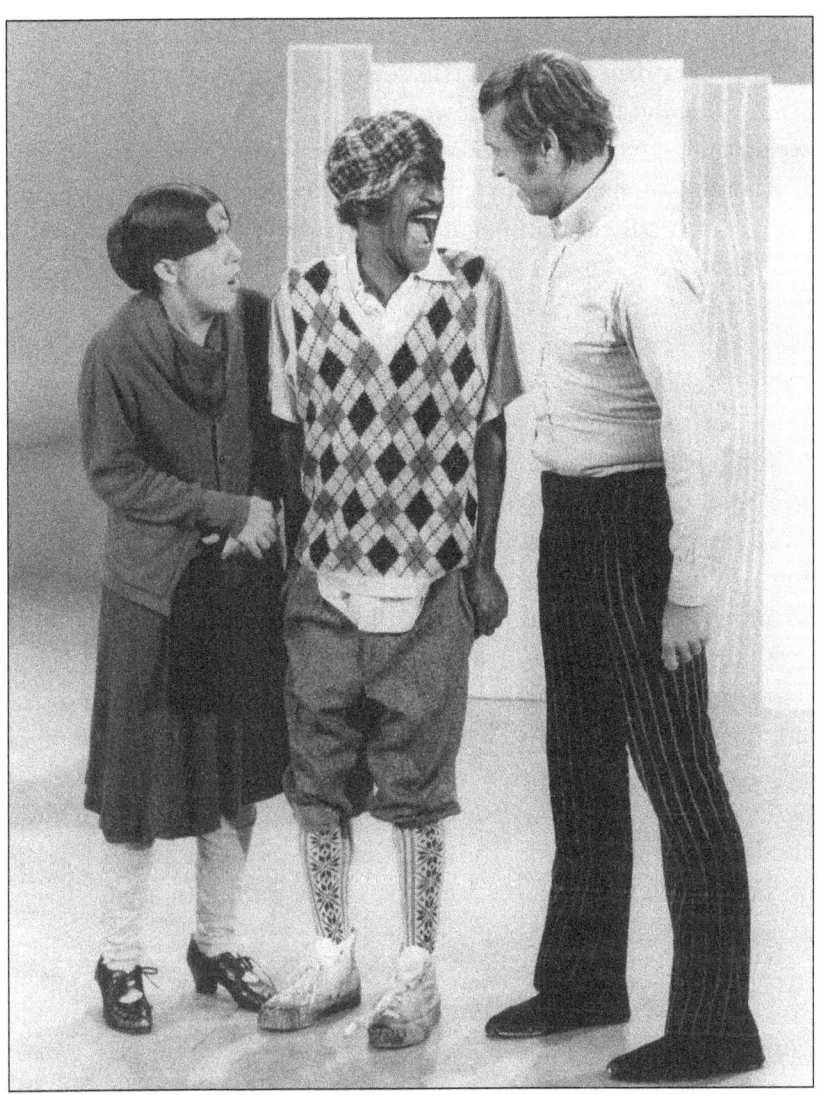

Ruth Buzzi, Sammy Davis Jr. and Alan on Laugh-In.

number one program on television with an average share of 31.8. "It all happened so fast," Alan recalled. "People recognized me everywhere I went. When you're in people's living rooms each week, the fans think they actually *know* you. They followed me, and they knocked on my apartment door. I was shocked."

Laugh-In was touted as an anti-establishment, counter-culture show. The format consisted of fast-paced editing with a "hip" music track and a psychedelic, colorful "Summer of Love" design. While tuxedo-clad Rowan and Martin seemed a bit anachronistic to the young demographic, the "flower-power" zeitgeist and the bikini-wearing go-go dancing girls with flowers painted on their undulating bodies were enough to appeal to young liberals and hippie kids. Schlatter originally campaigned for Digby Wolfe as head writer, but Rowan and Martin vetoed the idea and brought in Paul Keyes who had written *The Dean Martin Show*. Keyes' right-wing political views and long-time friendship with then-Republican Presidential candidate Richard Nixon would set the tone for any political satire the show presented.

Keyes was responsible for securing the appearance of Nixon on the September 16 season premiere episode, two months before the 1968 Presidential election. "All Nixon had to do was say, 'Sock it to me!'" Alan said. "But it took him hours to get one line right. Not surprising that he couldn't get his Presidency right."

At that time, *Laugh-In* was the most popular and talked about show on television. One in three American homes tuned in to the national love-in. It was a Monday night ritual, and the topic of "water-cooler conversation" every Tuesday. George Schlatter described the program as a "tsunami of youth and vitality." Alan loved the job, and his co-stars. The attention was as overwhelming as the work-load, but the $750 a week paycheck gave him a new-found sense of security.

"We had a 240 page script every week," Alan recalled. "We all were working five day weeks, except Rowan and Martin who would come in on Wednesday and work a few hours. Taping day for everyone else was very long, we could work till four or five in the morning. It was exhausting. I'd never worked that hard in my life."

Alan told Cynthia Lowry of the Associated Press, "The show is not for beginners. Our average shooting time is two days. The pace is so fast that most of us have to be our own directors—the director is pretty well occupied just setting up camera angles."

With very few exceptions, the cast worked happily and respectfully together. "We were all funny and creative," Alan said, "and you were never in competition with anybody else, just yourself. We didn't have a live audience. This show was made in the editing

Chelsea Brown, Byron Gilliam, Connie Stevens, Ruth Buzzi, and Alan on Laugh-In.

room. We had so much material each week, more than we needed. If the writers gave you something you didn't think was funny, you'd ad-lib to make it funny because you knew if you didn't, with all the stuff being taped and only an hour of television time to fill up, you

Publicity portrait from Laugh-In.

wouldn't make the final cut if you weren't funnier than the next guy. I think the main success of the show was George Schlatter, who managed to trick the censors. And he put a lot of talented people together on one show."

Like any artistic endeavor, the creation of a successful television show is a combination of skillful craft and serendipity. "*Laugh-In* was a series of accidents," George Schlatter explained. "Alan was one of my favorite accidents. I knew how funny he could be and he was perfect for the show. He was a free spirit, a real upper. When he walked on the set, everybody felt happy. He could be outrageous and irreverent, and he was a genuine 'love child.' He'd scold me when I got tough with the cast."

Despite the show's claim to be a show business bastion of counterculture, within months censorship became a problem. Paul Keyes, with the support of Rowan and Martin, was both sensitive and protective toward newly-elected President Richard Nixon. Keyes nixed jokes poking fun at the President, and toned down anti-Vietnam War sentiment on the show. "It seemed to defeat the purpose of satire on the show," Alan said. "And since Nixon, Republicans, and the war were all off limits, it limited the subjects we could joke about. The women's movement was powerful and politically correct then. We couldn't make jokes about African-Americans, either. That left one sub-group that seemed to be a prime and acceptable target. Homosexuals. And Keyes loved to make jokes about homosexuals."

The recurring characters that Alan became best known for on the show included a free-wheeling, and perpetually hung-over children's show host named, Uncle Al the Kiddies' Pal. Dressed like a clown on hallucinogenic drugs, he would drunkenly mumble into the camera, "Oh, Uncle Al had a little too much medicine last night, boys and girls."

The other fan-favorite character was Big Al, an effeminate, limp-wristed sportscaster who would ring a small bell on his desk and breathily exclaim, "Oh...my tinkle...my tinkle...I looove my little tinkle..." He also played an eyeball-rolling, rotund Tarzan who was literally tickled by the apes, and Julius Child, the flaming (literally and figuratively) version of television chef, Julia Child. "It didn't take long for me to see," Alan said, "that any and every queer character they could think of would be thrown at me. Even if I was playing a football player, a cop or a cowboy, I was directed to play it as queer as could be. At first, even *I* thought it was funny."

The Big Al character was Alan's favorite. "The sports announcers thought it was very funny," Alan said. "Frank Gifford even wrote and asked for an autographed picture of Big Al. So did Vin Scully. My

Alan Sues as "Big Al" on Laugh-In.

conception for the character was that he was absolutely confused. He's a guy whose uncle owns the newspaper but there wasn't any room for Big Al in the drama department—where he belonged—so he became, of all things, a sports announcer. As Big Al, I rolled my eyes and tinkled a little bell and acted pretty silly. Every sports term he read suddenly had a double meaning. I sort of understood this guy who found himself trapped in the wrong place."

"*The Rowan & Martin Show*" in Las Vegas.

Alan's eyeball-rolling, exasperated characterizations became hugely popular with the public. So effective was his role-playing that his free-spirited, unselfconscious flamboyance became part of the lexicon of *Laugh-In*. The television phenomenon made him a star.

Alan filmed an episode of *The Doris Day Show* in the fall. He played the part of a country-bumpkin relative of the farmhand who worked for Day's television character on the episode titled, "The Relatives," broadcast on December 31, 1968. "It was interesting," Alan said. "I had worked with Doris Day in a couple of films. I was a minor player, but now, with *Laugh-In* going great guns, I was treated very differently on her set. Her show struggled in the ratings and they actually brought me on in a guest-shot to help *her* out. The times were a-changing."

During the December holiday break from filming *Laugh-In*, Alan and fellow cast mates Ruth Buzzi, Jo Anne Worley and Dave Madden joined Rowan and Martin in a live *Laugh-In* stage show at the Copa Room in the Sands Hotel in Las Vegas. "No rest for us," Alan said. "It was unbelievable. We were a sensation. The place was packed at every show. Standing room only. We were the hottest ticket in town. I called my parents after our New Year's Eve Show in Vegas. They had moved again and now were living in San Rafael, California. They always knew how to take the wind out of my sails. They told me they hadn't even seen *Laugh-In*."

As early as January 1969, stories began to circulate in the press about trouble and in-fighting on the *Laugh-In* set. "We felt it,"

Alan said, 'but I denied it in the press. We all did." At the time, Alan told a reporter, "The rumors I keep hearing are a crock. I find it quite unusual that people who are together as much as we are get along so well. For example, Goldie Hawn may be innocent, but she's a smart one and she's very quick to soothe over hurt feelings among the rest of us. Jo Anne is the power of positive thinking. I've never heard her talk about anybody. Ruth is extremely neat. She wakes up at night, dusts off her husband and goes back to sleep. Judy Carne is the original 'doom' girl. I saw her knocked out cold twice. She's a great, fabulous gal. Artie is serious and a loner."

Alan later recalled, "We got along well, but the pace of the work really wore us all down. For me, comedy is attitude and timing. If I think something is funny, which is subjective, the next thing I do is apply timing. Timing is difficult to learn. People who have it are instinctive, not trained. Television kills timing. It sacrifices quality for speed, which is fatal. We tried our best on the show, but considering the cost of producing a television program, it's almost impossible to indulge actors with the time they really need to work."

Alan appeared with *Laugh-In* co-star Ruth Buzzi on the February 1, 1969, broadcast of the popular variety show *Hollywood Palace*. They recreated the prison sketch Alan had written and earlier performed with Edie Adams.

"I just simply loved him," Ruth Buzzi said. "I loved working with him because he was truly hilarious. He was even funnier off camera."

"All we had to do was look at each other," Alan said about Ruth, "and we'd laugh."

Ruth explained, "Alan was a smart comic actor. I think it's all about how a person looks at himself. And how honest and smart he is. You have to really look at yourself from afar, and be objective about who you are. Alan could see the value in his craziness, and he knew how to test an audience. He could feel an audience out very well and know where to go with material. The fact is, of all the funny men I worked with, Alan was the funniest guy to rehearse with. He was quick thinking and with great instincts. Once during a rehearsal on *Laugh-In*, he had me laughing so hard I collapsed on the floor and rolled into a ball. I just couldn't stop laughing. And he wasn't on script.

Ruth, Alan and James Coco on Laugh-In.

"Alan talked about his mother and father a lot," Ruth added. "His parents weren't very good to him, but he could tell stories and make you laugh and cry at the same time. We were all so individual and different on *Laugh-In*, but I think Alan was the funniest of all of us. The show was great for me because I love sketch comedy. It's my favorite type of comedy and Alan loved it, too. He always wanted to make it better and with his ad-libbing, it always *was* better."

In the spring, Alan and the *Laugh-In* cast recorded an album of the some of the show's comedy sketches which was released later that year. Not surprisingly, the Reprise Records LP titled "Laugh-In '69" (rs6335) was a best-seller. Soon, *Laugh-In* merchandise—including lunch boxes, thermoses, collector cards, comic books, paperback books, puzzles, pins, stickers, posters, paper dolls, body paint kits, coloring books, T-shirts, and toys flooded the market. "All the junk they manufactured made more money than the show," Alan said, "and the cast didn't earn a penny from it."

Huddled in his little NBC dressing room between filming and rehearsing, Alan wrote a screenplay for a silent comedy for himself, Ruth and Jo Anne. The story concerned a bum who worships a movie star and his clumsy attempts to get her autograph. "It was a tough sell," Alan said," but with the attention we got from *Laugh-In*, I thought we would do it. I'm a great admirer of the French actor/director Jacques Tati, and it was sort of in his style. I came close when Columbia optioned it, but it never got made."

Alan's brother and sister-in-law had moved to San Luis Obispo and opened a restaurant called The Cigar Factory. When he could, Alan drove to the small town to visit them and "get away from the noise." John always welcomed his brother, and besides, Alan's visits were good for business.

At the time, John said, "Alan's been in show business for twenty-two years. Mostly starving. He has had so many really crummy breaks. Like in plays. Either he would be fantastic and the play would flop, or the play would be great and he would flop. He's always lived an unbelievable life. Very funny things happen to him. I would like to be a free-thinker like he is, and he sort of looks on me as the cornerstone. I'm staid and establishment, and then there's my brother, rolling his eyes and ringing that little bell."

Alan's unwillingness to "self-edit" put his brother on the spot, however. In an interview with Dick Kleiner for the *San Luis Obispo County Telegram-Tribune*, Alan said, "John was always a food freak. He loves all kinds of food. So he opened a gourmet restaurant. Only trouble is he opened it up in San Luis Obispo. The people here aren't gourmets. They only want to eat steak. It's frustrating for my brother."

John's wife Yvonne recalled, "Alan thought he was being funny, but he nearly closed us down with that interview. He made it sound like we were surrounded by backwater dimwits. People in town boycotted us!"

When *Laugh-In* went on hiatus in the spring of 1969, the live stage version, which was introduced months earlier in Las Vegas, hit the road. "The cast members really didn't know what being number one on television was all about until we flew to San Diego for an appearance and there were seven thousand people waiting for us at the airport. It was like a rock concert! I thought a big political figure had arrived at the same time. I remember talking to Ruth just before that San Diego show and saying, 'Ruth, I don't think I know this material.' Ruth told me not to worry. 'There's gonna be two hundred people in the audience, tops. If you screw up, who cares?' Well, there were fourteen thousand people in that opening night audience!"

"The Rowan and Martin Show" opened at the Anaheim Convention Center on May 31, 1969. "The place was mobbed," Alan said. "We could barely get into the building without getting crushed. At the time, we didn't really know how popular the show was. We did shows with up to twenty-eight thousand people who came to see us. It was like a Rolling Stones concert." The show toured for the next six weeks, ending up at the O'Keefe Center in Toronto, Canada. "We were a huge hit in Canada," Alan said. "Being on the road was rough, but we were earning more money making personal appearances than we did each week on TV."

Alan spoke about his most popular characterization, Big Al, to the Canadian press. "First of all, I don't know a thing about sports. It's funny I got to do this. I've never been one to go to the games. Now I get sent tickets all the time. I even got asked to appear at both the USC and UCLA rallies before a football game. I couldn't make either, though, because I was out of town. I was at a basketball game to watch Wilt Chamberlain ... the, uh, what's the name of the team ... the Lakers? And everybody around me starts asking, 'Hey, Big Al! What's the score going to be tonight?' What would *I* say? I didn't know a *thing* about it. So I started saying, 'Rain.'"

"Big Al," Alan Sues.

He was asked if it bothered him that he was most associated with his Big Al character. "No, any recognition is great," he said. "I do other things on the show. You can always change your image. I'm glad I'm indentified with sports instead of, say, pot. Pot isn't my bag, whereas sports might be. It's made me more interested, anyway. In another town, I was doing a Big Al skit. I said, 'And Grabowski serves to his own end.' What I meant was to say, 'passes to his own end.' And when I said, 'Boy, I sure do love sports,' it broke everybody up. It came out accidentally."

While the cast made personal appearances and the bickering writers prepared for the new television season, word continued to leak to the press about more and more trouble behind the scenes. "When you're on top," Alan shrugged, "they want to drag you down."

Paul Keyes' control of the joke content on the show was quickly becoming apparent to the viewing public and especially to television critics. On June 13, 1969, Cecil Smith wrote about the show in his entertainment column for the *Los Angeles Times*. He felt some of the material was "dated," and actually suggested that the new television variety show *Hee-Haw*—*Laugh-In*'s country-style copycat—was more topical. About *Laugh-in*, Smith wrote, "I felt the homosexual jokes beat out the college militancy jokes in the final tally."

The idea to satirize homosexual men (homosexual women were rarely the brunt of television network jokes) was not plucked from thin air. Gay liberation became a national conversation following the so-called "Stonewall Rebellion" on June 28, 1969. On that hot summer night, a gathering of gay bar patrons and drag queens at the Stonewall Inn in Manhattan's Greenwich Village reached the breaking point when police entered the bar and began to harass the customers. For the first time, the patrons fought back and attacked the New York vice officers—chasing them out of the venerable gay bar. The huge media focus on the incident became a cause célèbre among outspoken liberals and young gays everywhere. "Gay Power to Gay People" and "Gay Liberation" protests were staged nationwide. The press, politicians, political pundits and educators became embroiled in the hot topic of gay sexual liberation.

"Don't piss off a drag queen," Alan joked. "They might be wearing falsies, but those girls are scrappers!"

While still writing for *Laugh-In*, Paul Keyes became more and more involved with Richard Nixon's image-makers. Chris Bearde was a talented writer on the *Laugh-In* staff. He managed to work as a mediator between the increasingly conservative and strident Keyes and the liberal, out-spoken George Schlatter. The pressure took its toll and began to boil over onto the stage at NBC Studios in Burbank. Bearde wanted an early release from his contract, which both Keyes and Schlatter fought for fear tensions would escalate if he was no longer working behind the scenes to keep peace. As feared, as soon as Bearde left to write for *The Andy Williams Show* in the summer of 1969, both factions on the *Laugh-In* set dug in their belligerent heels. The material suffered because of the feuding, and so did the television ratings.

"Chris was very funny. I liked him a lot," Alan said. "We were sorry to see him go. I did a bit for him for the premiere of Andy's new show." On the first episode of *The Andy Williams Show*, Alan carried a gigantic glass slipper and chased an elephant dressed as Cinderella across the stage behind the oblivious singer. Alan yelled out, "I'm getting a six-pack!"

"*That* my parents saw," Alan exclaimed. "My mother called and said, 'I can't figure it out. What are you doing with an elephant? You *never* liked animals.'"

As the "writer wars" continued behind the scenes, *Laugh-In* was still the number one show on television, though the network rating had fallen from 31.8 to 26.3. "We all just went to work," Alan said, "and we were sort of shielded from all the bullshit going on in the office."

On September 9, 1969, NBC threw a block party in "beautiful downtown Burbank" to celebrate the show's season premiere. A city mall was turned into a *Laugh-In* party zone and Rowan and Martin and the cast performed for an invited crowd. A public buffet dinner followed. "They all showed up for the free food," Alan laughed. "Actually, so did I."

Every major star bandied for a cameo spot on *Laugh-In*. Even Elizabeth Taylor and Richard Burton tried to arrange their schedule to appear on the show. Alan said, "It never worked out. There was no place to dock their yacht."

For many veteran performers, a guest-shot or even cameo appearance on the program could reinvigorate an otherwise forgotten career. "Jack Lemmon was the first to come on and make it the thing to do," Alan said. "Of course, those guest appearances only took them about forty-five minutes to do. They didn't have to stand around all day. We had great guests from Jack Benny to Rita Hayworth to Kirk Douglas to Greer Garson to Tiny Tim," Alan recalled. "I loved working with Sammy Davis Jr., Orson Welles, Sally Field, Eve Arden, Debbie Reynolds, Carol Channing, Truman Capote and Peter Lawford. My least favorite was Raquel

Alan with Peter Lawford on Laugh-In.

Welch who wouldn't come out of her dressing room and kept us waiting for hours."

Alan recalled, "My all-time favorite never made it on the show. I loved Mae West. I actually met her at a press party with some of the other cast members and they urged me to go over and talk her into coming on the show. She was a little tiny thing and she looked me over like I was a dust ball. But she was very nice, and she knew *Laugh-In*. She said she'd seen it! But it didn't take me long to realize this was one woman who couldn't be talked into anything."

One of Alan's favorite anecdotes about the show concerned the time veteran singer Kate Smith appeared as a guest. "She was playing some kind of royalty, like a queen or something," he recalled. "She was wearing a big hoop skirt and Henry Gibson and I played her footmen. We were taping the scene and she was awful. She was too serious and she just didn't get it at all. George Schlatter took Henry and me aside and told us to kid around with her to loosen her up. I said, 'How am I supposed to do that?' George said, 'Oh, you'll figure it out.' So we tried again. This time when I bowed in front of her I stuck my head up her dress. She grabbed her skirts and ran off yelling. Henry came up to me and asked, 'What did you see up there?' And I said, 'Irving Berlin.' *That* they should have put on the show!"

"I had a great time with Jonathan Winters, too," Alan recalled. In a scene set atop a snowy mountain in the Alps, Winters played the role of the "Swiss soft-cheese tossing champion of the World." Decked out in Swiss lederhosen, Alan's Big Al character was sent to the remote location to interview the champ. "There was a script," Alan explained. "I don't think we used a word of it. I tried, but Jonathan never let a script get in his way. He was a comic genius with turrets. I think we did fifty takes and it was never the same twice. By the time we were done, we had every NBC employee huddling in the shadows. And those janitors know a good joke when they hear one! It was exhausting."

Not all the ridiculous things wound up on film. "On one show, Ruth and I were wired up into the air. The director and producer got into a fight over which way we should go. They decided to settle it after lunch and everybody walked off and left us hanging in the air! Finally, some guy came back and got us down.

"Even though the work was tough and the hours long, it was fun. Very fast and frantic. Makeup and costume changes were always challenging. It was like playing dress-up on a rainy day. For the show with Capote, I changed seventeen times!"

Alan was often paired with Jo Anne Worley during their two years together on *Laugh-In*. "Doing sketch comedy is so fast," Jo Anne explained, "no time to over-think anything. *Laugh-In* was tightly scripted when I was on it. We were encouraged to contribute ideas, and after we shot a scripted sketch, we could add something on our own while we were still in costume if we thought of it. We waited a moment so they could edit, but we were encouraged which was something that doesn't always happen on television. Alan was especially good at that. But he had a problem with his physicality. He couldn't 'throw a punch.' He really hit you. I'd yell when he hit me. He actually hurt me sometimes. There was a sketch we did where he grabs me and throws me on the floor to kiss me and I was yelling, 'Stop! You're really hurting me!'

"Alan was best when he was working off the cuff," Jo Anne added. "He was quick on his feet and worked best without the constraints of a script and the pressure of a filming schedule. For him, the script was just a launching pad, really. He could run with the ball. George Schlatter was a task master, but he was always open to our input. We always over-shot the show. Many things and sketches were recorded for the film library archives, and each year George would edit together an entire show from the existing library of material previously shot that hadn't been used before."

The "writers' war" (then dubbed the worst kept secret in Hollywood) abruptly ended after the fourth episode of the second season was completed. Paul Keyes quit. He told a Hollywood reporter that *Laugh-In* had become "slanted, dirty and vulgar." Not surprisingly, Keyes became a media advisor for President Nixon. At first, the remaining writers re-introduced satirical attacks against the President and his Administration, but after several months an NBC emissary was dispatched from New York to Burbank to tell the *Laugh-In* producers they could no longer make political references of *any* sort in its comedy.

"But the homophobic jokes piled up," Alan explained. "Nobody was watching out for homosexuals. It was open season. And the jokes weren't funny anymore. They told me they were being *topical!* But it's all about presentation. Do you serve it on a shiny platter or a garbage can lid."

On October 13, Alan appeared on *Letters to Laugh-In*, a daytime comedy game show spinoff of *Laugh-In*, hosted by the erudite Gary Owens. Celebrities read jokes written and submitted by audience members. Whoever wrote the funniest joke won a prize. "Alan was a very talented performer who everyone loved having around," Gary Owens recalled. "He was hilarious, and we all enjoyed his stories. He was always funny, even when he wasn't trying to be. He was an upbeat person and he had a little wicked twinkle in his eye. Sometimes you didn't know where he was going with his humor, which was also part of the fun."

A day later, Alan made another memorable appearance on the variety show *Hollywood Palace* hosted by Diana Ross and The Supremes. Sammy Davis Jr. and The Jackson 5 performed on the show. Alan sang "Good Times are Here to Stay" in a large production number with backup dancers. In a very funny skit, Alan played Ross's fluttery butler/photographer/clothing designer. "Michael Jackson was just a little kid," Alan said. "He was very polite and so cute. And he was the most talented kid I ever saw."

Alan and Kaye Ballard joked around on the October 28 broadcast of *Della!*, the short-lived talk show starring Della Reese. "Kaye was terrific," Alan recalled, "and Della Reese was great, but don't get in her way. She had a good show with an improv segment that really worked. Too bad her show didn't."

The Hollywood Squares was an enormously popular television game show on NBC featuring nine celebrities in box-like cubicles stacked like a giant tic-tac-toe board. Most of the "squares" were filled by different guest stars each week. But the center square belonged to the acerbic Paul Lynde, who had become the stand-out star of the weekday game show. Alan appeared on the show for two weeks in November.

"I knew Paul, casually," Alan said. "We ran into each other around town now and then and I saw him in a bar once in awhile. I met him first in New York. He ran hot and cold. He was pleasant, if he was sober, but he couldn't hide an odd air of suspicion when he was around other actors. He was very funny, in a snide way, but it took a mean turn as he juiced up. He was great on that show, but he stiffened up if he thought someone else was getting a bigger laugh."

Joe Namath with "Big Al" on Laugh-In.

In January 1970, Alan published his first book, *Big Al's Sport Scene: Where Big Al Tells It like It Really Isn't*. The hardcover, comedic book was designed and illustrated by Nellie Caroll, an artist who designed costumes for *Laugh-In*. *Big Al's Sport Scene* was a collection of humorous riffs on various sports, as only Big Al could tell them. The book was a big seller, but Alan never saw any profits.

"All that marketing shit was such a scam," Alan said. "It was like pumping gas into someone else's car."

Since Alan and the other cast members were not entitled to share in the *Laugh-In* merchandising income, Alan decided to explore the market on his own. He wrote and provided the voice for a one-minute radio series called "Hickey High" that was syndicated to disc jockeys all over the country. Each episode provided news about Hickey High School and its football team, The Scared Chickens. He also formed a business called "Alan Sues Creations," and created a line of inflatable greeting cards.

Alan got the idea when he attended a birthday party. "I bought a cheap card someplace, and it was just a typical, boring card. I figured what if the cards did something funny, like what if they blew up? Sometimes the only gift you give someone for their birthday is a card, so what if the card was something imaginative and special? It was worth a chance, and worth a laugh."

The cards were manufactured in Los Angeles, and Alan eventually produced thirty-two different cards in the line. The vinyl cards were packaged flat, and blew up into various shapes. The recipient had to blow up the card in order to read each three-dimensional greeting. One card inflated to a small, colorful birthday cake which read, "At your age, you should have only one piece." Another blew up into a flatiron that read, "Don't press your luck!" The messages ranged from the square, "Hot Dog! It's your birthday!" to a then more timely, "If It Turns You On—Do It!" One of the biggest sellers blew up into the form of a silver coin which read, "Happy Birthday from a Big Spender!" The cards were distributed nationally, and sold well for a couple of years. The June 13, 1970, issue of *TV Guide* provided Alan with a great pictorial spread about his inflatable cards called "Inflation Hits the Greeting Card Business."

"Anyway," Alan said, "so many people are full of hot air and I figured they should put it to good use. I'm not really calling these people blowhards, but no one had any trouble blowing up the cards."

Alan's NBC contract permitted him to do other television programs, if time allowed. On February 6, Alan made his first appearance as a guest on *The Tonight Show Starring Johnny Carson*. In mid February, Alan was invited back to *The Hollywood Squares*. Paul

Alan publicity shot from 1971.

Lynde had become embroiled in a contract dispute and was jockeying for more money. During the negotiations, he did not appear on the show. The network thought Alan might make a good "center square" replacement in case no agreement could be reached with the petulant Lynde.

"I went back on the show, and the reason was really to give Paul a scare," Alan said. "I did well before on the show and I did great in the center square for a couple of weeks while Paul was on strike. When Paul saw that I was doing so well, he settled his dispute, and he had me banned from the show for the next couple of years! It certainly didn't endear me to him."

On March 31, Alan was a guest with Tommy Smothers and Rich Little on the popular interview program *The David Frost Show*, and on April 10 appeared with Nancy Wilson on *The Mike Douglas Show*. He then did a comedy bit on the syndicated show, *Playboy After Dark* on May 26. Hosted by *Playboy* magazine founder Hugh Hefner, the show appeared to be set in Hefner's penthouse apartment where he was surrounded by "Playboy Bunnies" and his performing guest stars. "I was *way* out of my element," Alan joked.

"There was a trade-off," Alan explained. "The more popular *Laugh-In* became, the more recognizable we all became and the less privacy we had. I hated it. It was hard to maintain a private life. It's hard for fans to see performers as separate from their roles. TV will do that especially. Fans think you belong to them in some crazy way. I had to go grocery shopping in the middle of the night so I wouldn't get swamped by fans. Once I was squeezing melons in a grocery at three o'clock in the morning and I got a standing ovation from four people in the produce department. I was always looking over my shoulder."

TV Radio Mirror printed a cover story about *Laugh-In* called "Private Love-Ins of the Laugh-In Stars" in the February 1970 issue. Alan had told reporters he "dated" Jo Anne Worley occasionally, which was far from the truth. When Alan was asked about his love life by the reporter, he said, "I don't want to get married again. I'm a great believer in temporary relationships."

"But what could I have said about my love life," Alan later explained. "I couldn't talk about who I was dating, but they always asked me about that. Fortunately I *had been* married, and I could just tell people I was divorced. The publicist loved that idea and told me that would throw reporters off. It all just pissed me off that I was living in the shadows."

In a UPI interview with Hollywood correspondent Vernon Scott, Alan said, "I've been going with two girls simultaneously. I try hard not to mention them to one another. I'm not the type of guy who likes to have his date drop by and fix dinner. Domestic type girls turn me off. I like swingers." He told the television editor of the *Houston Post*, "I think I'll be single for the rest of my life. I can't even make it with pets."

For legal reasons, it was impossible for Alan to talk about his private, romantic life. His NBC contract included a "morals clause," and any public revelation of his sexuality would violate his contract and allow the network to arbitrarily terminate his services. "I didn't want to talk about that stuff, *anyway*," Alan recalled. "It was too invasive and I just wasn't comfortable talking about my private life in public. I talked about my family and told funny stories about growing up, but that was it."

Alan knew if word got out that he was gay, it would be devastating to his career. "My agent told me not to go to gay bars," Alan explained, "and not to go out without a woman on my arm." His agent even arranged for Alan to make an appearance on the popular game show *The Dating Game*. Alan was one of three bachelors seated behind a screen who answered questions posed by a young woman who would ultimately choose—based on their answers alone—one bachelor to accompany her on an arranged date. Only the studio audience and television audience could see the three bachelors. After the requisite questions, Alan was chosen by the contestant.

"We went on a date to a restaurant in town," Alan explained. "We were seated for just a minute when I yelled out, 'I told you not to do that again! Don't pee on my expensive shoes!' The poor girl was mortified, and the entire restaurant was stunned. I gave that girl a date to remember!"

Despite his agent's and many of his peer's warnings, Alan frequented the few gay bars in Los Angeles. "It was a little like an AA meeting," Alan explained, "except everyone was drunk. What happened in the bar, stayed in the bar. There was an unspoken code, like everyone maintains anonymity in an AA meeting. First names only and you don't talk about who was there outside the meeting. Same in the bar world. You'd see people you knew or even worked with there, and you'd have fun, but never speak about it in public. And there was no paparazzi then. No one hanging by the doors waiting to take pictures. You *could* have a personal life, but it was sort of underground."

Updates about the *Laugh-In* stars' love lives did little to quell the news that there was discord on the set of the most popular show on television. The focus had shifted away from the bickering writers to who had "created" the show. Reporter Bill Davidson wrote an expose about the persistent rumors in the March 18, 1970, issue of *TV Guide* in a feature article titled, "What's going on in beautiful downtown Burbank?"

Davidson spent two weeks in cavernous Studio 4 at NBC observing the busy goings-on. Taping had dragged on for twenty-two hours on the first Tuesday he visited. On Wednesday, work began at noon and didn't wrap until two o'clock the next morning. "The cast is becoming testy," he wrote. "Big Al Alan Sues, shedding perspiration from his perch on a ladder during a musical number, growls mincingly at the bearded, indefatigable, omnipresent young executive producer, George Schlatter: 'We're not *machines*, you know.'"

Davidson confirmed the persistent rumor that Rowan and Martin were at odds with George Schlatter and his professional partner, co-producer Ed Friendly. The gist of the argument had to do with who claimed credit for the creation and continued success of the show. The writer tried to defuse the problem by reporting, "I found only the normal blowups and quickly forgotten snarling that afflict any large, unwieldy group of people working on a backbreaking schedule. It's not all sweetness and light. Part of the tension stems from the fact that everyone calls the program *Laugh-In*, instead of *Rowan and Martin's Laugh-In*."

Alan happily returned to the stage during the summer of 1970, starring in the comedy *Something Different* written by Carl Reiner. The story concerns a playwright named Sheldon Nemorov who is writing a play titled *Something Different*. The neurotic Nemorov has an Oedipal complex and can only work if his controlling Jewish mother is present. At first, he tries to get his wife to dress up like his mother. Then, after interviewing an odd assortment of females, he hires a strange woman to do the job. *Something Different* was first produced on Broadway in 1968.

Alan in Something Different.

The two-act comedy opened on June 23 at the Little Theatre on the Square in Sullivan, Illinois. Summer stock audiences embraced Big Al Sues. David Miller reviewed the play on June 24 in the *Decatur Review*. "Sues fits into the mold of a highly eccentric playwright with apparent ease and his temper tantrums are classic. Sues' timing, all important to successful comedy, is near perfect. Known as a successful ad-libber, Sues came through at least once, moaning, 'Oh, I hate this part,' when he was involved in a violent fight scene." The *Champaign News-Gazette* wrote, "Sues sort of plays himself—the way-out, confused ding-a-ling of *Laugh-In* that is—to perfection. And now, having seen his zany performance, it's hard to conceive anyone else as lead in *Something Different*."

"Alan Sues—Big Al fits him remarkably well—uncorked what has to be one of the funniest and most original performances to hit the Little Theatre in quite some time," wrote the *Urbana Courier* on June 25. "Sues tackles the difficult role of the wacky playwright. Sues himself is something different (Oh, is he different) as he portrays the guy with the 'mother thing.' The beauty of the performance is that, with few exceptions, Sues dominates the stage. He has long, straw hair, arms that reach from one side of the stage to the other, a voice that can whine like a baby or rock the theater, face made of rubber that stretches everywhere and a body—well, enough. He is both a sensitive and explosive actor."

Enthusiastic audiences greeted Alan at the Cherry County Playhouse and beyond for the following six weeks. "I loved this play," Alan said. "It was good for me, too. My first big step away from *Laugh-In*, and I felt good about it."

Fans had overwhelmed Alan at the stage door following each performance. "I'd never experienced that working in the theater before," Alan recalled. "When you're working on TV without an audience, you get boxed-in. You're not fully aware of who's watching you until you go out in public. And summer stock audiences are especially enthusiastic. It was fun. Summer stock is rustic, though. I could handle the resident dressing-room mice, but the mosquitoes with four-inch wing spans were too much."

Later that summer, Alan appeared on a few television game shows including *The Game Show* in July, and *It's Your Bet* on August 17. He was a guest on *The Dick Cavett Show* on July 14 with Harry Belafonte, and returned to *The David Frost Show* on August 20 with Zsa Zsa Gabor. On August 21, he visited *The Virginia Graham Show*.

"I really had it with my lack of privacy," Alan said. "I had to leave my apartment and find something more secure. I found a little Spanish-style house built in 1927 with wood-beamed ceilings in West Hollywood. Right after the *Laugh-In* season premiere [on

September 28, 1970], I went to George and asked him about it, and he said, 'Don't do it! You don't know how long this job will last. Don't tie yourself down!' It was one of the few times I *didn't* listen to George. I bought the house on Dorrington Avenue for $32,000, and the first thing I did was build a wall around it. I'd lived in one room apartments forever. I had the idea in my head that artists always live in one-room apartments. Well, forget it!"

"You know you've arrived when people have to guess who you are," Alan joked. In October, he was the "Mystery Guest" on the popular quiz show, *What's My Line?* On November 5, he appeared on the NBC hit variety television program, *The Dean Martin Show*. Like all the *Laugh-In* stars, Alan commanded a $7,500 guest-star fee for other television shows. "That's where the money was," he said. "We supplemented our little salaries with guest-star spots."

Alan did a comedy bit with Dean Martin and his voluptuous dancing girls euphoniously dubbed "The Gold Diggers," and recreated his gladiator skit with Ernest Borgnine and boxing champion Sugar Ray Robinson. "I had a good time with Dean," Alan recalled. "He wouldn't rehearse. He just showed up on the taping day and did it. He was so smooth and I think of all the people I ever worked with, he was the most at ease in front of a camera. Completely natural and he could roll with whatever you gave him. He was easy to work with and he loved to laugh."

Dean Martin loved playing off "fluttery" male characters on his show. He was a master of the double entendre, and he was always in on the joke. "He was the perfect straight 'straight man'," Alan said. "He cracked himself up and was very comfortable playing against type. Paul Lynde, Charles Nelson Reilly and Dom DeLuise were regulars on his show. I wish there had been room for me. The comedic interplay was not as sophomoric as it was on *Laugh-In*."

Alan again appeared on *The Tonight Show with Johnny Carson* on November 16, and guest-starred with George Gobel on *The Glen Campbell Goodtime Hour* on November 29. In a sketch called "Bachelors Anonymous," Alan and Gobel hilariously try to save Glen from marriage.

Love, American Style had premiered on ABC in September 1969. The popular comedy anthology series showcased a collection of short comedic "playlets" dealing with the subject of love. The list of actors who appeared on the series read like a "Who's Who" in Hollywood. Alan first appeared on the show in an episode titled "Love and the Intruder" with George Furth, Abby Dalton and John Astin. Broadcast on December 4, 1970, the story concerned a man who burglarized his ex-wife.

George Furth was gay, and perfected the role of a put-upon milquetoast with a nervous smile. In addition to his frequent film and television appearances, Furth was an accomplished playwright. He wrote the book for the hit musical *Company* which opened on Broadway a few months earlier that year. Based on Furth's collection of one act playlets about relationships, *Company* boasted music and lyrics by Stephen Sondheim.

"I became good friends with George," Alan recalled. "He looked like Paul Lynde, but his style was milder. And he wasn't mean like Paul. But those nelly roles were just about the only parts any of us could get then. But George was smart. He won a Tony Award for *Company*, and he was a terrific writer. I love smart people. George was smart. And he was a gossip queen. He had the best showbiz stories. Whenever we'd see each other, he'd begin by saying, 'There is so much going on. I can't talk about it.' And then, without me asking, he'd just start talking and he'd tell me everything he said he wouldn't talk about."

Alan returned to *Love, American Style* in the episode titled "Love and the Baker's Dozen," broadcast on February 12, 1971. He played the role of a chef who becomes the hapless referee when three couples fight over an enormous wedding cake. The highlight of this classic is a colossal food fight involving six dozen frosted cakes and cream pies.

While work continued on *Laugh-In*, Alan became happily preoccupied with redecorating his new home. He painted murals on the kitchen and dining room walls, and built a brick patio in the backyard. He planted lush gardens surrounding the house and spent what little spare time he had hunting for antiques, rugs, English china and other furnishings. "Once the walls were up," Alan explained, "I had some privacy at last. People would just come to my

Alan as the Easter Bunny with Peter Lawford on Laugh-In.

door at my old apartment, now they couldn't get that close. And I really didn't like that attention. I wanted to live my life."

Alan's weight battle came to a head one day on the set at NBC. "Being fat isn't funny," Alan said. "I was always aware of how I looked and I couldn't stand to watch myself on tape." He sat in the NBC commissary and watched Ruth Buzzi unpack a small food scale, and canned tuna fish and some vegetables. She told him about an eating program she followed called "Weight Watchers." After she explained the diet, Alan said, "Oh, I can't do that." Ruth answered, "Yes, you can." So, with trepidation, Alan joined the "Weight Watchers" program and lost thirty pounds. "I was so excited about it," he said, "I was interviewed for *Weight Watchers* magazine." Alan's story, "Fat People Aren't Funny," appeared in the April 1971 issue. "It was an important subject," Alan recalled, "and I got so much fan mail from that article."

While dealing with weight loss, Alan also tackled his drinking problem. "The drinking issue was easier to deal with," he said. "I could stuff my fat face with food all the time I was working, but I couldn't work with a hangover. I just couldn't. I needed overeaters anonymous but I didn't need alcoholics anonymous. I cut the

Cliff Robertson, Robert Stack, Alan, Dinah and Gregory Peck, 1971. "I took eleven pounds of cake with me when I left."

drinking on my own." Physically, Alan was feeling very good. He began to play tennis regularly. "It was good exercise," he said, "but it was also relaxing." Still, his residual self-loathing was stifling at times. He continued to see his psychiatrist twice a week.

On March 1, Alan appeared with Richard Benjamin and Paula Prentiss on *The Dick Cavett Show,* and he made a special appearance on *Dinah's Place,* at the star's request, to celebrate her fifty-fifth birthday. Hollywood leading men Robert Stack, Cliff Robertson and Gregory Peck were also guests. The producers surprised the star with a six-hundred-pound cake that was sixteen feet tall! "When I wasn't on stage with Dinah," Alan said, "I stood just out of camera range and blew kisses. She couldn't keep a straight face. Then I'd move to another spot and blow more kisses. They stopped tape a few times because she couldn't get a grip. Finally, she said, 'Alan, stop blowing me kisses!' I said, 'I'm not blowing *you* kisses, they're for Gregory Peck!'"

If Alan wasn't working on *Laugh-In,* or busying himself around his house, he took dancing and singing lessons. "There were a few auditions on the horizon, and I wanted to be ready," he said. But being a good singer or dancer was no guarantee a performer could successfully navigate an audition and land the job. "They can teach you how to sing, or even to act, after you get the job. The question is *how* you get the job. I always thought somebody ought to teach a course in how to get the job. I took classes from a guy named David Craig. He was a great teacher and specialized in musical theater performance. My friend, Nancy Walker, was married to him. He also taught a course in how to handle yourself during an audition. Once you're working, you might have no trouble with the public audience, but the guy who hires you is the most dubious audience of all.

"Casting decisions are made by people who specialize in their particular theatrical area. You could be auditioned by people who worked at their specialty in the day. They go home at night and relax, turn the television on, and watch a late show. That's how they became acquainted with many of us outside their bailiwick. You need to be secure about yourself to get the job. When I started in New York, I could hand over my picture or tell them my name, but I couldn't do both at the same time. You can do ten things wrong just walking out on the stage. You drop your eyes to the floor and you lose the audience, or whoever auditions you, right away. You look right at them and you seem secure even though you aren't."

When *Laugh-In* went on hiatus, Alan flew to Hawaii. The islands were a favorite place for him to get away, virtually unnoticed. He stayed with an old friend, Al Angier, near Diamond Head for a short time before traveling to Maui. Alan was relaxing at a resort in Hanalei Bay on Kauai when he got a call to return home for an important audition for a supporting role on a variety program to be produced in England for American broadcast called *Kraft Music Hall Presents The Des O'Connor Show*. O'Connor was a popular British entertainer and Alan desperately wanted to work with him. "It was a summer replacement series, and I could have done it with my time off *Laugh-In*," Alan explained. "I went in and read for Mort Lachman who was going to write and produce the show. Lachman wrote and produced Bob Hope specials, and produced

All in the Family. He hated me. I don't know why, I thought it went well, but he didn't want me. He hired Dom DeLuise instead."

Alan made the first of several appearances on the show *The Movie Game* on August 7. The format of the show was that of a parlor game of movie trivia. The questions concentrated on films of the 1930s and 1940s, and the celebrity guests were often legendary stars. Alan joined Roddy McDowell, Lee Grant, Gene Barry and Earl Holliman on the program.

One night in the summer of 1971, Alan met a man named Walter Finley at a gay bar in West Hollywood called the Gallery Room. Walter, who worked in the advertising business, was ten years younger than Alan, very tall, and very handsome. They dated for several months. "Alan didn't really like bars," Walter recalled, "but we went to the Gallery Room often. Lana Turner would show up and Alan always liked talking with her. 'She's one of the guys,' he'd say, 'but I could never pull off that gown.' We became friends with the clothes designer Nolan Miller there, too. Actually, I was sleeping with Alan and Nolan at the same time. When Alan found out, he said, 'At least you could have gotten yourself some new clothes out of it. Do you ever look in the mirror?'

"One night we were sitting at the bar," Walter said, "and a guy came up and said to Alan, 'Did anyone ever tell you that you look like Alan Sues?' 'Yeah,' Alan said, 'my mother.' We were feeling the booze, and a woman came up with a couple of her friends and said to Alan, 'Oh, I like you on *Laugh-In*. Say something funny.' Alan looked at her and said, 'You're a very beautiful woman.' He was much funnier off the clock."

Walter had acting aspirations, which he discussed with Alan. "Alan told me, 'It won't work for you. You like *things* too much. And the income isn't steady for an actor.' I told him *his* income was pretty steady, and Alan snapped, 'Yeah, well, I'm not buying you any *things!*'"

Alan took Walter to the *Laugh-In* set a few times. "They didn't have a real audience, but cast members could invite friends to watch," Walter explained. "Rita Hayworth was the guest one week and I watched them all work with her. Alan was actually a little bit star-struck, which was unlike him. She was struggling with her lines, and Alan was very kind to her and tried to relax her."

Alan with Joey Bishop on Laugh-In.

Walter said that Alan began to feel his professional oats when they first met. "He loved *Laugh-In*," Walter recalled, "but he also wanted to do other things, to stretch himself a little bit." Alan's television contract obligations made it impossible for him to star in a planned production of *A Funny Thing Happened on the Way to the Forum* at the Ahmanson Theater in Los Angeles. Alan recalled,

"The producers contacted my agent and asked me to come in for *Forum*. It's a great show and I wanted to do it, but I couldn't." Phil Silvers played the role in October and November, 1971.

"Alan and I went to see the show and saw Phil Silvers afterwards," Walter recalled. "Alan knew Phil and introduced me. They had a few laughs. Alan was very disappointed he missed out on the part."

Other *Laugh-In* cast members had left the show earlier to pursue more ambitious projects. Goldie Hawn completed the motion picture *Cactus Flower* during her 1969 hiatus. The film was released that December. She left the show a few months later to begin a successful career as a movie actress. Jo Anne Worley left the show at the same time for other television and theatrical projects. "Jo Anne and Goldie did it right," Alan said. "They left the show when it was number one to take advantage of their immense popularity, and they rode that wave. Put that on a cracker."

Lily Tomlin first appeared on *Laugh-In* in January 1970, and became an instant fan favorite with her character Ernestine, the prickly telephone operator. Lily recorded an album of her Ernestine monologues in 1971 called *This Is A Recording*, which became the highest charting album by a solo comedienne, and won her a Grammy Award.

"Lily was the most interesting person on the show," Alan said. "Her humor was intelligent and provocative. She was so much bigger than *Laugh-In*. She had studied with Charles Nelson Reilly who introduced her to the work of a famous monologist named Ruth Draper. I saw Draper in New York at the Vanderbilt Theatre when I was doing *Tea and Sympathy*, and she was fantastic. She could transform herself into an array of characters on the stage with just a few wardrobe items or hats. She wrote her own material and her monologues were funny in an odd, subtle way. She made observations about life through the eyes of her different characters. I went back several times to see her. I was quite influenced by her, and Lily was very inspired by her, too. We talked about Draper a lot.

"After about a year on the show, Lily came over to my house in tears. She was tormented. She had met a writer named Jane Wagner who had helped her create the Edith Ann character on the show. She was working on a new album and some television specials. She wanted to pull together a stage show of monologues, too. It was frustrating. Also, she fell in love with Jane and didn't know what to do. Lily had been involved with her manager Irene Penn and felt very conflicted. And of course she wanted to protect her privacy. She was sort of a loner. We had sort of an unspoken bond. I knew there would be no stopping her professionally, but, for me—I felt the writing was on the wall."

Laugh-In's fifth season premiere was broadcast on September 13, 1971, with special guests Bob Hope and Johnny Carson. By that time, *Laugh-In* had earned 105 Emmy nominations and won a staggering twenty-five Emmy Awards. Although Richard Nixon and his Administration could not be the subject of satirical attack, certain "outsiders" were not immune. Martha Mitchell, the bombastic wife of Nixon's Attorney General John Mitchell, had made a name for herself with her outspoken and controversial political observations. The Administration considered her an embarrassing problem, and John Mitchell couldn't seem to control her very public rants. Mrs. Mitchell was a guest on the season premiere. Her appearance on the show was taped in August. Each cast member had a comical go at her. Wayne Warga, a reporter for the *Los Angeles Times*, covered her visit to the program. On August 20, he wrote, "Alan Sues who can at once be daft and daffy, zoomed in for his turn [with Mrs. Mitchell] and slipped on a peel called Freud. 'Lissen, Mrs. Missile ... Oh, my God ...' There was a long uncomfortable pause and no one laughed until Mrs. Mitchell did."

On September 23, Joyce Haber wrote about *Laugh-In* in the *Los Angeles Times* in a scathing piece titled, "A Blemish in Beautiful Downtown Burbank." She reported that Paul Keyes, who had left the show because he objected to "a show which was all anti-Nixon and anti J. Edgar Hoover," was about to return. The bickering on the set now had to do with the question, "Who created the show?"

George Schlatter told Haber, "Digby Wolfe and I wrote a whole presentation that's on file at the Writer's Guild two years before Rowan and Martin were even considered for it." Schlatter's producing partner, the normally silent Ed Friendly said to the reporter, "Who the hell cares who created the show? The entire argument is ridiculous because the show wasn't created by anybody. It evolved out of a lot of people including George, Dan Rowan, Dick Martin, Digby Wolfe, Paul Keyes, Carolyn Raskin and myself. All having the sole pupose in mind of doing an all-comedy show. And the show I don't think could have evolved without any one of those people. It never would have happened without the performers. Arte Johnson brought three or four of his characters. Ruth Buzzi's characters. And Alan Sues brought some of his characters, too."

Haber's newspaper feature only made matters worse on Stage 4 at NBC.

During writer Paul Keyes's absence from *Laugh-In* the ratings had plummeted from number one to number seven to number twenty-two. Keyes returned to the show in the autumn of 1971 at the invitation of Rowan and Martin, and to the consternation of George Schlatter. Back in the hands of President Nixon's friend, the show which suffered the earlier loss of fan favorites Goldie Hawn, Judy Carne and Jo Anne Worley, now relied on bathroom humor and more pointed homophobic gags. What began in 1968 as a show rife with political satire, became little more than an exercise in cultural satire.

The often rancorous national discourse regarding gay rights had come to a proverbial head in the summer of 1971. To commemorate the second anniversary of the "Stonewall Rebellion," gay rights protests and parades were staged in New York City, Chicago and Los Angeles. "It was all over the news," Alan said. "It was the big debate. It was relevant and it brought out the best and worst in people. Unfortunately, it brought out the worst in Paul Keyes, whose jabs at homosexuals evolved into demeaning homophobic representations. He played to the lowest common denominator.

"I didn't stand a chance," Alan added. "They even dressed me in drag as Jo Anne for the 100th episode special where they brought in Keyes' pal, John Wayne, who drunkenly stumbled through the whole show. I got so sick of the homo sketches they threw at me, many times I'd just fuck up the lines over and over again and say, 'Gee, I'm sorry. I don't know what's wrong with me tonight.' Finally, they gave up the shot. I was wasting too much money, but it kept the shot—and me—out of the show."

A year earlier, a diminutive Broadway singer/dancer/actress joined the cast of *Laugh-In*. Barbara Sharma had appeared in *Hello Dolly*, *Sweet Charity* and *Last of the Red Hot Lovers*. "My first scene on *Laugh-In* was with Alan," Barbara recalled. "He was playing a judge and I was playing a woman who was brought before him. We looked at each other and started to laugh. Before I knew it, we tore the set apart and tore each other's clothes off. George stopped the cameras and asked if I was all right!

"Alan was brilliantly talented," Barbara explained. "It was his mind and his view of things. I worshipped him and he was great to me on the show and we became life-long friends. But he was very frustrated with the material. There were too many gay jokes and the producers didn't seem to know what to do with him. When we were given a sketch to do, if we didn't like the material, we'd just start tap dancing around each other on the set. And let me tell you, we did a lot of tap dancing."

"Rowan and Martin squelched a lot of talent on the show," Alan said, "such as Barbara Sharma. She's one of my favorite people and she's a fabulous performer, but they never scratched the surface of what she can do. It was that way with many of the kids on the show."

Lorne Michaels (who later created *Saturday Night Live*) was a new addition to the *Laugh-In* writing staff and took George Schlatter's approach to political humor. He immediately felt the wrath of Paul Keyes. Any wisecrack he proposed about Nixon was cut short by Keyes. Even if Michaels managed to slip in an anti-Nixon joke, Keyes' staff neutered it before it hit the air.

"That fall was tough on the set," Alan said. "The writers were still at odds, but the new fight was over who invented the damn show. There was a lot of shouting, stomping and door slamming. But by that time, it made as much sense as people fighting over who built the Titanic as it was sinking."

Alan appeared as a guest on *The Merv Griffin Show* on October 1, and again appeared on *The Movie Game*, on October 11. One of Alan's favorite actors, Paul Henreid, was a guest on the same episode.

In the fall, Alan signed a lucrative advertising contract to play the role of Peter Pan in print and television commercials for the Swift

Alan in a Peter Pan Peanut Butter advertisement.

& Company owned brand Peter Pan Peanut Butter. Dressed as Peter Pan, Alan appeared in several television commercials featuring him crashing through a kitchen window, tripping over a couch, and dancing about as he promoted the product. In one television spot, he interrupted a mother as she prepared peanut butter sandwiches for her young son and daughter. As Alan sputtered, rolled his eyes and climbed over the kitchen sink to make his exit, the little girl said, "He's weird but he makes a good sandwich."

"One of 'em never made it on TV," Alan recalled. "We shot one where I fell out of a tree and landed on a picnic table. There was a big bowl of potato salad that spilled all over the family eating peanut butter sandwiches. Never made it past the cutting room. They thought that one was too sadistic."

The special 100th episode of *Laugh-In* was scheduled for broadcast on November 1, 1971. John Wayne and Tiny Tim were the special guests, and many old faces returned for the special episode. Alan joined Barbara Sharma, Ann Elder, Judy Carne, Ruth Buzzi, Jo Anne Worley, Johnny Brown, Henry Gibson, Gary Owens, Larry Hovis, Teresa Graves, and Richard Dawson.

"One of my favorite people was Tiny Tim," Alan said. "He was sweet and shy and soft spoken, and his stardom defied logic. He spoke formally on the set and he always called me Mr. Sues. He wasn't exactly a fashion plate, but somehow the guy got every girl around! It was hilarious."

To promote the special anniversary episode, Alan was interviewed by Joan Fontaine on NBC's *Monitor* radio show. "It was funny," Alan recalled. "Joan kept looking at me strangely, and asking all kinds of way out questions like she had never seen me before. After an hour and a half, I reminded her that I worked with her on Broadway in *Tea and Sympathy*. Without missing a beat, she said, 'Of course you did, now what about this peanut butter business.' It was perfect."

Alan was interviewed by Harry Harris for the *Philadelphia Inquirer TV Week* magazine on October 31, 1971. "I had been talking non-stop for hours with reporters," Alan explained. "This interview was about the twentieth one I did at the end of the day and I was exhausted." The latest story about the behind the scene machinations on the *Laugh-In* set concerned the return of Paul Keyes as head writer and the rumor that he had entirely supplanted George Schlatter as producer.

"I always hear and read in fan magazines that the cast is *shaking* because they're afraid *Laugh-In* is about to blow up," Alan told the

The cast of the special 100th episode of Laugh-In.

reporter. "You've got to expect some tension when people work so closely together, but there's been no real outbreak. For instance, there have been rumors that Rowan and Martin don't get along. They're very professional. In fact, I always thought I'd like to see some of this excitement I keep hearing about! Paul Keyes is a sharp writer and a great on-your-feet gag man. The hardest thing in sketch comedy is to get that last funny line. What I'd like to see is Schlatter and Keyes working *together*.

"I think this argument about who created *Laugh-In* is childish. I was in a pilot a few years earlier, Jay Ward's *Nut House* at CBS that was exactly like *Laugh-In*. Everybody contributes characters and jokes. I must have done fifty interviews, and no one has *ever* asked me about Dick and Dan. They've made a tremendous amount of money for doing the same monologue week after week, while others, like Ruth Buzzi, Lily Tomlin, Arte Johnson and myself, have brought in new things all the time. Do I resent that? No, I think it's *terrific* to make a fortune that way!"

The reporter, who described Alan as "surprisingly fluttery off screen," then asked Alan if he felt Rowan and Martin were dispensable. "I wouldn't say *that*. Anyone who rocks the boat when he has such a good thing going needs looking after, but I don't consider the rest of us as second bananas to Dan and Dick. They're the first bananas only in pay, not in popularity. I think a Lily Tomlin monologue has more impact on the public, and in fan mail certain people outdraw them completely. I'd rather not say who, but it does happen. When Goldie Hawn was on, she was head and shoulders above everyone else."

Alan then explained what the anniversary special was about. "The new people and the old were mixed in sketches," he said. "As someone who's worked with *all* of them, I was curious to see how they'd blend. It was *great*! It was interesting to see what the people coming back would be like, if they had changed, if they would have a *put-down* attitude. Everybody was *glad* to be back. At the rehearsal hall in Burbank on Thursday at noon, everybody made an entrance. But Dan and Dick weren't there. They come in on Wednesday, taping day, and only work about four hours—their monologue, the cocktail party and once in a while a sketch—and leave. The rest of us work a five-day schedule, and taping day is *very* long, sometimes as late as four in the morning. At a thousand dollars a minute in costs, no one is fooling around. All that pressure makes the rest of the group a little tighter. We see each other a great deal socially."

For the special, Alan appeared in drag, dressed as Jo Anne Worley. "When Alan dressed like me in curls, a boa, a dress and false eyelashes, he looked better than me," Jo Anne said. Judy Carne was a "Judy" doll and repeatedly had buckets of water tossed at her

Alan in drag with Jo Anne Worley in Laugh-In.

on stage. Henry Gibson and John Wayne had a poetry-reading contest, and Arte Johnson's old man character Tyrone again wooed Ruth Buzzi's old woman Gladys on the park bench. Gladys dreamt of marrying John Wayne, and Teresa Graves danced as a part of sultan Tiny Tim's harem.

"I think every performer on the show always wants more to do," Alan told the reporter. "You never know how many spots you're in

Sandy Duncan with Alan on Laugh-In.

until the show is actually on the screen. I like Uncle Al, the Kiddie's Pal the best, and the put-down homosexual jokes the least. Camp is great, but I don't think it's necessary to lay very heavy on the homo jokes."

Alan's interview was considered explosive. "I was already on Dan's shit-list," Alan recalled, "because I beat him at a game of tennis. He invited me to play him at his house. Everybody told me, 'Don't play tennis with Dan. And for God sake, don't win!' But I played tennis with him and I won. He went nuts on the court, slamming his racket down and breaking it. 'It's just a game, Dan', I said. 'Fuck you!' he yelled at me, and he stormed into his house. From that moment on he barely acknowledged me on set."

On December 6, Alan appeared with singer José Feliciano on *The David Frost Show*. Game shows then dominated Alan's professional calendar. On February 7, 1972, he appeared on *The Movie Game* with Barbara Sharma and one of his idols, Myrna Loy. He also taped an episode of Ralph Edwards's *Remember Me?*, which aired later on May 18.

"Paul Lynde had settled his contract dispute and he was back in the center square on *Hollywood Squares*, "Alan explained. "I went back to the show, and Paul appeared on *Laugh-In*, but he wouldn't speak to me and avoided me completely." Alan appeared as a guest star on *Hollywood Squares* during last two weeks of February.

"The atmosphere on the *Laugh-In* set was heavy in the last couple of months of the season," Alan recalled. "You felt it when you walked into the building. I knew they were out to get me when I was doing a sketch with Sandy Duncan. It was one of the last shows that year. We were running around and a camera moved in close very fast. We got slammed up against the set and whole damn thing fell on us. I was okay, but Sandy got bumped up pretty good and had a lump on her tiny little head. Thank God she fell on top of me and saved me. They gave us about a minute and a half to get ourselves together and finish the scene."

In February, NBC dropped a bombshell when the network announced that George Schlatter was essentially off the show for the upcoming 1972-1973 season of *Laugh-In*. Rowan and Martin bought his interest and appointed Paul Keyes as head of programming.

Alan Sues was fired.

Walter Finley recalled the day Alan heard the news of his dismissal. "I dropped in on him, which he never liked," Walter recalled. "He came to the gate to let me in and said he just heard he was dropped from *Laugh-In*. The producers said he could handle it any way he wanted, and the show would back up his statement. Alan said something like it was time to 'move on.' He complained

Ruth Buzzi with Alan on Laugh-In.

about the material they gave him on the show all the time, but this really hurt him deeply. Lily Tomlin was good friends with Alan and she was having issues on the show with the gay jokes, too. She spoke up in the press, but they didn't do anything to her."

In an interesting turn-about, Paul Lynde made his first appearance on *Laugh-In* on January 31. He appeared once more on February 21. "They were feeling him out to replace me," Alan said.

"But Paul was not a team player. He was very funny, but was not good in repertoire. He was not a generous actor to work with."

Charles Nelson Reilly also appeared for the first time on *Laugh-In* in January 1972. He made two more appearances in March. "I didn't realize at the time that Keyes was looking to replace me—shopping around," Alan said. "Charlie was also very funny, but by that time, the show was gasping for air. The ratings were in the toilet. They even brought in Dom DeLuise, and Rip Taylor—who simply tried to copy me—for guest shots in the last season, but it was too late. They tried out every gay comic actor they could find. They thought we were interchangeable."

On March 15, 1972, Joyce Haber reported in her *Los Angeles Times* gossip column that Alan had told her, "The show was wonderful for me and I was wonderful for the show. But you did whatever you were told to do, and everybody wants to do more." When Haber asked him how he felt about the *Laugh-In* regulars he was leaving behind, Alan said, "I loved George Schlatter."

Merv Griffin invited Alan back on his show on March 27 to talk about his departure from *Laugh-In*. Former *Laugh-In* regular Jo Anne Worley joined Alan and together they delivered one of Griffin's highest rated shows of the season. Alan quickly became one of Griffin's favorite guests, and often appeared on the show on short notice when another guest dropped off the schedule.

Months later, as *Laugh-In* prepared for its first season without Alan and Schlatter, ABC-TV scheduled the Oscar-winning film *Patton* to go up against the *Laugh-In* premiere. During an NBC press conference announcing the fall television schedule, Paul Keyes complained that he didn't know how they could compete with the hit film. "How do you combat it?" he asked. "We're going to pass out documents explaining that George C. Scott is a fag. A commie, pinko fag!"

"I was so happy to be off the show," Alan said, "away from that homophobic shit." Once the number-one show on television, *Laugh-In* didn't even place in the top thirty rated shows during the 1972-1973 season. The once talked about, groundbreaking comedy-series went out with a whimper and was cancelled in early 1973.

Alan in drag as Jo Anne with Dick Martin playing Tiny Tim.

"There was so much going on and so much talent on *Laugh-In* that it sort of revolutionized television because it made people watch the show," Alan said. "With most other shows, you could get up in the middle of it and get a beer or go to the bathroom. With *Laugh-In*, you didn't want to miss *anything*! Once other shows started to mimic that kind of pace—and they did—it was no longer a big deal.

"I was thankful to George for giving me the opportunity," Alan explained. "*Laugh-In* gave me a new life. But as time passed, I took issue with the material they threw at me. And in a way, it hurt me professionally because I was typecast. I did one hundred and four episodes. Casting agents saw me as Big Al and the only acting parts I was getting sent out for were flaming gay characters."

Act 2
Scene 3

1972–1976 "This role is definitely a career move."

Even though Alan felt relief to be free of *Laugh-In*, his dismissal played havoc with his ingrained low self-esteem, and he fell into a deep depression. He stayed in bed for days, and left his house only to visit his psychiatrist four times a week for a couple of months. "People thought we were going steady," Alan said. "*I* thought we were going steady."

Yvonne Sues recalled, "We never really talked very much about work with him. I don't think he ever really told us he was fired."

"Alan had mixed feelings about it all," Walter Finley recalled. "Mostly, he was afraid he'd never work again. Around that time, I had a terrible fire in my apartment and lost everything. Alan came over and looked around and said, 'Ahh, you're just trying to make me feel better. Well, I told you to redecorate in burnt orange, but this is too much.' He took me out for dinner at Cyrano's Restaurant that night. I had nothing but the clothes on my back. He handed me a little gift box. It was a toothbrush. But he was kind enough to let me stay in his house until I got on my feet."

Fortunately, Alan had a good professional team to help him. He hired Gene Yusim to manage his career, and the Ben Pearson Agency to represent him. About Ben Pearson, *TV Guide* had written, "*the* man to see if you need a TV star in your theatre."

"Alan hit the road in a play," Walter said, "and I stayed on to house-sit and take care of his dog, Lois. Six weeks of house-sitting turned into two years."

In April 1972, Alan packed two large trunks (which he had purchased at antique stores and faux-painted to look like Gucci luggage) and traveled to Dallas, Texas, to appear in the play *Catch Me If You Can* at the Windmill Dinner Theater. Described as a comedy-mystery, the complex story revolves around the disappearance of a woman from her Catskill Mountain honeymoon cottage, and the sudden appearance of a mysterious lady who claims to be the vanished bride. Alan played the distraught and confused groom.

Catch Me If You Can opened on May 31 and played four sold-out weeks. John Newille reviewed the play in *The Dallas Morning News* on June 2, 1972. He wrote, "The choice of Alan Sues in the lead role could not have been a happier one. But, those who come to see 'Big Al' roll his eyes and ring his little bell, will be let down. He doesn't. Sues proves to be a fine 'book' comic actor. He never overdoes it, even in his highly nervous bits. The scenery remains relatively unchewed as he sketches in the comic-tragic figure of a newlywed bereft of his bride and seemingly in danger of his life! Sues gets all the laughs, does it legitimately and shows us a side different from the small tube image."

Alan searched for material he felt was appropriately suited to his talents or could be adapted to his comic style. He found a then fifty-year-old musical-comedy titled *Good News*. Written by Laurence Schwab, with music and lyrics by Ray Henderson, B.G. DeSylva and Lew Brown, *Good News* had been a giant Broadway hit that opened in 1927 and played almost six hundred performances. The story is set in a small college in the midwest and centers on the adventures of the football team and its hero as they prepare for the upcoming big game of the year. The story was trite, but the score was upbeat and engaging and included songs which became such standards as "Life Is Just A Bowl Of Cherries," "I'm Sitting On Top Of The World," "The Best Things In Life Are Free," "Varsity Drag," "You're The Cream In My Coffee," "Button Up Your Overcoat," and "Good News."

Alan's agent, Ben Pearson, booked a ten-week summer tour of *Good News* beginning at the Falmouth Playhouse in Falmouth, Massachusetts. Alan starred as the hapless football hero, Bobby Randall. "It was a big cast," Alan recalled, "and we had about one week to rehearse. The play was old-fashioned. I wanted to do something distinctive with my character. I wanted to liven it all up. So, I made him a sissy. What's funnier or more unexpected than a sissy *football* hero!" Pearson also began tedious negotiations with the representatives of the various writers' estates to secure the rights to later co-produce (with Alan) a Broadway revival of the musical.

The *Cape Cod Standard-Times* reviewed *Good News* on July 12, 1972. "Comedian Alan Sues is really *Good News* at the Falmouth Playhouse this week. The near capacity audience of 525 Sues fans responded warmly to his antics in the old college musical of the 1920s, which a large, energetic youthful cast brought to life with fun, non-stop singing and dancing and revived old gags. Alan Sues ran the gamut of facial and body gimmicks he's noted for in *Laugh-In*... and that's what the audience wanted."

The *Falmouth Enterprise* dismissed the show as "trite," but praised Alan's exuberance. "Those who have enjoyed Alan on *Laugh-In* found him equally funny as the somewhat bumbling, slightly sharp, double-taking perennial student. Mr. Sues proved himself to be a pretty good dancer in some fast company, a good match dueting 'You're the Cream in My Coffee,' a quick man with a leer or a joke, and a genial enough personality to keep the whole thing moving briskly and cheerfully toward the grand finale."

On July 17, *Good News* opened at the Playhouse in the Park in Philadelphia, Pennsylvania. The *Philadelphia Inquirer* wrote, "*Good News* is performed with irresistible exuberance and unflagging energy. Alan Sues is starred as a perpetual student who stays in college to avoid life's responsibilities. Sues' encounters with a football toughie who almost kicks apart Sues' jalopy; with a lovely young woman in a clinical kissing experiment, and with the game of football are hilarious!"

Alan talked about his career path with a reporter for the *Philadelphia Sunday Bulletin*. About his years working the nightclub circuit, he said, "It's like working in a circus with booze. People come and go but you're stuck listening to the bartender and his cocktail shaker. It's the toughest form of entertainment there is, but you can get a concentration with your work in nightclubs you can't get anywhere else."

He didn't care to talk very much about his *Laugh-In* years, but he did say that his characters, Big Al and Uncle Al were particular fun. "I developed the role of Uncle Al by watching my brother with his kids when he had a hangover."

About starring in *Good News*, Alan said, "The humor is all very rah, rah, and there are tons of songs, including, "Varsity Drag." I've reached the point I like to do what makes me happy. I'm happy on the stage, because I love live audiences.

"I like comedy better than serious drama, because it's harder. It's one thing to say a line, and it's another to say a line and show through it an attitude that will make an audience laugh. It's a delicate balance. If the audience is seated wrong, you can lose a lot of your laughs. In comedy, an audience has to understand what you're saying all the time, because laughter always starts down front and moves back in a rippling fashion."

Alan told the reporter he intended to return to television work, but censorship was detrimental to creativity. "Everyone is nervous [about censorship] in California where TV is a mainstay of existence. It's one of the reasons I prefer living in the east. I'm more eastern than western. One of the big things I like about the east is city life. I've never been one to be wild about nodding off at the beach all day long—a big day out there."

On July 24, *Good News* opened in Syracuse, New York, at the Famous Artist Playhouse. The *Syracuse Post-Standard* wrote, "What do you do with a show that creaks with age? Simple. You oil it with Alan Sues, the bug-eyed sportscaster of Rowan and Martin's *Laugh-In*!"

The cast of Good News.

The musical was reviewed in the *Syracuse Herald-Journal* on July 25. "Alan Sues is rip-snorting his way through Nostalgialand. Sues' tour-de-force ignites the spark needed to fire up *Good News* and turn it into a blazing bonfire. The show's humor is badly dated. Sues knew this so he wisely perpetuates his TV image by 'camping' it up madly. It is the ideal vehicle for him and vice versa. The show cannot bear up under a 'straight' performance. Sues' swishy style isn't everyone's cup of tea. Yet, amid the trappings of the Twenties, he is likely to win over some of the dissenters. He comes across like one of the prancing Russian bears and just as friendly as a puppy dog."

While Alan was in Syracuse, he entertained an enthusiastic crowd of ladies at the "Stars at Luncheon" at the Corinthian Club. Stars who appeared in summer stock and regional theater productions were obligated to make appearances in the community to promote their shows. Alan dutifully attended such events, but rarely enjoyed himself. "They always expected you to be funny," he recalled, "to say something funny. It was awful." He told a few funny stories about his family, and then answered questions posed by the ladies at lunch. Asked if working on *Laugh-In* was easy, Alan said, "Somewhat." He said he was working on a comedy album, and wanted to revive *Good News* on Broadway. When he was complimented on his slender appearance, he said, "I don't diet all the time at all. And I don't attend Overeaters Anonymous. Overeating comes from anger. I must have some hostility." He explained it was often lonely touring with a show. He worked on needlepoint, he explained, and scoured the local towns for antiques. "In Dallas, they're into wood," he said, "so antique glass is cheaper. In Syracuse, they're into drinking, so, bottom's up!"

Following his engagement in Syracuse, Alan flew to Columbus, Ohio, to satisfy a three-week engagement with the famous Kenley Players, founded by a notorious theatrical producer named John Kenley. His summer-theater empire included three large theaters in Ohio.

"John dressed in drag," Alan recalled. "He was a tiny little man and the story was that he was a hermaphrodite. During the winter he lived as a woman in Florida. He loved movie and television stars, and he *loved* the theater. He was great to work for. He had an adorable, white miniature poodle he carried around in a basket on the bike he rode around backstage. The actors' contracts called for them to meet and greet the fans after the show. We stood on the stage for hours signing autographs.

"The only problem with working for Kenley was that he had his own favorite actors he cast in the shows," Alan said. "Karen Morrow and the New Christy Minstrels joined *Good News* in Ohio, so we had some intense rehearsals in a short time. It was like relearning the show with new actors and a new director."

"I knew Alan before *Good News*," Karen Morrow recalled. "We had mutual friends and I'd see him now and then. We were both on the Weight Watcher program and we laughed about that all the time. Alan said if you ate the food off the store shelf or in the car on the way home, the calories didn't count!

"He was one of those people who could size up a situation in a minute and he could make it funny. He was so quick. He was not subtle. He was unique, nobody was like him. I was worried when I found out we'd be working together. I thought, God help me, I can't ad-lib. But he was very considerate. He always went off book, but not enough to throw me off. I'll never forget the big bunny slippers he wore on stage. Hilarious.

"We both loved John Kenley. I really admired John very much. He wore a green corduroy suit—in the summer—and he had flaming red hair. He used electrolysis to shape his eyebrows. He had a closet of his gowns backstage. He didn't like one of my costumes so he took me back there and gave me a beautiful black satin gown, which worked great! Alan and I had dinner with John when we could, but Alan spent his free time antique shopping. He'd show me all these treasures he found every day. He was really a delight and so funny."

Alan arrived in Ohio to begin rehearsals about ten days before the show opened. On July 30, he attended the final performance of the Kenley Players' production of *Last of the Red Hot Lovers* starring his friend Dom DeLuise. After the show, he visited with DeLuise in his dressing room. "We were going out for drinks," Alan explained. "Dom had some cute, but unsavory, young guys with him in the dressing room and he wanted to celebrate the end of the show. He always left his wife back in California, and he loved Italian looking guys. Anyway, I left the theater and walked to my rental car in the parking lot. I got in the car, and was attacked."

The Associated Press wire service reported the news. "Two unidentified men knocked two teeth out of Alan Sues' mouth and stole a courtesy car the comedian was driving here Sunday night. Sues told police he had just pulled his car out of the parking lot about 11:30 p.m. when 'these two guys came up. One of them stuck his hand into the window and pushed something against my neck.' Sues doesn't know what the object was and doesn't remember what was said to him."

Alan was taken to a nearby hospital for treatment. The truth of the incident was especially disturbing. "They had a gun," Alan said. "They hit me in the face with the butt end of the gun and punched me, and pulled me out of the car. They beat the shit out of me. I was in World War II and never got a beating like that. They called me a queer and a faggot, spit on me, and punched two teeth out. They left me on the pavement, and I got myself back to the theater to call for help. In the heat of the moment, I thought one of the guys who attacked me had been in Dom's dressing room. I couldn't tell that to the police, though. There would have been a scandal. It would have been all over the papers. I was afraid to tell them what the guys said to me. It really shook me up. It gave me something else to talk to my shrink about. I looked over my shoulder for years afterward."

One of the residual physical effects of the beating was a painful problem Alan suffered with his jaw and upper teeth that lead to the premature replacement of all of his teeth with dentures. Until he returned to Los Angeles for dental care in September, he worked in constant pain, and relied upon prescription pain-killers for relief. For weeks, he also nursed a badly bruised knee. These injuries were especially challenging since he was required to sing and dance in every show.

At the time, Phyllis Diller was appearing in the comedy *Everybody Loves Opal* in Columbus. Diller shared her first professional success at the Purple Onion in San Francisco with Alan and his wife, Phyllis, and appeared with Alan numerous times on *Laugh-In*. "I liked Alan very much," Phyllis said. "He was funny and wildly frantic. Very, very good."

Throughout her long career, Phyllis worked with most of the comic actors including Paul Lynde and Charles Nelson Reilly. "I have a theory," Phyllis explained. "I think comedy comes from loneliness, feelings of inadequacy and abandonment. It can even come from self-loathing. Comedy is a form of self-defense. It's a coping mechanism. Alan wanted to be noticed and loved, so he made people laugh. He turned his humor on himself. He tried to make sense of things that seemed to make no sense at all.

"Paul Lynde turned his humor on others. He was always on the defensive, and he could be retaliatory. Charles Nelson Reilly was trying to make himself laugh. He liked being the center of attention. They were all very funny, very original, and truly different.

"It takes guts to be funny," Phyllis said. "A person has to be as brave as he is talented. But comics rarely consider themselves brave. They develop comic personas as a means of defense. Most of the funny men I knew had deep sadness buried inside, and they felt like they were outsiders."

In spite of the vicious attack, *Good News* opened in Warren, Ohio, at the Packard Music Hall on August 8 to a sold-out audience. Critics loved the show. The following day, Carol Williamson wrote in the *Youngstown Vindicator*, "*Good News* couldn't lose at Kenley Players Tuesday with a lively, eager audience greeting talented Alan Sues. Every time Sues walks on the stage he's a hit, whether wearing his pink and purple flowered pajamas and pink bunny slippers with floppy ears or defending himself against the school bully. One of the funniest scenes in the show takes us into the football locker room at half time. He's all dressed up for the big game and is pouting because he hasn't even left the bench. When the coach finally lets him play, Sues is in heaven. 'Oh, isn't that nice,' he coos, crossing his legs and swinging one orange-stockinged foot. And when, before stepping out for his big moment, he brushes his hair and sprays on cologne, the audience doubled up in their seats laughing."

The *Cleveland Press* wrote, "Alan Sues was one of the main reasons why an old chestnut like *Good News* came off as a very entertaining evening. Just how much liberty was taken with the original script is still top secret, but Sues' brand of humor of special material convulsed the opening night populace. In the role of the completely defeated athlete, *Laugh-In*'s 'Big Al' and the nut in the peanut butter commercials finds a new dimension. His eyes roll like drunken ping-pong balls and his face contorts in fits of mock anguish."

"Kenley's theaters were cavernous, converted auditoriums," Alan explained. "They really weren't meant for theater, but the audiences there didn't care. They packed into those sweat-lodges and had a ball. The audiences there were terrific!"

Miriam Hawkins reviewed the show in the *Youngstown News* on August 9. "The clownish absurdities of frolicsome Alan Sues are complemented with vocal intonations, which bring more laughs in the huge auditorium than any preceding comedian. He is truly the most durable, versatile and unflappable funny man to play a Kenley vehicle: a true master of caustic comedy. Comedy walks a delicate line between the bawdy and the funny. It is one of the most serious forms of entertainment and has to be handled by a real professional to be good. Anyone can tell a vulgar story and get laughs but it takes Alan Sues to present it in good taste, and that's *Good News!*"

The *Herald* newspaper in nearby Sharon, Pennsylvania, wrote, "Sues really saved the show from causing the audience to lapse into a dead slumber. The character of the sissified Bobby Randall is perfect for the lanky comedian who really 'does his thing' throughout the show, whether he's wearing his flowered pajamas and rabbit slippers in a racy bedroom scene or 'prancing' for the big touchdown in the second act."

On August 16, the *Dayton Daily News* reported, "Producer John Kenley sent Dayton some really "Good News" Tuesday night at the Memorial Hall. Kenley also sent the biggest news—Alan Sues. *Laugh-In*'s loss is summer theatre's gain—and Alan Sues gained about 2,500 rabid rooters last night as he camped, cavorted, cutup and just generally raised merry hell with his role in the Kenley Players production of *Good News*—about the campiest musical comedy ever devised. And if I were to name the single standout star of the current season so far, it'd have be Alan Sues who took all of us by storm—not surprise—last night! We all knew Sues had it. We never knew how much. Alan Sues takes off where Paul Lynde left off!"

Alan and company's next stop was the cavernous Vets Memorial Auditorium in Columbus, Ohio. In an interview with the *Columbus Dispatch* on August 25, Alan tried to make light of the attack he suffered there a few weeks earlier. While he was in the emergency room, he said, the doctor asked for his autograph and the attendant nurse said, "You're the guy in *Laugh-In*, aren't you? Roll your eyes for me."

"Summer theater is a place to have a good time," Alan explained, "and a good time only. It's not a place to dress up, or to notice what everyone else is wearing—or showing off. We all are having a great time doing the show, and we're working hard at it. We had a few rough moments on opening night here, but stuff like that is to be expected. The whole show is on the beam now."

The interviewer wrote, "Alan Sues has logged thousands of miles in his life. He has made many people laugh and happy, but is he the traditional clown who bears grief under the mask? 'To be honest,' Sues confessed, 'I would have to admit I'm not a happy man.' Serious or silly, Sues is pleasant company—and he's no 'poor man's Paul Lynde'."

The reporter may have assumed Alan was being "silly" when he said he wasn't happy. How could he not be happy with such a critically acclaimed, audience-pleasing show? Sadly, Alan was serious.

Normally, Alan was not interested in being compared to any other comedians, least of all, Paul Lynde. He had first met Paul in 1951 in New York. He felt he and Paul were not alike at all. But he did take some satisfaction in being praised in Paul's most appreciative stomping ground—the Kenley circuit in Ohio. Paul Lynde worked for John Kenley each summer, and famously packed the theaters. Alan was thrilled to be held in such high esteem by the local Ohio press.

While Alan was in Dayton, he appeared on the popular television talk show, *The Phil Donahue Show*. Earlier that year, Alan's parents, Pete and Alice Sues, moved to what would be their final home, a ranch in Solvang, California. "They were too old to do anything but watch TV," Alan said. "Finally, they saw me on the tube."

Ever since *Laugh-In* made Alan a popular guest on television talk shows, he had told funny stories about his family. "It was therapy," Alan joked. "Doctor's orders." While always funny, some of his stories had a bite, and his parents took offense.

"I was on the Donahue show," Alan recalled. "It was a very, very popular show—one of my mother's favorites. Days after the show aired, I got a letter from my father."

Pete Sues pointedly wrote, "We want you to know the self-satisfaction that your tremendous success in *Good News* has given us. The *Laugh-In* show did not display the diversity of your talent. I'll have to confess Alan that it flatters your parents to be referred to on national television. On the other hand, I'll have to point out that your old man is still capable of being bugged. True, the old man moved you and the family around plenty. The reference to moving is fine with me but in the interest of supplying some new material as your audience is getting tired of that one, I'm going to give you a fact or two that may be of some interest that you may utilize.

"I've got to confess that I was deeply hurt by one comment you made on the show. I don't care about a national audience but my friends and associates of many years may have gained an impression which I would prefer for them NOT to have as the result of your foolish comment that your father was so German that if he had his way, Hitler would have won World War II. Undoubtedly, I am at fault for not properly apprising you of your antecedents. True, they were all of German descent on my side of the family but the heritage was considerably in the background so far that I have a tremendous pride in the comfort that we are a family of patriots of the U.S.A. As you may know, your mother and father were born right here in California. My mother and father were born in the U.S.A., too.

"As to your old man, there may be a thing or two that may be of more interest to your audience than the number of times he moved the family around, if only to show that you are not exactly a descendant of dumbbells. When I retired, I didn't go into a tailspin or immediately deteriorate.

"Although during my business career I ran a successful business, I was also identified with considerable associate work having served as President of the Pacific Coast Electrical Association and the Los Angeles Electric Club among many others. As you may recall, I had a real interest in horses since childhood and at the time of my actual business retirement, I was President of the Thoroughbred Breeders Association of California. I left business to indulge in my real interest which was the breeding of good thoroughbred horses. I could write many pages about your little old mother, but all I will say is that for the last fifty years she has dedicated her life to one and only purpose, that is, worrying and caring for and loving three people. So, Alan, if you want to refer to us, lighten it up. Dad."

"He didn't even send the letter directly to me," Alan said. "He sent it in care of my brother at his Manhattan apartment. I guess the biggest surprise for me was realizing that they had actually seen me on television. They never acknowledged it before. I never talked to them about the letter. And I never stopped talking about them on TV, either."

Good News returned to the Playhouse in the Park in Philadelphia on September 1 for a two-week, encore engagement. Reports were that they turned away as many as five hundred people a night during the show's first week in Philadelphia. "One funny thing happened during that summer tour," Alan recalled. "Fans would bring jars of Peter Pan Peanut Butter for me to autograph. The playhouse staff in Philadelphia gave me a case of peanut butter on opening night with a card that read, "Tonight on the stage you're our man, but in giving a gift we've no plan. Since booze you don't drink we were prompted to think that you might just enjoy Peter Pan. P.S. They were all out of the kind with nuts.""

While Alan was in Philadelphia, his friend James Coco was co-hosting the *Mike Douglas Show*, which was taped in the city. "Jimmy came to see *Good News*," Alan said. "He loved the show and raved about it on *Mike Douglas*." Alan appeared as a guest-star on the talk show at his friend's request. He performed a comic song and dance routine with Douglas and Coco.

Good News played its final two-week engagement at the Playhouse in the Mall in Paramus, New Jersey. Critic Susan Santangelo wrote, "I guess first prize for pure entertainment would have to go to the show's star, *Laugh-In*'s very own 'Big Al,' Alan Sues. He is nothing short of hysterical from the very moment he makes his first entrance. Sues proves beyond any doubt in this production that he is not only a gifted comedian, but a talented singer and dancer as well. He is absolutely perfect. Every minute he is on stage, he is hamming it up, mugging right and left, and doing otherwise completely outrageous things that, coming from someone else, you might think was simply too much. But Sues can get away with it. Get away with it? The audience just loved it! And the scene with him in his pajamas and pink bunny slippers is one of the funniest things I've ever seen in my life!"

"I loved the show," Alan said. "We worked so hard to secure the rights for a Broadway run, but after months of negotiations, we couldn't do it. I was very disappointed. I thought this was a perfect vehicle for me."

In the early 1970s, a nostalgia craze swept over Broadway. Producer Harry Rigby staged hugely successful revivals of *No, No, Nanette* and *Irene*. In 1973, he struck a deal to produce *Good News*. Rigby later admitted that Alan's successful summer tour and rave reviews inspired him to pursue the theatrical property, but he had no interest in having Alan recreate his role. After a national tour lasting almost a year, and fifty-one preview performances, *Good News* starring movie veterans Alice Faye and Gene Nelson eventually did open on Broadway in December of 1974. The expensive musical was an unmitigated flop and closed after just sixteen performances.

Alan in Good News.

"I wasn't bitter," Alan said, "but I sent Rigby a funeral wreath when *Good News* closed."

Alan returned to Los Angeles to film a CBS television special called *Imagination: Folk Heroes and Tall Tales* which aired on November 23, 1972. Burl Ives hosted the music and comedy revue profiling legendary figures in American history. The all-star cast included Jo Anne Worley, Jonathan Winters, Frank Gorshin, Vicki Lawrence, Pat Carroll and Stubby Kaye.

Alan appeared on *The Merv Griffin Show*, and worked on a game show pilot called *Foursome*, with Jo Anne Worley and Ann Miller.

More importantly, he had several meetings with a producer who had offered him a television situation comedy for NBC. "There's very little imagination among the people who cast TV shows," Alan told a reporter for the *Minneapolis Tribune* a few months later. "*The Bob Newhart Show* was a hit. So they offer me practically the same show, only I'm a lawyer instead of a psychiatrist. It doesn't make sense. Paul Lynde plays a TV lawyer. What kind of mind would create a show for a marvelous freak like Paul, and then put him on there with an uptight, conservative family?"

Walter Finley recalled, "Alan was happy to be home for a while. He worked on the place and planted some beautiful flower gardens and fruit trees. He tried to cultivate orchids and even got a hybrid orchid named after him. While he was away working, he shipped boxes of antiques from back East. We had a good time arranging things in his house.

"Alan and I had dated on and off," Walter added, "but when things got too serious, he'd back off. He wasn't comfortable with that, except in a way, I think it was something he craved. He encouraged me, and I took some acting lessons, and then began to model. I even did a nude centerfold for *Playgirl* magazine. That really took off for me, and I eventually moved to New York to pursue modeling."

On November 22, 1972, Alan began a five week engagement in the play *Send Me No Flowers* at the Alhambra Dinner Theatre in Jacksonville, Florida. *Send Me No Flowers* is the story of a hypochondriac who overhears his doctor discussing a terminal heart patient with another doctor on his telephone, and mistakenly assumes that he is the subject of the disheartening phone conversation. He is convinced he has only two weeks to live, and sets about preparing for the welfare of his "widow-to-be." Alan played the role of the frantic hypochondriac.

Send Me No Flowers was a smash. On November 23, *The Florida Times-Union* wrote, "Sues had ample opportunity to do what he does so well: bounce double-takes and verbal nuances off each passing bit of dialogue. It was a kind of comic sonar and Sues' neurotic gropings were a delight." *The Jacksonville Journal* concurred; "Sues, the husband who decides to provide his 'widow' with a second husband after he is gone, bumbles his way through one catastrophe after another with consummate skills. He is able to skirt the edge of absurdity, using a fluid face and a mop of lawn mower-coiffed hair to good comic effect."

In an interview for *The Florida Times-Union* newspaper, published on November 26, Alan ruminated on the differences between drama and comedy. "In comedy, the important thing is to keep it loose. You're sort of playing for individual points. With serious drama, you can devote a whole scene to building a mood without losing your continuity. People don't realize how much different it is to play comedy. It's harder, really, to score those points with the audience and still keep things together."

Send Me No Flowers began a four-week engagement at the Friar's Dinner Theater in Minneapolis, Minnesota, in late February 1973. Alan was happy on stage, but dinner theater had its own drawbacks. "Theater is much easier than TV. There's not all that technical stuff to worry about like which mark you're supposed to stand on. And the stage is leisurely by comparison. Summer theater audiences were the best. But doing dinner theater was challenging. It's hard to be funny in dinner theater, because you're competing with people crunching on celery sticks and tinkling ice cubes in their glasses."

His time in Minneapolis was especially tiring. "I'd had my fill of rubber chicken dinners at Rotary Clubs, Lion's Clubs, Chambers of Commerce, and Ladies with Bad Hats Clubs. All the radio interviews asked the same questions, and the lead-in was the hit song at that time, "Killing Me Softly with His Song." Just kill me now. At one of the interviews, the DJ's secretary rang a cow bell as a joke and nearly blew out the sound booth. The Shriner's Circus was in town at the same time, and they had me doing a press conference with Chug Chug the gorilla from the circus. How they got that fez on his head I'll never know. At least the gorilla could dance the hula, which was a nice diversion in Minnesota."

In the summer, Alan booked a couple of appearances on *The Merv Griffin Show*, and returned to work with the Kenley Players in *How the Other Half Loves*. He spent the month of July at the Columbus, Dayton and Warren, Ohio, theaters. The critics were not as enthusiastic about Alan Ayckbourn's comedy as were the audiences. The

Alan in 1973.

bedroom farce concerns three couples, and the problems that occur when the boss employs the two younger men, one of whom is having an affair with his wife.

Alan's co-stars included George Maharis, Diane Baker, and Stephanie Powers. "I'd never met anyone with a bigger sex drive than George," Alan said. "His dressing room should have had a revolving door. It seemed like he hooked up with any good-looking guy he met, anywhere he met them. There were a few guys working at the theater and I saw George, wearing a towel, reach out of his dressing room and yank the guys in when they walked by. I don't remember a thing about Diane Baker, but Stephanie was terrific. That girl could laugh. She was vivacious and funny, and we played tennis together every day.

"It was always so boring on the road. I spent time shopping around for antique knick-knacks, books and silver wherever I was. I had my dog, Lois, with me. I found a lot of art books in old book stores and practiced drawing with watercolors and things. I even enrolled in local singing and dancing classes to give me something to do."

Alan spent some time with his brother and sister-in-law in Manhattan, and again guest-starred on *The Mike Douglas Show*, which was broadcast during the first week of September. "That was a free-for-all," Alan recalled. "All sports – right up my alley. Don Meredith was co-host." Alan then arranged for someone to rent his West Hollywood home for a few months before flying to Florida to begin rehearsals for another dinner theater engagement.

Love is a Time of Day is a 1969 Broadway flop written by Pulitzer Prize-winning playwright John Patrick. Patrick's numerous plays include *The Hasty Heart* and *The Teahouse of the August Moon*. The story of *Love is a Time of Day* concerns a pretty college girl who has learned how to fend off amorous suitors. A graduate student named Skipper Allen becomes enamored with the young woman and tries to finagle a way to move in with her. The casting was perplexing. Alan was forty-seven years old and his leading lady, veteran character actress Patti Heider, was fifty-five!

Alan was feeling introspective when he was interviewed by the St. Petersburg newspaper *Evening Independent* on September 12. "Comics are a very freaky breed," he told the reporter. "They project one thing and are another thing completely. I'm a Pisces. I think I'm very split. One minute very out-going, one minute very quiet and wanting to be by myself. I think I'm definitely shy. Some people turn me off if they come on too strong."

Alan admitted that *Laugh-In* provided him with stardom, but it wasn't an easy road. "There was no security," he explained. "And we worked from 9 a.m. to 4:30 a.m. the next morning, two days a week. That's a long day, a lot of hard work, and you were expected to be funny the whole time. If I had to do it all over again, I think I'd go into some other area. Not because I don't like the public. I do. But the people running the business, particularly in TV, ruin it. They have a lot of childish motives."

He said he preferred theater work. "I like it. I like to see people laugh. I'm amused at that, telling a joke and seeing people laugh. Who doesn't? Comedy is like a ball game. You throw something out and the audience throws it back by laughing."

The *St. Petersburg Times* profiled Alan on September 13. Michael Marzella wrote, "Sues is the tallest elf in captivity. His swivel-eyed lallygagging seems to come naturally, because it erupts like a popping cork in the middle of a relatively sane conversation. 'Tennis is what I play, but my game is off,' Alan said. 'You have to play it every day to stay with it, and some days I don't get to play at all.'

"That's tame enough," Marzella wrote. "The aquiline nose and the blue-gray eyes are placid, fixed in a tall, angular face. But then he says, 'Then I get a great SURGE of it,' and he lunges, eyes bugging, nose flared and arms flailing, to demonstrate the rush of pent-up tennis. It surprises the heck out of you! And that's what he meant to do; turn on the humor was a surge of surprise. He'll sneak up on you with it!

"Crazy things happen when Sues is about. There was a time at the Minneapolis airport. Sues and a friend waiting for a plane noticed a woman's garish wig, lifted by the wind, tumble toward a plane on the runway. 'We see this pile of dead hair rolling along and suddenly the security guard runs out and *shoots* it!' That breaks him up. Sues pitches and yaws in his chair."

Marzella continued, "Sues says he is a simple man, a stay-at-home sort who'd rather have a few friends over than linger in nightclubs. He prefers quiet, conservative things, such as cantaloupe and tomato salad with mayonnaise. 'It's great, really,' he exclaims. 'The longer you leave those flavors together, the better it gets. Actually, it isn't. I'm just angling for a mayo commercial.'"

In an interview with the *Clearwater Sun* newspaper on September 16, Alan said if he had to start out in show business all over again, he wouldn't. "When you're working, it's fine. But you have to be two people; you have to adjust when you're not working. It's like hurrying up to wait when you're in the Army. The constant changing of gears in your head all the time is rough. When you study show business, you don't study *that*! But I'm in it now. And I guess I've been pretty lucky. I haven't stopped working since *Laugh-In*."

Love is a Time of Day was advertised as "a youthful sex comedy." Alan explained, "Comedy is a great indicator of what people in this country are thinking. I learned that on *Laugh-In*. For people to laugh, they have to understand. But I don't understand censorship. I think the public is very hip. But people in the industry are not so hip. If they're going to do a Big Brother number, why don't they go all the way and pay my taxes? Why stop in the middle of the joke? Go ahead and run it through to the end. If these network people find things offensive, isn't that their problem that it bothers them? The most violent things are in TV and movies, and you read the most violent things. I went to a movie and a guy got riddled by a machine gun. The audience laughed hysterically for at least a minute. I don't know why that's funny. Stuff like that is okay, they say. But we can't talk about sex. I mean, we don't all come out of salt shakers.

"Students can be difficult audiences. You have to do humor with things people know about, and some students in California are so politically oriented, they don't respond to a lot of things I was doing. Sex jokes always get laughs, but I hate to do just that. It's too easy. People are funny about humor. You can take the same booze joke in Vegas and substitute pot for a college crowd and get laughs from the same material.

"Dinner theater gets to be exciting. We can say, 'let's do this,' or 'let's do that.' We can try things out. You can't do that on TV. Things are budgeted so tight and everything is handled so closely that you don't get into it at all. So actors who can do it take jobs on the road to open themselves up."

The resident director at the Country Dinner Playhouse was a twenty-six year old handsome, blond man named Jack Stillman. "He was young," Alan said, "but he had a good instinct for directing. He was a knockout. I had a little fling with him once the show got off the ground. Second act . . . slow curtain." In a couple of years, Jack Stillman changed his name to Jack Wrangler. He became one of the most famous gay porno film stars in America.

The day before the play opened, Alan told the *Tampa Times*, "Patti is a terrific actress and we are in our seventh day of rehearsal. When she shuts up I start talking. But, it is really a three-part show, because we have a dog in the cast. I have my own dog here with me, Lois Lane, a miniature dachshund, but she flunked the audition. Just couldn't do it right. And I was hoping she could start earning her own way. We got sort of a poodle-type from the pound, and not meaning this to be a pun, but she's a real ham. I am well aware of what children and animals can do to a good actor on stage. You have to stay ahead of them at all times, and that's not easy."

The play opened a one-month engagement on September 19, 1973, in St. Petersburg. On September 21, critic Michael Marzella wrote in the *Tampa Times*, "*Love is a Time of Day* is a pointless sex comedy of so little literary merit, that it would likely perish without the energy and invention of Alan Sues. It's a perfect vehicle for Sues' loony sashaying. This is such a flimsy piece of whimsy, that you may forget about the plot altogether and enjoy the delightful presence of a skilled, and sensitive actor. Sues is darned funny. He struts, prances and flourishes with such abandon and variety, that the lunacy isn't tiring. Crazy things can happen onstage, in any play, anytime. Wednesday, a mannequin Sues carried disassembled itself unexpectedly. It just fell apart; torso, legs, head, hands and wig. Sues covered the small disaster beautifully, adlibbing risqué lines that fit as if they had been written for the spontaneous scene. You wonder how much of the hilarity is Sues ad-libbing and how much is from playwright John Patrick. Sues is the probable culprit."

In late October, the production moved to the Country Dinner Playhouse in Austin, Texas. "The trouble with that type of traveling show," Alan explained, "is you often have a different cast and director wherever you go. This was a two-character play and I had a new leading lady in Texas. We had to start from scratch with a new director and we only had a few days to pull it all together. It was tiresome."

Love is a Time of Day opened a four-week engagement at the Country Dinner Playhouse in Dallas on December 4. On December 23, Alan spoke with Bob Porter for the *Dallas Times Herald*. "I don't care what anyone says," Alan said, "comedy is the toughest thing to do. I can name you fifty comedians who can play a straight role convincingly, but there is nothing worse than seeing Bette Davis trying to play comedy." Alan laughed and rolled his eyes off to one side and upward, the reporter wrote. He asked Alan if people expect him to be funny. "Sure," Alan answered. "I give them enough of a certain image. I don't do Big Al, but I try to have something there recognizable on a certain level. I'll tell you for sure, I don't go out before a dinner theater audience and do *Virginia Woolf*."

When Alan finally returned home to Los Angeles in January 1974, he found that his house had been trashed by his short-term renter. "It was a mess," Alan said. "They didn't take care of the garden, and things were missing. I was exhausted. I needed to rest."

During the next few months, Alan appeared on *The Merv Griffin* Show four times, usually accompanied by his dog, Lois. "I loved working with Merv," Alan said. "He had an all-male staff, and everyone wore polo shirts and tennis shorts that were one size too small. I'm not sure what *that* was all about. Well, actually I *am*. Merv had a great sense of humor and the best belly laugh. He had a genuine television personality. In fact, he was more comfortable in front of a camera, than not. I liked him, and he was terrific to me. I appeared on his show about fifty times!"

On April 7, Alan appeared as the Easter Bunny in the primetime holiday special *Merv Griffin and the Easter Kids*. "It's tough working with animals and kids," Alan said, "even tougher when *you're* the animal." A few days later, Alan was reunited with Ruth Buzzi on Sandy Duncan's television special *Sandy in Disneyland*. The show had an all-star cast including musical guests Loggins & Messina and The Jackson 5, and was filmed live at Disneyland.

That spring, Alan began an affair with a UCLA drama student whom he met in the Gallery Room in West Hollywood. "It was terrific," Alan recalled. "He was a great guy, and cute as a button. He stayed with me all the time and left little notes for me when he left for school in the morning. He was very romantic, actually. We went to the movies and saw some theater. He was very interested in acting, and he was good, too."

Alan's psychiatrist discouraged the relationship. "But I didn't listen," Alan said. "I was lonely and at the time it filled a need. I

Alan in Sugar, *1974.*

think in my heart I knew it wouldn't lead to anything, but I liked his companionship. It wasn't his age that was so much the problem, but when I met his friends, it was too much. I felt so out of place, and I didn't understand them at all. But the biggest problem was Marlene Dietrich. He didn't even know who she was! And that was it. Over."

In July, Alan embarked on summer-stock tour in *Sugar*, the musical adaptation of the Marilyn Monroe film *Some Like It Hot*. With music by Jule Styne and lyrics by Bob Merrill, *Sugar* was originally produced on Broadway by David Merrick and directed and choreographed by Gower Champion. The story concerns a couple of musicians who accidentally witness a gangland massacre in Chicago in 1931. To escape their trigger-happy pursuers, they disguise themselves as women and join an all-girl band about to leave for a play date in Florida.

"It was a lousy, lousy time," Alan recalled. "I was depressed. I was lonely. I had a respiratory infection all summer. I was miserable."

After only six days of rehearsals in New York, *Sugar* opened on July 21 at the Ivoryton Playhouse in Connecticut. "It's a good vehicle that's a great audience show," Alan said. "That's important. It not only appeals to adults, but to kids as well." The musical-comedy was well received. The *Morning Record* wrote, "Anyone who thinks men running around in women's clothes are funny, with all the leers, innuendos and obvious mistaken identities will find *Sugar* hilarious! Bug-eyed Alan Sues, immediately recognizable as the bell tinkling sportscaster on *Laugh-In*, is the star of this package. Sues is ideally suited for this burlesque-styled comedy as he stumbles on his high heels, wards off the fanny-pinching advances of a doddering octogenarian, fixes a bra strap (with appropriate leers) for one of the 'real' girl musicians and sings a falsetto version of "I'm Engaged" while bouncing from bed to bed. Only the traditional pie in the face is missing." The *New Haven Register* reported, "Sues is a scream! Just watching him careen around the stage in high heels is enough!"

"Alan Sues, the Tinker Bell of *Laugh-In*, brought comedy and sparkle to the production of *Sugar*," Marge Ward wrote in the *Middletown Press*. "Sues' portrayal of 'Daphne' is side-splitting!" And the *Hartford Courant* wrote, "The production of *Sugar* does not the reach the greatest heights, but it does get off the ground enough for all but the toughest critics—thanks to a gutsy cast led by Alan Sues. Sues gapes, scurries, and pirouettes with such élan that he seems ready at times to skydive into the orchestra pit!"

Sugar opened on July 29 at the Lakewood Theater in Skowhegan, Maine. The historic theater was the main attraction at the lakeside

Alan in Sugar *at the Lakewood Playhouse, 1974.*

resort, which included a small marina, cabins, tennis courts and a golf course. A pine tree encircled courtyard separated the theater from a picturesque New England-style inn.

I met Alan at the resort, where I was working. With little to do in the evenings, I attended every performance of the show.

Alan played the leading role of Jerry, who disguises himself as Daphne. Jack Lemmon played the role in the film *Some Like It Hot*. The ruse plays itself out until the end of the musical. Alan shared the final scene with Chet Carlin, an actor who played the role of Osgood Fielding III, an eccentric millionaire who has fallen in love with Daphne. Joe E. Brown played the role in the movie. Mr. Carlin could not get his last—and funniest line—correct.

Fielding awkwardly proposes marriage to Daphne. Daphne declines and when Fielding refuses to take no for an answer, Daphne rips off her wig and exclaims, "I can't marry you! I'm a man!" Fielding is supposed to answer, "Oh, nobody's perfect!"

The first night Carlin said, "Oh. You are?" Alan threw his hands up, exclaimed, "Jesus!" and walked off the stage. The next night, Carlin said, "Oh. Well, that's all right." Alan slowly turned to look at him, and snidely said, "Really?" The third night, Carlin said, "I don't care." Alan shrugged and said, "Well, you're getting warmer." The audience never seemed to know the difference.

There was a small bar that adjoined the theater. After the show, the resort employees, actors and guests gathered for drinks to unwind. A pianist, guitarist and bass player played live music. On their breaks, a jukebox provided more danceable tunes. On the second night, a lively song played on the juke box and everyone jumped up to dance. It was a bohemian crowd so everyone was actually dancing together. Alan stayed seated at his table when his fellow cast mates got up. On a dare, I walked over and asked him to dance. He shrugged, didn't say a word, and joined me on the dance floor.

When the song was finished we headed back to his table. He turned to me and said, "Don't ever ask me to dance again until you learn a few steps! I'm a professional! I taught Sammy Davis Jr. everything he knows!" Then he asked if I would like to join him for breakfast at the café the next morning.

The following day, we met shortly after noon. Alan ordered two eggs sunny-side up with bacon and potatoes. We talked about art while we waited for the food to be served. He quizzed me about local antique shops. When the waiter served us, Alan gazed at the two large sunny-side up eggs on the plate in front of him. He slowly looked over at me and said, "Oh, well. It wouldn't have lived. The eyes are too far apart." We instantly became friends. Several afternoons, I drove him around in my friend's station wagon looking for antique bargains. "I buy stuff everywhere," he told me, "and ship it home."

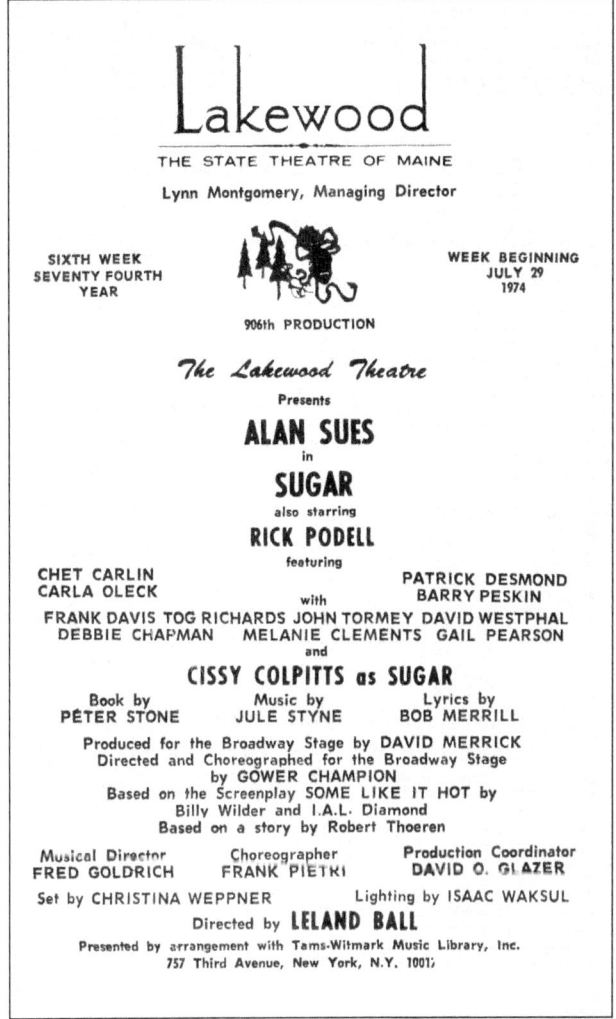

The cast of Sugar *at Lakewood, 1974.*

After a couple of days, Alan's friend, James Coco, flew to Maine to spend a few days on vacation at Lakewood. Coco stayed at the Inn, and for the several nights he was a guest, Alan joined him in the downstairs bar after the show. A gentleman played a baby grand piano and sang. Alan and Coco put on an impromptu recital of Cole Porter songs, and as the evening grew long and the drinks flowed, the lyrics became hilariously X-rated. Each comic tried to outdo the other with the raunchiest burlesque songs ever written. The owner of the theater complained that she should have been charging for the show because the small room filled to capacity each night to watch the dueling comics.

"No one could make me laugh like Jimmy," Alan recalled. "He didn't have to say a word. His face was so expressive. He looked like he was frowning, even when he was laughing."

Sugar fulfilled a week engagement at the Playhouse in the Park in Philadelphia before ending its tour at the Music Hall in Detroit. On September 13, while Alan was in Philadelphia, he appeared on *The Mike Douglas Show* with Loretta Lynn.

"Loretta Lynn was terrific," Alan said. "She didn't know what to make of me. I sat with her and Mike joking around and she just watched me—speechless. When we went to a commercial break, she said to me, 'Well, you're the kind a guy who could become president if someone don't shoot ya down first!'"

Other than a couple of appearances on *The Merv Griffin Show*, there were no television jobs for Alan in Hollywood when he returned in September. There were no feature film offers, either. "I got a voice-over agent," Alan said, "but I just couldn't get a job. It was very discouraging. The theater work was great, but it was repetitive. I never got a review for whatever I was doing that didn't mention Big Al, or *Laugh-In*.

"I didn't read reviews very often," Alan explained, "but some of the reviews for *Sugar* really pissed me off. The Tinker Bell shit was so boring, and *enough* with Big Al. That's what they wrote about me in a little farm town in the middle of nowhere. I wondered what they wrote about me in a market that really counted. Of course, I *was* doing a musical in drag. And I think, even though I had been working steadily, I had been playing comic characters over and over again. I needed a change. I thought New York could provide me with more opportunities. I needed to find a serious play and really step out of the shadow of *Laugh-In*."

Alan rented his West Hollywood house to a woman who was in the witness protection program. "I thought the cops might keep an eye on my little hacienda," he said. Alan's brother had sold his San Luis Obispo restaurant a couple of years earlier and moved to a spacious apartment on 48th Street in New York City.

"A crazy fan gets a traffic ticket after nearly running me over."

Alan flew to Chicago on October 1 to begin a six-week engagement at the Pheasant Run Playhouse in nearby St. Charles in the play, *Love Is a Time of Day*. "Fans always surprised me," Alan said. "I was in Chicago to do some interviews before the show opened and I was walking across the street with a photographer to meet a reporter in a restaurant. I was nearly run over by a car, and the driver pulled over and jumped the curb and jumped out and screamed at me that he loved me and wanted my autograph! Before anything could happen a cop pulls up and writes the guy a ticket, and then the cop asked for my autograph, too!"

Love Is a Time of Day closed after a sold-out run on November 17. Before Alan returned to New York, he flew to Toronto to record an appearance on the CTV variety show, *Funny Farm*. "It was a rural-style *Laugh-In*. In Canada! Confusing, but some other kids from *Laugh-In* did the show, so I signed up."

"The worst thing that ever happened to me was the time I hosted Macy's Thanksgiving Day Parade," Alan recalled. Alan was tapped to host the NBC-TV pre-Parade show on Thanksgiving morning, November 27, 1974. Actress Rita Moreno, then starring in the popular children's show *Electric Company*, and nine-year old child star Mason Reese joined Alan for the one-hour special, broadcast live from New York. The diminutive, red-haired Reese was best known for television commercials.

The program was circus-themed and included performances by Ringling Brothers clowns and a magic act by Doug Henning. "We started out at 77th Street near Columbus Circle," Alan recalled. "Rita Moreno got into a terrific fight with her young daughter who kept screaming at her mother, 'I hate you! I really hate you! I'll be glad when you're dead!' And, of course, we're live on television.

"They quickly moved me down Broadway and put me in front of Macy's in Herald Square where Mason Reese was waiting with his mother. The director had no experience with live television, and was frantically running around making the rest of us really nervous. The biggest problem for me was the cue cards had been printed by someone who not only couldn't spell, but the letters were either too big or too small and looked like an eye test. I couldn't read a damn thing.

"Then this Reese kid was a demon. Whenever the director said anything, the kid would say, 'He's an asshole. He's a God-damn asshole!' The kid had the filthiest mouth I'd ever heard in my life! And instead of trying to control her son, his mother kept saying, 'Oh, isn't he funny. He's so funny.' 'This is live,' I said to her. He's not funny. We're all going to do about five years in jail for this.

"Then a clown who was staggering around in big, floppy shoes fell down and a policeman had to help him up. The cop put the clown up on a horse. The horse spooked when some cymbals crashed and bucked the clown, and stepped on him. While I'm trying to commentate this disaster, the clown crawls over to me and cries, 'I'm bleeding! I'm bleeding! Somebody help me! I'm going to sue!' I said, 'Not now, not now,' and pushed him out of camera range. Of course, the kid thought it was all hysterical.

"I introduced Doug Henning, and unbelievably, the director was shooting Henning's magic acts from the side instead of from the front so everyone could see how he was doing the tricks. Henning said, 'You're shooting this wrong. You need to be in front.' And the kid says, 'He doesn't know what the fuck he's doing. He's an asshole.'

"At the commercial break, the director runs over to us and says, 'We have to do the whole thing over again! Go back to the start!' I said, how can we *do* that, the parade is already marching by. The kid says to the director, 'What a fucking asshole!' and finally gets hauled away. As they're dragging him off, we go back on the air just in time to see the kid turn to me and scream, 'You're a fucking cocksucker!' 'Welcome back,' I said smiling into the camera.

"I just tried to get through it. I was certain I'd never work again for as long as I lived. When we were done, I just handed over the microphone and walked back to John's apartment on 48th where I was staying. Of course, John and his wife had seen the whole fiasco on television. He said, 'I've never seen such a sad thing in my life.'"

"When Alan got home," Yvonne Sues recalled, "he was so upset, he stood in the kitchen and ate the entire turkey by himself. He picked it clean to the bone."

"I went to bed and slept for three days," Alan said. "I knew it was a disaster because everyone I knew had watched, and not one person ever said a word to me about it."

In February 1975, Alan flew to Edmonton, Alberta, Canada, to appear in the play *Boeing, Boeing* at the Mayfield Inn's Stage West Dinner Theater. *Boeing, Boeing*, a Tony Award-winning comedy, is about a successful American architect living in an expensive Paris apartment. With the help of his housekeeper, he juggles three fiancées who are all beautiful flight attendants. When he's visited by his old college friend, the delicate, deceitful balance is thrown into comical disarray. The one-month engagement, which began on March 18, was an audience pleaser. To promote the play, Alan appeared on several Canadian television programs including *The Tommy Banks Show*, and *Celebrity Cooks*.

Alan liked the play, the cast, the accommodations, and the beautiful theater. He told a reporter, "Edmontonians don't know how lucky they are." He talked about some of the "dumps" he'd played in, and recalled one in particular that was infested with mice. "On five different nights they ran across the stage—on opening night two mice ran right into the lobby. Everyone's a critic, but the mice too? The girl working with me almost went crazy. So they assured us they would take care of the problem. The next night, the stage manager pointed out dozens of mouse traps all around backstage. But we couldn't have a quiet scene because the traps kept going off. It sounded like castanets! I broke into a Spanish dance, which had nothing to do with the play."

A couple of years earlier, Alan had surrendered to his inability to control his weight, and joined Overeaters Anonymous. He dropped forty pounds. In analyzing his bad eating habits, Alan felt that it all boiled down to a basic anger he felt that was related to his career. He claimed to be unconcerned with reviews. For the most part, his reviews were very positive. But one bad review wiped out a dozen rave reviews. "Bad reviews bothered me," he said. "And a neutral review was just as depressing. One bad review could wipe out every good review I ever got."

He also realized, with the help of his psychiatrist, that he harbored resentment toward the people who met him offstage and expected him to be funny on command. "I never thought I owed anybody anything except a good performance," he said.

In an interview for the *Edmonton Journal* newspaper on March 29, Alan told reporter Jean Koenig that he felt the weight of that expectation and was afraid to disappoint people. He pointed out that many comedians suffer great depression in their personal lives. "I can handle bad reviews more easily now," he explained. "I'll be a compulsive eater till the day I die, but I'll be able to control it more."

Alan was also interviewed by Clarence Metcalfe for *The Ottawa Journal*. "It has always been difficult to find work," Alan explained. "The areas I want to get into are more in performing variety, and New York is a better place to be. And good comedy writers are difficult to find. I'm always looking for them. They can be great if they tune into you. It's a real marriage there. I know a comedian who was going great guns. He had a manager-writer relationship going and the manager died and the comedian's career dropped away down, and it never did recoup.

"On *Laugh-In*, I could tell immediately if they switched writers on me – although we never saw the writers. It would be somebody else who wasn't really into it, and immediately, I would have to start rewriting to make it work for me. And a lot of times you can write something and you think it is very funny, and it reads funny – but it doesn't play funny. And I'm a perfectionist. At least I've always tried. I don't like to slough off anything. There are some people who just come and take the money and run. If I'm going to be part of it, I want it to be good, or there's no point in doing it."

A few months later, Alan wrote a funny and informative article for the August 1975 issue of *Cosmopolitan* magazine, titled, "Fat Stay Away From My Thighs." "Dieting alone won't achieve a permanent pare-down for you," Alan wrote. "That calls for a deeper program, requiring delving into the *inside* you—the you that eats to stem anxiety over trying *not* to eat. In this area Overeaters Anonymous has been invaluable to me. I've learned from O.A. how reasons for eating can include moments of insecurity, repression, resentment, and anger. Every compulsive eater is goaded into gorging by one or more emotional motives. For many of us, overindulging is a form of self-punishment. We, consciously or unconsciously, use eating sadistically, as a weapon against ourselves. Or we look for the sheer instant—albeit *temporary*—gratification that comfort food can offer when we're upset. Just recognizing this destructive pattern of behavior in myself was a positive step forward. If you *don't* like being fat, give O.A. a try. Listen to Uncle Al. It just might be the best move you've ever made."

Alan received thousands of letters from overeaters and others battling weight problems. "Some sent me healthy recipes," he said, "which was kind of cute. And I got an offer for a commercial. For Oreo cookies."

Alan returned to New York in April 1975. As was his habit, he attended many Broadway shows, and was thunderstruck when he saw the Royal Shakespeare Company's production of *Sherlock Holmes (Being a hitherto unpublished episode in the career of the great detective and showing his connection with the STRANGE CASE OF MISS FAULKNER)* at the Broadhurst Theater. Written by Sir Arthur Conan Doyle and William Gillette, this seven-time Tony Award nominated play had been originally produced on Broadway in 1899. The current production was the seventh Broadway revival.

In May, English actor John Neville replaced the actor who played Holmes. While Alan had been working in Edmonton, he became acquainted with Neville who was the artistic director of the Citadel

Theater, a major venue for theater arts in downtown Edmonton. "He had six kids, and he was kind of nuts," Alan recalled, "but we became great friends."

"I was back in New York, trying to get some work," Alan explained. "I had dinner with Frank Dunlop, the director of *Sherlock Holmes*, which opened on Broadway six months before. Dunlop knew me from *Laugh-In*, which had been big in England, but he didn't really know what I did. They were in the process of re-casting the role of Professor Moriarty, and I wanted it. John Neville joined us for dinner. John suddenly spoke up, 'Alan is the only person who could play that part.' I was shocked. But Dunlop loved John, and what he said made a difference to him. I'm sure if Dunlop had been an American director, though, I would have had a very hard time getting a reading."

John Handy, who cast the original production of *Sherlock Holmes*, helped prepare Alan for the role. Alan also worked with a dialect coach to achieve a proper English accent. "It became an obsession," Alan said. "I was determined to get that part. I didn't want any more of the campy stuff I was doing. I wanted something serious. I was working a lot, but it was wrecking any chance I had of being taken seriously as an actor."

The Frank Loesser/Abe Burrows musical *How to Succeed in Business Without Really Trying* opened a one week engagement on August 4 at Starlight Musicals in Indianapolis. The production starred Dean Jones as J. Pierrepont Finch, Mamie Van Doren, and Alan. "Mamie had champagne for breakfast, lunch and dinner," Alan recalled. "She was my kind of gal. She dated Joe Namath, and I told her he flirted with me on *Laugh-In*, so we had a lot to talk about. She got a lot further with him than I did."

The *Indianapolis Star* reviewed the show on August 5. "The comedy lead is taken by Alan Sues, formerly of the Rowan and Martin *Laugh-In* hour on TV. Sues plays Frump, who calls his mother, who is the company president's wife's sister, to cut red tape and solve his problems at the office. He gives the part energy and broad humor."

The following day, the newspaper printed an interview with Alan. "Fans are a little bit afraid of me," Alan told the reporter. "I think people come up to me thinking I'm gonna jump! Actually, the op-

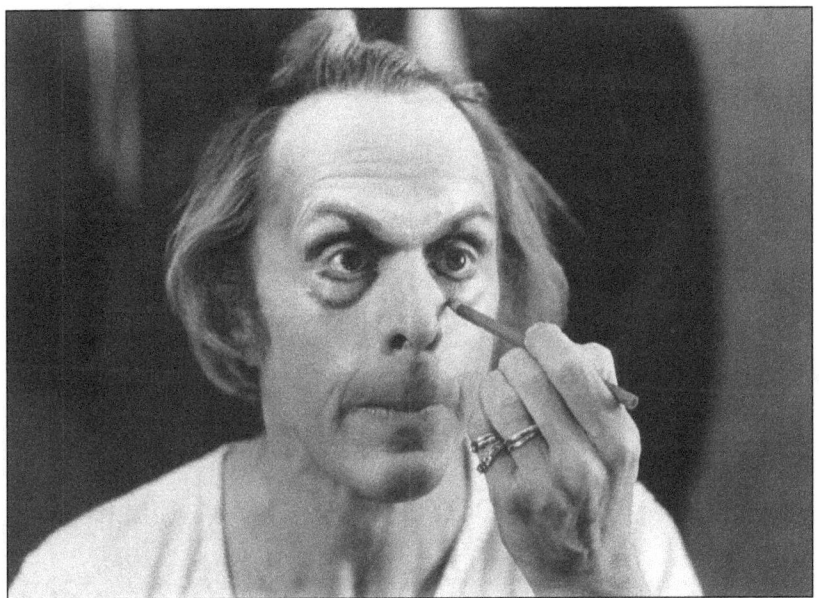

Alan transforms into Professor Moriarty.

posite happens and they scare me! I'm embarrassed when people ask for my autograph." The reporter asked what Alan was like off-camera. "I'm a frustrated architect. If I had my way, I'd be building things all the time."

Alan said the entire cast contributed to the success of *How to Succeed in Business Without Really Trying*. "There is no such thing as a star in this show," he explained. "All the parts are very well cast, even the parts that aren't particularly large. All the performers are very strong. They help the momentum of the show and keep it going."

He told the reporter that he hoped to spend his spare time "hitting antique stores for awhile if I can find out where they are." He added, "After this show, I'm going to New York to audition for a part I want so badly I'm too superstitious to tell you what it is. The part is very serious and represents a real departure from anything I've ever done."

Alan said superstition was subject to conjecture, but he did have a new set of "donkey beads" which he got in a Greenwich Village shop just before going to Indianapolis to begin rehearsals. "With all the lines I had to learn and five songs to sing, I figured I needed

> **BROADHURST THEATRE**
>
> James Nederlander, Inc.
> The Shubert Organization, Kennedy Center Productions, Inc.
> Adela Holzer, Eddie Kulukundis and Victor Lurie
> *present*
>
> *By arrangement with the Governors of the*
> ROYAL SHAKESPEARE THEATRE, STRATFORD-UPON-AVON, ENGLAND
>
> ## THE ROYAL SHAKESPEARE COMPANY'S PRODUCTION
> ## ROBERT STEPHENS *as*
> ## SHERLOCK HOLMES
>
> *a play by*
> ARTHUR CONAN DOYLE and WILLIAM GILLETTE
>
> *and* ALAN SUES *as Professor Moriarty*
>
> | GEOFF | DIANA | RICHARD | CHRISTINA | RON | ROBERT |
> |---|---|---|---|---|---|
> | GARLAND | KIRKWOOD | LUPINO | PICKLES | RANDELL | STATTEL |
>
> ARTHUR BURGHARDT   TOBIAS HALLER   MICHAEL HARTMAN
> MICHAEL HAWKINS   KIM HERBERT   JEFFREY HILLOCK
> PATRICK HORGAN   SUSAN MERRIL-TAYLOR   ROBERT PERAULT
> ROBERT PHALEN   FRED STUTHMAN   ELIZABETH SWAIN
> MATTHEW TOBIN   RICHARD WOODS
>
> *Music Arranged by*   *Lighting Designed by*
> **MICHAEL LANKESTER NEIL PETER JAMPOLIS**
>
> *Scenery and Costumes Designed by*
> **CARL TOMS**
>
> *Directed by*
> **FRANK DUNLOP**

The Broadhurst playbill, November 1975.

all the luck I could get. I'm thinking about moving to New York. I prefer the atmosphere, the basic creative energy, going on there."

Alan was cast as the replacement for the departing Philip Locke in the role of Professor Moriarty in the Broadway production of *Sherlock Holmes*. He worked for a couple of months to create a memorable characterization of the well known villain. "It took five hours to apply the makeup at first," he recalled. "I took my movements from vultures and condors and other birds of prey. Their large talons and beaks were made for tearing flesh, and I wanted to appear as predatory as those birds. It was a challenge to play such exaggerated movements with stealth on stage. Funny was the last thing on my mind. There was nothing funny about what I was doing."

He first appeared at the Broadhurst Theater as Professor Moriarty on November 4, 1975. By that time, his friend, actor John Neville, had been replaced in the role of Sherlock Holmes by another English actor, Robert Stephens. Long a celebrated theatrical star in London, Stephens famously co-starred with his wife, Maggie Smith, in the film *The Prime of Miss Jean Brodie*, and starred as the title character in Billy Wilder's 1970 film *The Private Life of Sherlock Holmes*.

"Robert was a mad man," Alan recalled. "He was a very heavy drinker, and seemed to be on the verge of a nervous breakdown all the time. I absolutely loved him. He was so great to work with. He introduced a comic element to Holmes that wasn't played by the previous actors. He sort of *swayed* through the part.

"I had a little party after my first performance as Moriarty, and Robert made a grand entrance into the restaurant wearing a cape and jumping on tables. He ran over to me and kissed me full on the

Robert Stephens with Alan in Sherlock Holmes.

mouth and yelled out, 'Delicious!' He was stoned drunk, but the most charming man in the world. I just loved him."

Business was brisk, and Alan was thrilled to be back on Broadway. He was especially happy to be in a dramatic play instead of a comedy. On December 20, Alan spoke about his coveted role with reporter Don Nelsen for the *New York Daily News*. "I took this role partly because nobody could conceive of me playing such a character. Because I was used to comedy, it was difficult to know how far to go in a serious part to get laughs. I worked damned hard on it. It took a month to get to know the character."

Alan continued, "For a while, I read Moriarty's lines with a sense of humor. Then I suddenly realized that he had absolutely *no* sense of humor at all. He's not interested in money, though he deals with it. He's fascinated by pure power. He doesn't care about anyone else but himself. Moriarty is king. He has total authority. I don't know whether I could be that way in real life. It's scary.

"I certainly feel more comfortable with Moriarty now. I feel my performances have gotten larger. This is not just another job. This role is definitely a career move."

In December, Alan was interviewed in the comfortable, new apartment he had rented on East 37th Street by Gerrit Henry for the prestigious entertainment magazine *After Dark*. He left summer stock and dinner theater to come to New York and "sweat it out," he told the reporter. "I wanted to act in front of *people* because I was tired of acting in front of the *eye* of a television camera. My manager at the time wanted to put me on game shows, but I wanted to do something totally different. God knows, the *Laugh-In* image shot off a tremendous amount of work for me, but I'm really, basically, a comic *actor*—comedian, but actor first."

On December 11, Alan tried his luck in children's television when he appeared as a guest star on *Captain Kangaroo*. "Bob Keeshan, who played the Captain, was one the nicest fellows I ever met, but I felt like a bull in china shop," Alan recalled.

The Broadway production of *Sherlock Holmes* closed on January 4, 1976, played a week in Philadelphia, and moved to the O'Keefe Center for the Performing Arts in Toronto, Canada, for a two-week engagement beginning January 14.

Alan with Lois Lane backstage at the Broadhurst.

On February 2, *Sherlock Holmes* began a week of performances at the Hamilton Place Theatre, in Hamilton, Ontario. *The Expositor* newspaper of Hamilton reviewed the play on February 3. "Holmes mania has hit our nation with a bang. The smooth-faced, pipe-smoking detective has been the toast of Broadway and London for some time now. The production, mounted by the Royal Shakespeare Company, along with a pick-up cast of American and English actors, stars one of England's most distinguished and sought-after actors, Robert Stephens. Professor Moriarty, that fiendish, plotting devil, is none other than Alan Sues. He attacks his role with glee, and gives a terrific performance. His make-up will fool you; for the camouflage that takes him two hours to apply turns an easily recognizable face into a stranger."

The Spectator of Hamilton raved about the production; "The travelling version of *Sherlock Holmes* is a very funny play, though it is a cultured comedy. No sex jokes, no slapstick, no clichés, just a thoroughly good-natured satire on Arthur Conan Doyle's Superman detective and on the stylized acting popular at the turn of the century. Alan Sues was impressive as Moriarty. He is a tall man, though lighter than when he appeared as a regular on *Laugh-In*. There is little that is funny in his brusque, sinister portrayal of the underground emperor. He relies too heavily on loud angry shouting to scare his audience, but it is a tendency he fortunately checks with lower insidious tones and the pure threatening power of his size."

The show's next stop was the Fisher Theatre in Detroit, Michigan, where it opened a one-month engagement on February 9. "It was freezing cold in Detroit," Alan remembered. "The theater was beautiful but it was as cold inside as it was on the street. Everyone in the audience was wrapped up in fur coats. I was wearing long johns under my costume. There was a violin trio that played "I Love Paris" in the lobby and they were all wearing gloves! Ever heard anyone play the violin with gloves?"

Sherlock Holmes was an expensive production. Five scenes of sets and props including two living rooms, a gas chamber, a doctor's office, and Moriarty's underground den weighed a collective forty tons. Two forty-five-foot tractor-trailers carried the show from one booking to the next. And it took a full stage crew forty-eight hours to unpack the sets and props and set up the stage. When the cast, sets and crew arrived in Detroit, there was one thing missing—the leading man. Robert Stephens left the show to fulfill another commitment. Leonard Nimoy, (television's Mr. Spock) assumed the role of the legendary sleuth.

"I was very, very upset," Alan said. "I really loved working with Robert. We clicked on stage. Leonard Nimoy was completely different. Where Robert overplayed it for laughs, Leonard played it very straight. Where Robert was a joy to be around, Leonard wasn't. For my taste, he was an elitist, and he was humorless. He worked drunk. He moved like he was sleepwalking. We barely spoke off stage and didn't socialize at all."

On February 15, Jay Carr wrote in *The Detroit News*, "Leonard Nimoy is new to the role of Holmes. This may account for his lack of authority and command. Not surprisingly, Moriarty comes close to walking away with the evening. Sues is on the verge of a juicy portrayal of the Napoleon of crime. He has the fingers for the role. They are long and they twitch convulsively as Moriarty lusts after Holmes' destruction in a voice of lunatic doom."

The *Monday Morning Sun* newspaper wrote, "As Holmes' archenemy, Alan Sues is a vision of terror. With disarrayed hair and

Alan as Professor Moriarty.

riveting bulging eyes he's a menacing Professor Moriarty. He commands the underworld of London with a hand of steel, and has people killed off with the ease of raising his long scraggly fingers. Sues is especially effective."

The college newspaper, *South End*, praised Alan's performance. "The plot is a typically complicated one, involving a network of evil headed by the Napoleon of Crime, Professor Moriarty, convincingly conniving as played by Alan Sues. His ruthless stare and cold, calculating nature is pure evil. Sues' calculating portrayal of this villain is perfect."

"The critics were dismissive of Leonard," Alan recalled, "and he was infuriated by my good reviews. All of a sudden, it was every man for himself on stage. We began to have technical problems, too. The fog machines worked intermittently, sometimes blowing fog at the wrong time. In Detroit, the flat set walls didn't fit properly, and the audience could see what was going on back stage. The show had changed. Warren Enters took over direction when we went on the road. He turned it in a different direction, but Leonard was flat and so boring on stage, it was like letting the air out of a balloon."

After a five-day stop at the Hanna Theatre in Cleveland, *Sherlock Holmes* began a six-week engagement at the Shubert Theater in Los Angeles on March 23. Since Alan had previously rented his house, he now rented an apartment in West Hollywood while he was in California. One afternoon, Alan received a call from the West Hollywood Sheriff's office. The neighbor who lived next door to Alan's house on Dorrington had admired Alan's front garden and taken photographs of the flower bed. Alan's tenant, who was in the witness protection program, panicked at the sight of a stranger taking pictures, and called the police. Fortunately, Alan was in town and could vouch for the veracity of his hapless neighbors. "Of course," Alan joked, "it *was* a beautiful flower garden!"

Any hopes he had that the role of Moriarty would redefine his career were dashed by the Los Angeles critics. "It was vicious," Alan recalled. "It seemed like they were out to get me. I really couldn't believe the way I was attacked. It was depressing, and reinforced my feeling that the only real work for me was in New York."

On March 27, theater critic Dan Sullivan panned the show in the *Los Angeles Times*. About Alan, he wrote, "Alan Sues as Moriarty is callow to the core, assuming there is one. No force, no voice and lousy makeup. Boo! Oh, it's just Alan. If that's the joke, it's an extremely private one. Moriarty as Mr. Bluster just doesn't play, especially when there's no bluster. Sues seems to be doing Saturday morning children's TV, the kind you don't let them watch."

The *Los Angeles Herald-Examiner* found the play to be "leaden." "*Sherlock Holmes* has opened at the Shubert, but this response is not a review—it's a lament. Leonard Nimoy is Holmes and Alan Sues is Professor Moriarty; Sues used to ring little bells on *Laugh-In*. But no bells ring at the Shubert. Sues' nemesis Moriarty looks like a flamboyant Kabuki character missing only his kimono and clappers. His interpretation and particularly makeup is drawn with color crayons."

The final blow was effectively delivered by *Daily Variety*, one of the most read and important entertainment trade periodicals in show business. On March 29, they wrote, "While Los Angeles theatre in recent years has been struggling to lose the reputation of being just another stop on a road company's tour, along comes a third-rate production of *Sherlock Holmes*. The atrocity at the Shubert Theatre is exactly the kind of thing the L.A. theatre community has been trying to shake off for the past 10 years. And it's the kind of thing that has kept people away from theatre for even longer than that.

"Sues wrecks the role of Moriarty in more ways than one. Starting with his grotesque make-up, which detracts from about everything else on stage. Sues plays the evil professor as a fey felon rather than the arch criminal menace Doyle would have him be. And Sues adds his own broad *Laugh-In* shtick which just doesn't fit 19th Century London."

Alan was stunned. "I couldn't fucking believe it," he said. "It was so depressing. I was certain I'd never work in Hollywood again. I ate every God-damn donut I could find. I put out two thousand dollars in tickets for casting people and producers to come see the show. It didn't do a damn thing. Nobody even came backstage. I couldn't wait to get out of Los Angeles. The rest of the tour was miserable. Leonard and I barely spoke. When I started the tour, I left my dog with Walter Finley who was staying in my Manhattan apartment, and I was so lonely."

Sherlock Holmes opened a five-day stand at the Auditorium Theatre in Denver, Colorado, on May 5. The *Rocky Mountain News* dismissed the performance of Leonard Nimoy, but praised Alan's work. "Nimoy's time-warp characterization throws the play out of balance and opens the way for others to shine. Some do. Alan

Leonard Nimoy as Holmes and Alan as Moriarty.

Sues, his red eyes ringed by sinister strokes of mascara, is a splendidly gaunt and vampirish Dr. Moriarty, installed with his devious genius in a paranoid chamber equipped with the production's greatest mechanical attraction—an elaborate door with enough clanging bolts and grinding gears to dazzle the back rows of the balcony."

The Shubert Theatre in Chicago hosted the final performances of *Sherlock Holmes* which began a one-month engagement on May 10. On the opening night, in the middle of the second act, an anonymous telephone bomb threat was called into the theater. The stage manager interrupted the actors and calmly asked everyone to clear the building. "It was a perfect ending," Alan said, "very appropriate. If I'd known that old trick would work, I'd have phoned in a few while we were in Los Angeles."

The *Chicago Sun-Times* was not impressed with the show. On May 13, their review read, "In New York, it was a Royal Shakespeare Company production, hailed for its classy style. This version is the kind of road show that we thought we had stopped tolerating. For one thing, the director doesn't know whether to patronize the script, parody it or play it straight. So he does all three styles, and as a result it ends up with no style at all. Leonard Nimoy of *Star Trek* does all the things Holmes is supposed to do. But the voice is weak and there is no flair, no melodrama, no mood. I wouldn't send him out to find my lost puppy. And is Alan *Laugh-In* Sues as the villainous Professor Moriarty scary? The Napoleon of crime? They must be talking about the dessert."

On May 14, the Northeastern Illinois University newspaper, *Print*, panned the show, calling it "a probable impossibility." The reviewer did enjoy Alan's performance, however. "Many who had seen the New York production just knew that Allen (sic) Sues, star of *Laugh-In*, would blow it as the present Moriarty. Not so, not so! Allen Sues and his make-up man did a fine job. He was a believably sinister, astute, villainous Moriarty."

Alan said, "The one passable review I got in Chicago and they didn't even spell my name right! The only good thing about my bad reviews was that Leonard began to say hello to me in passing backstage."

Act 3
Scene 1

1976–1986 "You could play gay if it was funny and not sexual, but you couldn't be gay."

The bell-tinkling, eyeball-rolling, hands-fluttering character Alan had created on *Laugh-In* was proving to be nearly impossible to overcome. Even when he was playing it "straight" in the role of a villain, most reviewers referenced his years on *Laugh-In*. His television game show assignments and frequent talk-show appearances seemed to perpetuate the "character" he was trying to distance himself from, and it created a familiarity with his audience that compromised his ability to act any role other than the one loved by his fans.

Alan's "witness-protection" tenant moved out as quietly as she had moved in. "She disappeared into thin air," he said. Alan moved back into his house, and remodeled the kitchen. He worked with an architect to enlarge his bathroom and create an open space shower with a tiled floor and walls. During the summer of 1976, he taped appearances on the television game shows *Cross Wits* and *Celebrity Sweepstakes*.

In the mid 1970s, Gay Liberation reared its surfer-boy, blonde-haired head with determination. At the time, the "gay scene" in Los Angeles was becoming more and more talked about. Gay men's culture informed social life, politics and pop culture. The gay population wasn't interested in hiding any longer, or even blending in

The kitchen at 9014 Dorrington.

as a means of acceptance. Young gay men and women wanted to flaunt their new-found freedom verbally and physically.

Like Fire Island in New York, Provincetown in Massachusetts and Key West in Florida, West Hollywood, California, (nestled between Los Angeles and Beverly Hills), became a popular and important gay oasis as "liberated" homosexual men became more visible. Boutiques, design shops, restaurants and bars sprung up in the community soon dubbed "Boys Town." It measured less than two square miles, and it was estimated that more than 40 percent of the population was gay.

Alan's house on Dorrington Avenue was two blocks from Santa Monica Boulevard, the center of all the commercial activity. Alan enjoyed the boutiques, the food and the bars. Ah, Men was a popular men's clothing store nearby. Famous for see-through pants, mesh underwear, revealing bathing suits and low-rise slacks, Ah, Men attracted an eclectic crowd including upwardly mobile gay men, bodybuilders, porn stars, and Hollywood celebrities. Alan was a longtime friend of the founder, Don Cook. The entrepreneur was a graduate of the Pasadena Playhouse, and owner of Numbers Bar and Restaurant on Sunset Boulevard. Numbers catered to a gay clientele.

Alan posed with his friend Richard Deacon, who had starred in *The Dick Van Dyke Show*, and Cook for publicity photos to promote the clothing store. "It was hardly a coming out event," Alan said, "but some friends of mine were actually upset that I did that. The photos appeared in the newspaper and my agent wasn't thrilled with it, either. But I knew Don for years and I went to Numbers quite a lot. And Sammy Davis Jr. shopped in the store for Christ sakes!"

In spite of many advances, there was still a strong wave of conservatism that defined the times. In 1975, an actor named Michael Kearns's previously closeted life came to a sudden end when he posed for the cover of a gay book called *The Happy Hustler*. Kearns had been cast to play John Boy's older brother in the family-friendly television series *The Waltons*, but when he was revealed to be the Happy Hustler on the book cover (some in the press wrongly assumed he *was* a male hustler), his acting career was derailed. He didn't act again on television for seven years.

A couple of years later, Robin Tyler and her lover, Patti Harrison, had a successful feminist comedy nightclub act. Fred Silverman, the head of ABC-TV, saw their act and gave them a television series of their own. When they expressed concern to Silverman about the ever-present and dreaded "morals clause" in their contract, he assured them that everything would be fine—"Just don't act up publicly." Tyler and Harrison hosted *The Krofft Comedy Hour* on July 29, 1978. After the Sid and Marty Krofft production was broadcast that evening, Robin Tyler appeared on the eleven o'clock news, speaking at a gay rally. Fred Silverman exercised the "morals clause" and dropped their contract.

Alan explained, "You could *play* gay if it was funny and *not* sexual, but you couldn't *be* gay. I was never really ashamed of who I was or the roles I played, but when your acting career is full of nancy boy characters, then it's hard to do anything else. And when an audience or the critics love your *performance*, but the world has a different opinion about your *private* life, then you have a problem dealing with all the emotions.

"Some of us dug the new freedom," Alan recalled, "and some of us didn't get much of a benefit." "Camp" quickly fell out of fashion. Youthful culture informed the gay liberation movement, and a lot of the "old school" closeted homosexuals were shut out of the party. "I wasn't sure where I fit in," Alan said. "My style of comedy was criticized more than it was praised in certain sectors of the gay community. It seemed to represent a repressed time, and young gay men were more uninhibited. They didn't come out of the closet so much as run out of the closet like a pack of wild horses. I thought it was great for them. But it was overwhelming for those of us who had led double lives for so long. When I was young, I didn't know how to express my sexual feelings. There were younger gay men who distanced themselves from us older guys because we represented a time of shame to them. I think we should have been *more* embraced just for that reason."

In 1974, what would become one of the most successful gay nightspots in California opened in West Hollywood. With room for 1,500 patrons, Studio One on North LaPeer Drive quickly became the premiere disco in Los Angeles. Leonard Grant, one of the own-

Alan in 1976. Photo by Martha Swope.

ers, created a nightclub called the Back Lot adjacent to the disco. His longtime experience as a Hollywood agent with clients such as Ann-Margret and Liberace gave Grant access to top talent. As a result, he became the booking agent for the Back Lot, and opened the showroom in January 1975 with a performance by Peggy Lee. Stars quickly lined up to appear at the popular spot including Chita Rivera, Joan Rivers, Phyllis Diller and Eartha Kitt, and some of the best female impersonators in the business including Craig Russell, Jim Bailey, Jimmy James, Kenny Sacha, and Charles Pierce.

Alan frequented the Back Lot, and was there with other *Laugh-In* friends for Ruth Buzzi's opening night. "Everybody was playing the Back Lot," Alan recalled. "I wanted to do an act there, too. I saw Charles Nelson Reilly and Rip Taylor there, and they were great. I talked with Leonard Grant many times, but he hated me. I offered to go in and do a bit just for him, so he could see what I did, but he wasn't interested. I didn't do wacky stand-up like Rip, but Charlie was a story-teller, and I felt I could do that. It would have been a good spot for me, but it never happened."

On November 8, 1976, Alan flew to Edmonton, Canada, to begin rehearsals for his starring role in the Woody Allen-penned comedy *Play It Again, Sam*. The play opened November 23 at Stage West Dinner Theater in Edmonton to rave reviews. After six sold-out weeks, the comedy moved to the Community Theater Harbor Playhouse in Corpus Christi, Texas. The one-week engagement opened on January 12, 1977. The *Corpus Christi Caller-Times* wrote, "Big Al—Alan Sues of *Laugh-In* really gets into the swing of his part in Woody Allen's romantic comedy about a comically inept hero in search of romance after his wife leaves him. A funny, wacky performance."

Alan returned to his 37th Street Manhattan apartment in February 1977. "I realized the kind of roles I wanted were not going to be offered to me," he said. "I had written my own material for years, and it just hit me that I should go back and write again."

Alan enrolled in writing classes, and frequently saw his friend, actress Barbara Sharma. "I was going back and forth between coasts," Barbara said, "but eventually was cast in the Broadway musical *I Love My Wife*. Alan and I had lunch almost every day. He really was my best friend. He was working on material and bounced stuff off me all the time."

Based on the classic children's stories, *Raggedy Ann & Andy* was an animated feature film written by Patricia Thackray and Max Wilk. Joe Raposa, who wrote music for *Sesame Street*, *Electric Company*, and the Broadway musical *You're A Good Man, Charlie Brown*, wrote seventeen songs for the film. Alan provided the voice of the Loonie Knight, and sang "Because I Love You." The four-million-

Alan with Shelley Berman in Room Service.

dollar production, which had taken two years to complete, was released to excellent reviews in the spring of 1977.

On March 2, Alan began a one-month engagement at Illinois's Arlington Park Theater in the 1937 John Murray-Allen Boretz manic, backroom farce *Room Service*. The screwball comedy concerns a penniless producer who finagles free room and board for his twenty-two member cast in a Times Square hotel while trying to raise money to produce his show. *Room Service* had been made into a film in 1938 starring The Marx Brothers. The cast of the play included Shelley Berman and Ron Palillo, who starred on the hit television comedy *Welcome Back, Kotter*.

On March 11, the *Arlington Heights Herald* reviewed *Room Service*, calling it "an old-time farce, generously sprinkled with slapstick." The newspaper wrote, "The play is filled with clichés and stale dialog that would bore you to death unless you concentrated on how it is said. Discover it, and you're definitely in for some offbeat, ludicrous fun. Ron Palillo, on hiatus from *Welcome Back, Kotter*, plays a wet-behind-the-ears young playwright who gets pushed around all the time. Alan Sues, in much the same kind of role he plays on television in *Laugh-In*, is the eccentric director who can't think with his clothes on. Shelley Berman behaves on the stage like the veteran pro he is. Sues contrasts Berman's straight-man role with continuous tomfoolery. The three—Berman, Sues and Palillo—work very well together. Timing is everything."

Alan later recalled, "I hated Shelley Berman. He was impossible, and terrible to the other actors in the show. The script meant nothing to him. I'd be engrossed in a scene and then I'd realize Shelley had gone completely off-book and was doing some kind of improvisation. It was like a counterpoint duet gone horribly wrong. And the more I complained to him, the worse he got. It was awful.

"But Ron Palillo was terrific. He was very mild-mannered, like his character. He was gay and quite reserved. Always smiling. He packed them in. Most of the audience was there to see him. They loved him on his TV show. You couldn't get out the stage door, there were always a hundred kids waiting for him."

Following his successful run in *Room Service*, Alan returned to California. In July, he appeared on *The Merv Griffin Show*, and on July 19 he attended the star-studded opening night performance of his old friend Charles Pierce at the Back Lot in West Hollywood. After the show, he hosted a cocktail party at his home.

"I had a full house," Alan explained, "a lot of old friends like Richard Deacon, Dom DeLuise, Alice Ghostley, and Charles Nelson Reilly. Charles Pierce arrived in drag wearing a glittering, full-length gown. He walked up the driveway arm in arm with Bea Arthur. The nosy couple who lived next door watched all this from their front door, and Charles waved and yelled out to them, 'It's just like Noah's Ark, two by two!' Charlie was behind them and yelled out, 'More like the Titanic!' Dom yelled, 'Up periscope!'

"We had an impromptu show in the living room. I stood at the front door and had everyone empty their pockets when they left. I could have been picked clean that night. Alice Ghostley was tiny but she tried to get out with a service for three in her purse."

In August, Alan was cast in a stock production of the musical *The Pajama Game*. With music and lyrics by Richard Adler and Jerry Roos, *The Pajama Game* had been a long-running hit on Broadway in the mid-1950s. The story concerns labor troubles in a pajama factory where workers demand a seven and a half cent pay raise. Some of the popular songs from the show include "Hey There," "Steam Heat," and "Hernando's Hideaway."

The Pajama Game opened August 16 for a two-week engagement at the Melody Top Theater in Milwaukee, Wisconsin. The 2,200 seat theater-in-the-round was in an enormous, circus-style tent in a meadowland on the outskirts of the city. On August 17, the *Milwaukee Journal* enthusiastically reviewed the show, "The musical brings to mind a pajama party attended by teenage girls. It is rollicking and occasionally raucous, effervescent and unusually fast moving. Rousing rounds of applause were common and culminated in a standing ovation. As the fastidious timekeeper who is forever wound up, Alan Sues just did not stop. The star of television's *Laugh-In* hit top speed as a comic when doing a slapstick segment. His modeling of buttonless pajama bottoms put the audience in stitches."

Jay Joslyn, writing for the *Milwaukee Sentinel*, didn't appreciate the production, but acknowledged Alan's performance. "The audience knocks itself out laughing at the fey swishing of the unregulated, bug-eyed Alan Sues!"

A few days later, Alan was interviewed by Anne Mason for the *Milwaukee Journal*. He was still sensitive about the critical thumping he took while appearing in *Sherlock Holmes*. "Critics seem to know road shows," he explained. "And they seem to be more critical in, say, towns that don't get so many shows. But then, Philadelphia is known for its slanderous critics, to the point where productions are now bypassing the city for Washington. There is a real need for good critics. It's so easy to slash without being constructive afterwards. Many critics don't even critique the show, they just describe what the show is about. And take John Simon, *New York Magazine* critic. He talks about how ugly people are, about physical attributes that people can't control!"

Mason asked Alan if he read what the critics wrote about him. "If I'm doing something I've done quite a bit before and know the audience likes it, then no, not really," Alan explained. "But if I'm making a departure and want to see the reaction, then sometimes. Mostly, it's how I feel about what I'm doing. How I feel when I'm going in to it."

Alan in 1976. Photo by Martha Swope.

Super Night at Forest Hills was a one hour music/variety television special produced and directed by Marty Pasetta. Broadcast on September 9, 1977, the program was hosted by Sammy Davis Jr. and Andy Williams. Alan and Zsa Zsa Gabor provided the voices in an animated sequence involving two tennis balls conversing on the court. Alan also appeared as a celebrity panelist on the game show *Liars Club*, and guest-starred on *The Merv Griffin Show* on October 10.

On November 22, Alan starred as The Metric Monster on a CBS television children's special called *The Great Metric Mystery*. Producer Ted Field recalled, "I had met Alan at a Christmas party on the coast, and I said in a joking way that if he was ever free, maybe he could work on a kids' show for us."

At the time, it was a CBS policy for local stations to produce children's shows. The Federal Government was contemplating a conversion to the metric system of weights and measures. "I had it in mind to do something on metrics," Field explained. "Finally I got around to batting out a plot one weekend."

Alan's fellow cast mates included a detective, a flamingo, and an assortment of puppets. The story concerned the flamingo's search for his lost inch-ruler. The detective suspected foul play, knowing that the metric system was taking over.

"Alan had some very difficult lines," Field said. "First he had to learn the metric system before he could even learn his lines. This show is very visual and funny, it's not too preachy. But Alan had to convey a lot of information."

"I taught myself using an antique grocery scale I bought in Massachusetts when I was doing summer stock," Alan said. "I used it for cooking all the time. It cost twenty dollars, but three hundred to ship it home. Now I could write it off!"

In makeup and costume resembling Professor Moriarty, Alan frantically waved his arms and rolled his eyes while repeating his mantra, "the pint is passé, the gallon is gone, the ounce is bounced, nothing could be sweeter than measuring by meter."

"This was made for the local television market in Philadelphia," Alan explained. "I had a great time on the show. I thought it could get me into Saturday morning television. The critics said I was terrific, but I scared kids. But I thought, wasn't that the point?

"Sid and Marty Krofft had a pretty good thing going with children's programming. Charles Nelson Reilly worked for them on *Lidsville*, and Rip Taylor was on *Sigmund and the Sea Monster*. Even Ruth had a show with them called, *The Lost Saucer*. I couldn't get anywhere with them."

Sid Krofft recalled, "I knew Alan and we thought he was great. On camera, he was as animated as a cartoon, and that's what we always looked for. It was more about timing, really. He wasn't available when we were putting certain things together. He fit the mould, though. He would have been great. I always liked Alan."

While he was in Los Angeles, Alan visited his parents in Solvang. "I wrote to them," he said. "I always told them what I was doing, but I never heard anything back from them. I drove up without calling, and when I knocked on the door, my mother didn't know who I was. Like a fool, I told her I was her son, and she reluctantly let me in."

Before returning to New York, Alan had several network meetings in regard to a television pilot he had written for himself and Ruth Buzzi called *Cater to Murder*. Alan and Ruth would play siblings who try to operate a catering business left to them by their recently deceased mother. "I wrote it as a feature film first," Alan explained. "Then I was told to turn it into a television pilot, which I did. I had a lot of good meetings, but couldn't get it off the ground. Then I met with a producer who looked like some kid selling lemonade on a street corner. I think he went to work on roller skates. He didn't know who I was, and he didn't know what *Laugh-In* was. He told me I should turn it into a play. I wished him luck with his mid-term exam, and went back to New York."

For the next few years, Alan lived a bi-coastal life. An old friend needed a place to live, so Alan rented his West Hollywood house again, and sublet a small Studio City apartment to use when he was in Los Angeles.

Alan appeared as a guest star on *Super Night at the Super Bowl* on January 14, 1978. The ninety-minute special, broadcast on CBS on the eve of Super Bowl XII, was highlighted by songs and skits about football. The program was hosted by Joe Namath and Andy Williams, and filmed live at the New Orleans Theater of Performing Arts.

Alan appeared on *The Merv Griffin Show* in February and again in March, and later that year, guest-starred as an effete decorator named "Andre Massoon" in an episode called "Cinderella Girls" on the popular anthology show *Fantasy Island*, and as a neurotic florist on the police-themed television series *CHiPS*, in an episode called "Neighborhood Watch."

Peter Pan *playbill.*

Alan appeared in the dual roles of Mr. Darling and Captain Hook in an ambitious production of *Peter Pan* at the Melody Top Theatre in Milwaukee in June 1978. The classic play by James Barrie about a mischievous boy who can fly and refuses to grow up was first produced in 1904. The musical adaptation of Barrie's play premiered in 1954 with music by Mark Charlop and Jule Styne, and lyrics by Carolyn Leigh, Betty Comden and Adolph Green.

The special effects and technical stunts proved too overwhelming for the Milwaukee theater. The announcement of a tornado warning at intermission cleared the opening night audience. "That was one of our highlights," Alan joked. Nancy Dussault starred as the perpetual youngster, Peter Pan. The reviews were withering. On June 21, the *Milwaukee Sentinel* reported, "Alan Sues was a rehearsal or two away from being prepared. Once he learns his lines and music cues, his Captain Hook may work." *The Milwaukee Journal* was less kind. "A startling disappointment is Alan Sues, who has large comic gifts and a deliciously villainous costume as Captain Hook. But Sues first proves erratically uneasy as Mr. Darling and then becomes a distracted, constricted Hook, with only a couple of ideas how to run with a great role."

Nancy Dussault recalled, "Alan went crazy with Captain Hook. He was so well cast in the role. He was wonderful. And he loved the costume! He was loaded with ruffles and lace and bangles. He even decorated his hook! When we opened, he was distracted by the costume, always fluffing the ruffles, and he struggled with his lines. I got the company together and told everyone to learn his cues and lines so they could help him out if he got stuck. He got it down in a short time, and was delightful. He was so funny, he made me scream. Every time I walked past his dressing room he was ironing. He had his dog, Lois Lane, with him and said he was taking her to the Elizabeth Arden Salon. We'd have lunch together and go antique shopping all the time.

"He had a beautiful home filled with things he bought on the road. He was so creative and he decorated it beautifully. My husband and I rented the house for a short time when I was in Los Angeles to shoot the movie *In-Laws* that fall. Alan was so proud of his house, and it was really lovely. It was an extension of him."

On July 10, *Peter Pan* opened a one-week engagement at the Sacramento Music Circus in California. The technical kinks had been worked out, and Alan was better prepared for his roles. Audiences loved the show and the critics were a bit kinder.

Alan as Captain Hook.

Rankin/Bass Productions was an American production company best known for its seasonal television specials using "animagic," a stop-motion animation process using figurines. Some of their best known and best loved specials include *Rudolph the Red-Nose Reindeer*, *Frosty the Snowman*, *The Little Drummer Boy*, and *Jack Frost*. Romeo Muller, responsible for more than fifty feature films and television specials, wrote *Rudolph and Frosty's Christmas in July* as a feature animated film for Rankin/Bass. The movie featured the voices of Red Buttons, Ethel Merman, Shelley Winters, and Mickey Rooney. Alan provided the voice of Scratch the Reindeer.

"Mickey was the voice of Santa Claus," Alan recalled, "and he's about as far away from Santa Claus as you can get. He was impossible to work with. He analyzed every word, every line, and wanted to rewrite everything. I thought I would lose my mind. He would arrive with his new rewrites, and now the other actors' lines had nothing to do with what his character was saying. The director objected and said, 'Mickey, this doesn't work, the other lines don't work with what you've written.' And Mickey's attitude was 'so what, just cut them out.' That went over really big with the other actors. Mickey and Shelley nearly got into a fist-fight in the recording booth. Actually, they did. I was able to crawl out on all fours. Mickey was a scrapper, but Shelley was just too big for the little guy, and she beat him down. Now, that's a Christmas special!"

Rudolph and Frosty's Christmas in July flopped as a feature film when it was released on July 1, 1979, but was broadcast to acclaim on ABC-TV later that year, and has since become a perennial television holiday classic.

While on the west coast, Alan appeared as a guest-star with Jerry Stiller on the television series *Time Express*, in an episode called "Garbage Man/Doctor's Wife." Vincent Price and his wife, actress Coral Browne, hosted the "Time Express" which was a train that took its passengers back in time to relive a moment in their lives.

"They were a real *Hollywood* couple," Alan said. "Vincent was terrific, an old-school gentleman. Always gracious. He had been on *Laugh-In* a few times. He had a spooky reputation, but he loved to laugh and he was very funny. For *Time Express*, he and his wife had dressing rooms at opposite ends. Coral Browne had a long-time affair with a British actress named Mary Morris. Vincent was always entertaining handsome young guys. He was surrounded by muscle men in his dressing room, and Coral was surrounded by beautiful lesbians dressed in leather in her dressing room. When Vincent and Coral passed each other on the set, they'd nod and smile and both say, 'Hello, darling,' like they were casual acquaintances. I'm not sure they even arrived in the same car."

The cast of Beane's of Boston.

In the spring of 1979, Alan filmed a pilot called *Beane's of Boston*, an American version of the British television hit *Are You Being Served?* Produced by Garry Marshall, and directed by Jerry Paris, the pilot was written by David Croft and Jeremy Lloyd who had written the original British show, and veteran comedy writers Sheldon Bull and Bill Idelson. The cast also included Tom Poston, John Hillerman, and Charlotte Rae. Marshall had two enormously popular situation comedies on the air concurrently, *Happy Days* and *Laverne & Shirley*. Considering the talent involved in the production, Alan had high hopes the pilot would sell to a network.

"I was very disappointed *Beanes* didn't sell," Alan explained. "Garry was the biggest guy in TV at the time and we did a great pilot. Someone told me the network liked it, but Garry was too overwhelmed with his other shows and dropped it. Whatever happened, it was a fucking shame."

"Alan was very funny," Charlotte Rae said. "This was a good pilot with a very good script. We were all disappointed it didn't make it. I think Alan wanted to be back on TV. He was a lot of fun to work with. Entertaining on and off."

Alan suffered another disappointment when he was hired to guest-star on a new show starring Redd Foxx called *Sanford*. The thirty-minute comedy was a midseason replacement, and a sequel to Foxx's hit series *Sanford and Son*. Alan was cast as a Gucci salesman in an upscale department store who has a run-in with Foxx's character, Fred Sanford. "I had a terrific scene with Redd," Alan said. "We got along great, and had a good time. I did my lines of dialogue and Redd did his lines of cocaine. But Mort Lachman struck again. He was the executive producer. I didn't know that and he showed up on set a couple days into filming. At the end of the day, I left. When I got home, my agent called and said I was fired, but not to worry because they would pay me anyway. Mort hated me, I never knew why. He cut me out of a job years before, and he did it again. It was embarrassing."

In the summer, Alan played the role of the comic reporter Benjamin Kidd in The Muny Theater production of the 1926 Broadway musical *The Desert Song*. With music by Sigmund Romberg and book and lyrics by Oscar Hammerstein, *The Desert Song* concerns the 1925 uprising of Moroccan revolutionaries who rise up against French Colonial rule. The hero, who falls in love with a beautiful girl, disguises his true identity by assuming a milquetoast persona. Through the years, the musical had been adapted to the screen three times and was presented as a live television special in the 1950s. "It was very old-fashioned," Alan explained. "Originally, it was very steamy, but all the suggestive things were taken out. I was the comic relief. I had a great number called "It." A lot of sheiks running around and a huge cast, it was fun."

Starring Ann Blyth, *The Desert Song* began a one-week engagement on July 23. Steve McQueen's wife, Neile Adams, played Alan's sidekick, Susan. "Ann Blyth was wonderful," Alan recalled. "She walked around with a big smile plastered on her face, and carrying flowers all the time. I never saw anything like it. She played a young French lass and she was fifty years old! I liked her, but Steve's wife was more fun. Swore like a longshoreman."

Beginning in the mid-1970s, Benji the dog was the star of a string of feature films. In late 1979, Alan was cast in a new Benji film called *Oh, Heavenly Dog*. Starring Chevy Chase, Jane Seymour,

Omar Sharif, and Robert Morley, the movie was shot in Canada and France. Like all the other Benji films, *Oh, Heavenly Dog* was directed by Joe Camp. The plot was simple. Chevy Chase played a murdered private investigator, reincarnated as Benji, who is hired to investigate his own murder.

Alan filmed his scenes in Montreal, Canada. "Chevy Chase was a bully," Alan said. "He was an asshole and constantly made fag jokes. But I loved Omar Sharif. We stayed in the same hotel and I had drinks with him in the lounge every night. I imagined we were honeymooning. The first night we were there, I ran into him in the hotel lobby. He took my arm and said, 'Oh, Alan, join me for an aperitif. We need a respite from this dreadful assignment. Who could imagine such a situation? What will we do about agents who put us in movies starring dogs? Just look at us, we need each other to make all this bearable.' *You ain't just whistling Dixie*, I thought.

"He wore the most beautiful, tailored Italian suits and turtleneck sweaters. He was very classy, and so charming. He had an incredible accent. 'Oh, Alan,' he said to me at the bar, 'have some of these peanuts. They're so delicious and fresh roasted. Oh, Alan, have one of these pretzels. It has the perfect crunch. It's marvelous.' Omar was a real sweet-talker."

Although the Benji film franchise had been very successful, *Oh, Heavenly Dog* was not. It opened in July 1980, and bombed. "I never even saw it," Alan said.

In the summer of 1980, Alan appeared in a supporting role in the Kenley Players production of the Lerner and Loewe musical *Brigadoon*, the story of a small, enchanting Scottish town that appears for only one day in each century. The show starred John Gabriel and the Cleveland Ballet, and opened at E. J. Thomas Hall at Akron University on July 8. *Brigadoon* also played in Columbus and Cincinnati.

On July 17, the *Cincinnati Enquirer* wrote, "*Brigadoon* is hollow at its core. Alan Sues employs all the mugging, eye rolling and spastic schtick which made him famous to get his laughs. It's just that he is in no way the character of Jaded Jeff as written by Lerner and Lowe. Gabriel is at a disadvantage; he can neither act, sing, dance or walk. Since Sues is busy effecting a drunken stagger worthy of Soupy Sales, the pair suggest a couple of out-of-control muppets."

Alan said, "Bad reviews, bad experience, but of course there was John Kenley riding around backstage on his bicycle in drag, and me standing in a kilt signing autographs for an hour after each show. Luckily I had the legs for it. A few days after we opened, I met a writer at John's party and the guy said to me, 'I would have reviewed the show, but I couldn't stand it and left after the third number.' I told him if I'd known that, I would have joined him."

In August, after appearing on *The Merv Griffin Show* to promote his upcoming theatrical engagement, Alan arrived in Sacramento, California, to appear as Prince Dauntless the Drab in the Music Circus production of the musical comedy *Once Upon a Mattress*. The farcial fable was based on the classic Hans Christian Andersen story "The Princess and the Pea." The story concerns a medieval King and Queen who put a girl named Winifred the Woebegone through an impossible series of tests to see if she is fit to marry their son, Prince Dauntless. Jo Anne Worley played Winifred. The cast included Roger Perry, Russ Thacker and Jackie Joseph.

"Alan was a delight," Jackie recalled. "The show had a very talented cast. The audience got their money's worth. Alan was wonderful to work with. A rascal. We did benefits together through the years. I always enjoyed him. His humor was unexpected. It would pop out like a champagne cork pops. And like me, he *loved* animals."

Mary Rodgers wrote the music and Marshall Barer wrote the lyrics for *Once Upon a Mattress*. The creative team was also responsible for *The Mad Show* in which Jo Anne and Alan had appeared. *Mattress* opened a one-week engagement at the Music Circus on August 11, 1980, and did brisk business.

At his mother's request, Alan drove to Solvang to visit his ailing father. Pete Sues had been diagnosed with Alzheimer's disease. "In the early stages, he was very mean and argumentative," Alan said. "I told my mother if that was Alzheimer's then I think he had it since I was a kid. I stayed in touch with them with calls and notes, but before long, my father completely lost it and became bedridden. On my next visit, he barely knew who I was. He stayed that way for ten years until he died in 1990."

In the fall, Alan filmed a guest-shot in an episode of *Brady Brides* called "Cool Hand Phil," which was broadcast months later in April 1981. He also had a small role in the all-star cast of a television movie called *The Great American Traffic Jam* that aired on October 2, 1980. Also known as *Gridlock*, the film starred Desi Arnaz Jr., and concerned the many mishaps caused by a series of traffic jams on Los Angeles freeways.

The CBS Library was an anthology series that presented animated and live action versions of children's books. Alan provided the voice of The Reluctant Dragon in an episode called "Misunderstood Monsters." The twelve-minute cartoon also featured the voices of John Carradine and Louis Nye. "Misunderstood Monsters" aired several months later in early 1981.

Alan settled into his apartment in Studio City, and worked on the one-man show he had tinkered with for years. There was no work for him in television, theater or film, aside from his frequent appearances on *The Merv Griffin Show*.

In March, he turned fifty-five years old. "Hollywood is about youth," Alan said. "Ruth Webb represented me at the time, and I went on auditions, but people making decisions were kids. I couldn't get anything. It was frustrating and depressing."

Occasionally, Alan met a man at a bar, but dating was sporadic. He was attracted to younger men. Often they were aspiring actors who thought Alan could help them professionally. "The scene was very sexual," he explained. "I was more interested in romance. I just wanted someone to kiss. The men that I met in the bars were very young, and nobody wanted anything steady. One night I asked a guy I met if he'd ever been in love or if he wanted a relationship. He looked at me for a second and said, 'No, not really. But sometimes I think it would be nice to have someone to go to Magic Mountain with.' I thought that was a euphemism for sex, then I found out it was an amusement park!"

Jerry Jackson, Alan's longtime friend, said, "Alan's problem had to do with trust. He didn't really trust anyone. He didn't even trust himself, or his own judgment. If he got close to anyone, he would nitpick and find the most inane reasons to break up. I think the chance of real intimacy frightened him. He didn't know how to deal with that."

As the holidays approached, Alan returned to his 37th Street Manhattan apartment in November to be near his brother and his family. "I always felt more creative in New York," Alan said. "Even with all the distractions, I always felt inspired there."

Alan had been referred by his Los Angeles psychiatrist to a hypnotherapist in New York City to help with his latest bout of depression. The urge to drink or overeat was always in his mind, but his issues of low self-esteem boiled to the surface again as his career opportunities seemed to all but evaporate. He was intrigued by the hypnosis his new therapist used to treat him. He researched the development of hypnosis and found that the process evolved from the theories of a German-born physician named Franz Anton Mesmer. Mesmer theorized that there was a natural energetic transference that occurred between all animated and inanimate objects that he called "animal magnetism." Mesmerism, named after Mesmer, emphasizes the movement of life "energies" through distinct areas of the body. In 1843, a Scottish physician named James Braid introduced the term "hypnosis" to describe a technique derived from the direction of these "energies" through the power of suggestion.

Inspired by what he thought were the immediate benefits of his new hypnotic therapy, Alan wrote a one-man show he called *Mesmerize, Mesmerism, Mesmerizer—The Story of Dr. Franz Anton Mesmer*. The work gave him the opportunity to play seventeen different characters. Within a year, Alan was performing the piece in workshops in Manhattan with the hope of booking his show on a college tour. "I wore a powdered wig, and a frilly Lord Byron shirt," Alan recalled. "It was a serious subject, but I wrote it as a comedy."

For the next couple of years, Alan stayed in New York and concentrated on his own writing projects. "I had no interest in going back to Los Angeles," he said. "I went back to California to visit my folks, but that was the only reason for me to go back." He worked on a cabaret act with a musician named Carl Eugster, who had written music for a couple of films in the 1970s, and was best known for his 1958 comedy album *Songs for Bashful Lovers*. They wrote a dozen songs about a struggling performer who fails an audition but in desperation, refuses to leave the stage until the producer hears a repertoire of his own compositions. Some of the original songs included "Contacts" and "The Goddess of India."

The centerpiece of the production was a song written by Alan called "I'm So Mediocre." The composition wasn't hit material, but Alan's lyrics were very revealing.

I'm so mediocre I could never be a threat!
The minute that they look at me
They all agree
There's got to be a place
For a face

I'm so mediocre
I make everyone look good!
I smile and do my walk-on bit,
My one-line part
No one ever calls it art
And no one ever could . . .
'cept maybe Hollywood!

I'm so mediocre,
So nothing and so blah,
I'm just the type they always need
To watch the lead
Work all the problems out
And then shout,
You've done it! Wow! Hurrah!

I'm so mediocre,
So un-chic and under par,
There's nothing I can really do especially well,
I'm only good enough to sell
An ointment in a jar . . .
Or maybe be a star!

During this creative phase, Alan also wrote a comedy pilot for himself called *The Honeymoon is Over*. The story concerned the domestic adventures of a man and woman in their fifties who decide to marry. Alan's character owned a bakery and was the director of the local faltering community theater.

To deal with his emotional issues, Alan continued to see a psychiatrist. His prescription anti-depressants exacerbated his mood swings, and he struggled to maintain friendships and enjoy social gatherings. "I never talked about it," he recalled. "It was so boring and no one really cares. They never really want to know how you feel when they ask you how you are. And how does talking about depression make it go away? Anyway, I didn't want anyone to know, and it would have interfered with being cast in anything. There were insurance issues and all kinds of problems. Gossip."

The drugs also profoundly suppressed his sexual feelings. "Those drugs probably saved my life," Alan said. "Those were crazy, freewheeling days. Gays were really swinging then. There was a lot of sex happening. A sex scene. I wasn't that interested in sex, though.

"I had some friends in the Hamptons and on Fire Island," Alan recalled. "I'd been going to Fire Island since I first lived in New York in the 1950s. I'd take the ferry over for the weekend. I had a friend who had a great house in the Pines there, and sometimes I stayed a few days. That's where I first heard about AIDS in the early 1980s. Gay men were getting very sick. And they died within months. Nobody really knew what was going on. There was so much talk about it, and people were calling it a gay cancer since only gay guys were getting sick then. It happened so fast. I knew many people who got sick and died. Everyone got very paranoid, including me. It really changed things for me because I was scared to death. That really ended a certain part of my life. I was afraid to be with anyone since we didn't know how you caught it. It hadn't touched any celebrities yet, but it scared the hell out of me."

The death of Paul Lynde in January 1982 was a sobering event for Alan. "We were the same age when he died," Alan recalled. "He was found dead in his house by a gay porn actor he was dating. The newspapers said the police found drug and alcohol evidence in his bedroom. The gossip was terrible. It didn't matter what the truth

Alan with Judy Carne at a Laugh-In *reunion in 1983.*

would ultimately be, his entire life's work was eclipsed by salacious gossip. We had never been friends, but I felt sorry for him, and it was disgusting when many of his so-called friends suddenly spoke badly about him. Nobody's perfect, but he was very funny, and all of that good stuff sort of went out the window. Show business is a lonely business."

Alan finally returned to work in the summer of 1984 with a star-turn in *Charlie's Aunt* at the Stage West Dinner Theatre in Winnipeg, Canada. *Charlie's Aunt* is a classic farce about a couple of young men who invite their lady-loves to meet one of the fellow's rich Brazilian aunt. When the aunt sends word that her visit will be delayed, the playboys convince their friend, Lord Fancourt Babberley (Alan Sues) to impersonate the aunt. *Charlie's Aunt* was first performed in London in 1892. Through the years, the play enjoyed great success, and was adapted to the screen to star Jack Benny. The musical version, *Where's Charley?*, was a Broadway smash starring Ray Bolger.

Charlie's Aunt began a successful, extended engagement on July 4. This was the first serious theatrical job offer Alan had received

Alan in Charlie's Aunt.

in three years. "I was back in drag, but I liked this play a lot," Alan said. "I had some misgivings because it was the stuff I was trying to get away from. But it was campy and fun, and that's what the audience seemed to want from me."

Irene Joyce reviewed the play for the *Winnipeg Sun* on July 5. "If you want to laugh, I mean the knee slapping, tear-producing guffaw variety, then reserve a front row table and pay close attention to Alan Sues' facial expressions. The former *Laugh-In* funny man bounds around the stage, bellowing, shrieking, and carrying on in an obnoxiously unladylike fashion. What can I say? You'll either love it, or hate it. I adored it and resigned myself to an evening of light-hearted ridiculous banter."

While Alan was in Canada, he had sublet his New York apartment to one of his nieces. His landlord took advantage of his extended absence, and exercised the clause in his lease that denied him the right to sublet. While Alan was out of town, he was evicted and his possessions were actually dumped on the street.

After *Charlie's Aunt* closed in Winnipeg, Alan returned to Los Angeles. He had previously rented his West Hollywood house, so he leased a small apartment on Fernwood Drive for a short time.

"I had a few auditions," Alan recalled, "but I wanted to see how my parents were doing so I stayed in California for a couple of months. They were in Solvang. I always had to go to them, all my life. They never once stepped foot in my house. I invited them, but they never saw my place. Of course, I bought a one-bedroom house that couldn't really accommodate overnight guests. Maybe that's why I bought it."

Alan was disconcerted to see that his father's condition had worsened. "My father was completely blotto," Alan said. "He didn't know anything. He didn't talk, he didn't move. He just laid in bed. I'd sit with him and talk, but I was talking to the wall. We just never connected. Whatever my feelings for him, he had always been such a strong presence that it was hard to see him like a vegetable. And my mother was stuck taking care of him around the clock. I actually felt sorry for her."

Alan sublet a small apartment at 1492 2nd Avenue in New York in October 1984. It was so tiny that he hardly had room for a day bed, his travel trunk and his dog. "You had to climb over one or the other to get to the bathroom," he said. "But I preferred living in New York."

That winter, Alan made a film on location in Park City, Utah. He received top-billing in the teen-sex comedy titled *Snowballing*. "I play a professor who gets involved with three guys who want to make it with all the girls," Alan explained. "It's a ski movie and was done by the same director who did *Silent Night, Deadly Night*, that Christmas classic about a murderer who dressed up like Santa Claus. He also directed *Grizzly Adams* and a bunch of science fiction documentaries. Go figure.

"I've never seen *Snowballing* so I don't know if it's funny. All I know is that I almost died it was so cold in Utah where we were shooting. We were standing out in the snow up on a hill with no dressing rooms, nothing. And you could just die.

"I was up to my ass in snow for *weeks*. The icicles were as long as I am tall. And on top of it, I never got *paid*!"

A short time later, Alan accepted an offer to work in a play in Pennsylvania. "My psychiatrist actually prescribed work for me. It was the first prescription that didn't come in pill form." Alan needed something to do with his time, and he needed money. The tenant who had rented his West Hollywood house had become a non-paying burden.

On February 1, 1985, he arrived in snowy Pittsburgh to begin rehearsals for the comedy *Room Service*. The play began a one-month engagement on March 6 at the Theodore L. Hazlett Theatre for the Pittsburgh Public Theatre Company. "I was paid six hundred bucks a week, but it was a job," Alan said.

Reviews were very good. The *Tarentum Valley News* wrote, "Alan Sues as the beleaguered brother-in-law would steal the show if he were not working with such a strong supporting cast. He used his exaggerated moans and groans, rolling eyeballs and grimaces made famous when he starred on TV's *Laugh-In* to best advantage in the role. Just when you think he can't possibly be any better, Sues outdoes himself in a scene where he tries to tiptoe out of the room as his boss discovers another bounced check—one for 15 grand. His attempted exit is nothing short of grand itself."

Bruce Steele wrote in the *Tribune Review*, "Alan Sues proves to Pittsburgh theatergoers that he is a gifted comic stage actor, not just the answer to a Trivial Pursuit Question."

On March 12, the *Observer-Reporter* wrote, "Alan Sues as Joseph Gribble, the befuddled hotel manager, gets better and better with each act. Sues' double takes and doubletalk are reminiscent of his old

Laugh-In roles, but this play allows him to expand on the character and make each line, each smirk, each roll of the eyes memorable."

"I did my best to stay in touch with my parents," Alan said, "because *they* sure never did." He sent them a copy of a Pittsburgh newspaper interview he had done with a note. "February 10. Dear Mom and Dad. Same old jazz about me, it's always interesting to me how these interviewers ask all these questions and always print the same stuff. Well, maybe it will sell a couple of tickets. Business seems to be up for this show. Alan"

On February 12, he wrote, "Dear Mom and Dad—I was wondering if Dad can still write letters. I don't remember if he was able to when I was out there—if I go to Kansas this summer maybe I can go on to Cal. and see you as it would pay for some of my trip. Hope all is well. Alan."

"Talked to John yesterday," Alan wrote to his parents on March 7, "and he says that he has been in New York a lot. Will see him Tuesday. That should be great. Too bad his business is dragging on so it seems. Never ending. Trying to get to the next point. Send mail to 315 E. 68 and tell me what's going on. Alan."

He sent a note attached to a favorable newspaper review of *Room Service* to his parents on March 9. "I am trying to read three plays before I leave here as they have asked me to come back. We shall see. Things are about the same—it's been raining a lot here, I hope not tomorrow as I want to go to the antique show in the afternoon and get home for a nap before the show. Can Dad still go on his walks. Let me know how you're doing. Alan"

On March 13, he sent another great review to his parents. "It was nice to get such good notices—which helps business which helps me coming back," he wrote. "Still haven't heard about job in Kansas City. Keep taking one step forward and four back. Trying to get my one man show together. Hope all is well. Alan."

"Dear Mom and Dad," Alan wrote on March 16. "Here is another review—all the notices were good which [sic] you know this game by now—is catch as catch can. I really am amazed most of the time what goes thru these guys minds. We got one notice that was fair and the producer said he howled during the show. I certainly didn't hurt business as I really don't think that people read the paper anymore. They just watch TV. Send a note when you can. Alan."

Alan's mother never answered his many notes.

In the spring, Alan played the role of General McKinley in a film titled *What Has Four Wheels and Flies* for a Polish producer named Andrzej Krakowski. Originally conceived as a television movie, the project was filmed in the summer. "I don't know if the movie was finished. I don't remember if it was a pilot. I don't know what the hell we were doing. Warren Berlinger and Pat Morita were in the cast, and some pretty chicken who was screwing the producer. It was her first and last film, I'm sure. I don't think it ever aired on television or was even shown here. I know I didn't get paid for it. But I heard we were really big in Poland."

On September 18, 1985, Alan began a six-week engagement in *Windy City* at the Paper Mill Playhouse in Milburn, New Jersey. The production was a musical adaptation of the Charles MacArthur and Ben Hecht award-winning play *The Front Page*. With music and lyrics by Tony Macaulay and Dick Vosburgh, *Windy City* was optioned by a Broadway producer during its opening week. Like the play, the musical version revolves around the lives of hard-boiled newspaper reporters in 1920s Chicago. The cast included Gary Sandy, Judy Kaye, and MacIntyre Dixon. Alan played a supporting role. "It was nice to work with Alan again," MacIntyre recalled. "He was as funny as ever. One day we had made a date to have lunch. I had to cancel because I got an audition. When I told him I couldn't make it, he slapped my face! He was playing, I *think*. He always made me laugh."

Windy City met with mixed reviews. The *Courier News* wrote on September 23, "Alan Sues' portrayal of prissy reporter Bensinger recalls his exaggerated and effective comic style in television's *Laugh-In*." On October 2, The *Independent Press* reviewed the show. "Alan Sues is great as persnickety Bensinger."

Critic Alvin Klein of the *New York Times* completely dismissed the production as "mediocre and mundane." However, he wrote that the reporters in the courtroom "are vividly depicted, especially by Alan Sues as the whiny Bensinger who sprays everything in sight with disinfectant."

Alan as Moonface, Public Enemy #13, in Anything Goes.

One reporter wrote, "The real star of the Paper Mill production is the three-story set constructed with intertwining catwalks, offices, newsroom, a jail and a backdrop of the city of Chicago." Alan concurred. "Reviews were okay, but a lot of people called it a poor man's *Chicago*. There was talk that the show would go to Florida for tryouts—not my favorite spot. And then New York. But it went nowhere. We all thought it needed work."

Laugh-In was released in syndication in 1985. Critics and audiences found it very dated. "We all sort of had mixed feelings about it," Alan said. "There was some money, but it just reintroduced the characters we were all doing fifteen years before. It was old news. The show was so topical originally. It was written literally up to the minute then. What was so hip back then seemed old-fashioned now."

In December, Alan joined his brother and sister-in-law on a European vacation. "We had a wonderful time in London," Yvonne Sues said. "We spent Christmas in Chelsea then we went to Paris and spent New Year's Eve there. John and I stayed at the Grand Hotel and Alan stayed on the Left Bank. We went to museums and did some shopping. We had a marvelous dinner at the Grand Hotel. One of John's daughters went to school in Paris. She joined us for dinner. She was so loud and complained about everything. She said the Louvre Museum was a dump, and she put the French people down. She was very obnoxious, and we were mortified. Alan was absolutely disgusted. He really didn't talk to her again after that."

Anything Goes opened a one-week engagement on March 21, 1986, at the Lobero Theatre as the first offering of the annual Santa Barbara Theatre Festival. The story concerns the wild cavorting of a colorful assortment of real and fictional characters on a London-bound luxury liner. The classic American musical introduced songs written by Cole Porter including "Anything Goes," "I Get a Kick Out Of You," "You're the Top," and "Blow, Gabriel, Blow." Alan played the role of Moonface, Public Enemy #13, and sang "Friendship" with his co-star, Cheryl Ladd. The cast included Didi Cohn, and Alan's friend Fred Willard.

News-Press of Santa Barbara raved about the show writing, "*Anything Goes* has bright choreography, a good cast, lovely costumes, and Alan Sues (Officer, arrest that man—he stole the show!). A melodic highlight was Sues singing the comic "Be like the Bluebird"."

Act 3
Scene 2

"1986–1991 "People still think I'll jump out of a cake."

After nearly a year of pleasing audiences at the George Gershwin Theatre on Broadway, *Singin' in the Rain*, the popular musical adaptation of the film classic, closed on May 18, 1986. Alan was cast as the movie director, Roscoe Dexter, in the national touring company, and began a grueling, 52-week cross-country tour on June 10 at the Music Hall in Dallas, Texas.

"I auditioned for the part and they thought I was cute as a button and they cast me," Alan said. "He's a director, and he's just *full* of himself. He's been doing silent pictures and when the switch is made to talkies—well, *everything* falls apart. He's working with this star who has this *terrible* voice. It wasn't the major role, it was really small, but it was a very funny role. Except for *Laugh-In*, I'd never worked so hard in my life."

The original Broadway production of *Singin' in the Rain* had been directed and choreographed by Twyla Tharp. Her post-modern version had closed in the "red," losing money for the producers. Major changes were made to the national touring production, including new direction by Tony-Award winning Lawrence Kasha, and all-new choreography by Tony-Award winning Peter Gennaro. The only road company hold-overs from the Broadway production were the two leading men, Don Simione and Brad Moranz.

Kasha, who also produced the hit television series *Knot's Landing*, explained his approach to the musical. "We went back to follow the movie. In New York, they added numbers that didn't make sense. Why mess with a classic? This is a new production—new scenery, new costumes, new musical numbers. Our version follows the essence of the film, the concept."

Singin' in the Rain tells the story of Hollywood's difficult transition from silent pictures to talkies. Alan's character tries to teach a shrill-voiced actress how to use a microphone. "I sang in shows before," Alan explained, "but I didn't sing in *Rain* and I was glad. Singing always makes me nervous probably because I rely on comedy timing. I flounced all over the stage and did everything except stand on my head. I can judge the audience to improvise comedy and timing with physical comedy, but it's nearly impossible to do that with songs."

The Dallas premiere of the national touring company was met with acclaim. *Variety* wrote, "Overall, this Dallas Summer Musicals production has the look and feel of an old-fashioned, traditional musical comedy. And, the old-fashioned term 'lavish' is the only word for the mounting of the show. The Musicals, flush from its most successful season ever last summer, budgeted the show at $800,000, highest in its 45-year history. It's a very entertaining, spectacularly mounted and winning version of the nostalgic-flavored show that should play very well in the nation's heartland."

On June 24, *Singin' in the Rain* opened at the Muny in Forest Park, St. Louis, Missouri. The show drew small audiences to the massive outdoor theater. Missed cues and sound problems plagued the production. Reviews were mixed. The *St. Louis Globe Democrat* reviewed the show on June 25. "Former *Laugh-In* regular Alan Sues is delightful in his role as the harried director Roscoe Dexter, stealing every scene with almost each appearance." The *St. Louis Dispatch* panned the production, and wrote, "Alan Sues brings some comic relief, but also tends to over-act."

After a week at Wolftrap in Virginia, the production opened at the Hilton U. Brown Theatre in Indianapolis on July 7. "Alan Sues milks every laugh possible out of his role as the swishing director," wrote Charles Staff for *The News*.

"This was a genuine road tour," Alan recalled. "I'm not sure I realized what I had gotten myself into. We traveled like a band of gypsies—without their flashy fashion sense."

Singin' in the Rain opened on July 22 at the Carpenter Center in Richmond, Virginia, after a week's engagement in Atlanta, Georgia. The Richmond theater could not accommodate the rain machine. Jerry Williams, the local theater critic, was impressed with the show, but for all the wrong reasons. He called it, "one of the most troubled opening nights in the city's theater history." The curtain went up one hour late. There was no rain machine, and the sets either didn't descend far enough down from the fly gallery or came crashing to the stage.

After stops at Shae's Theater in Buffalo, the O'Keefe Center in Toronto, the Shubert in Boston and the State Theater in Cleveland, the production opened at the historic Chicago Theater in Chicago on September 30. The *Daily Calumet* reviewed the show on October 3. "Alan Sues as the director," wrote Donna Kiesling, "was surprisingly noticeable in a small role, and quite funny." Alan told the reporter, "The show has thirty dancers and spectacular costuming. What's incredible is how these kids can keep their arms up with all the beads. It took eight different specialty shops two and a half weeks to make the costumes. And to keep any performers from catching a cold, the water used in the rain machine is warmed."

Alan was interviewed by the *Herald* in Seattle on October 30, two days before the show opened at the Paramount Theater. "We started this show in May in Dallas and worked our way through the heat wave. We've done it in rain, without rain. In Richmond, Virginia, we couldn't get the rain machine into the theater! So we went without. In St. Louis the temperature hit 109 degrees and we were performing outdoors in wool costumes. The girls had furs. I don't know how they stood it."

When he was asked if it was lonely on the road during a long tour schedule, Alan said that he was too tired to get lonely. "I take my miniature dachshund, Lois Lane, with me. It's nice to have her waiting for me after a show. The discos have passed me by. But she's there, usually on the phone. I've had her fourteen years, and she's traveled more than most humans.

"It's funny. One of the guys in the cast was saying he felt bad because he didn't have any pets. The other day we were running for the plane, and I looked behind me. The same guy was trying to carry a bowl of goldfish through the security gate. It gets desperate on the road."

As much as Alan liked the work, the physicality of the role was demanding for any sixty-year-old man. After several months on the road, he felt the wear and tear. "I'm in my golden years and I'm getting a little too old for it. People still think I'll jump out of a cake. We wind up in Baltimore. I hear there are good hospitals in Baltimore."

Alan enjoyed a brief respite from traveling when *Singin' in the Rain* played several weeks at the Orpheum Theater in San Francisco. "Most of our stops were for one week," Alan said. "It was

Alan in Los Angeles promoting Singin' in the Rain.

nice to stay put for a while, and I always liked San Francisco. The audiences there were just great. They loved the show."

A star-studded crowd greeted the show when it opened on December 9, 1986, at the Pantages Theater in Hollywood. Movie veterans Ann Miller, Jane Withers, Julie Harris, Fred Astaire, Red Buttons and Cesar Romero mingled with the cast in the theater's elaborate lobby following the performance. Alan, wearing a sequined caftan and a wild "fright" wig, greeted his *Laugh-In* friends Jo Anne Worley, Ruth Buzzi, Barbara Sharma and Larry Hovis who were also in attendance.

Alan was not surprised by the mixed reviews he received in Los Angeles. *Variety* wrote on December 12, "Credit in this show should also go to Alan Sues who grabs his share of laughs as the studio head's yes-man. He milks more broad laughs than you might expect." Dan Sullivan wrote in the *Los Angeles Times*, "I don't remember who played the director in the film, but Alan Sues is getting some pretty cheap laughs with him now." *Star News* reported, "Alan Sues as the frenetic movie director grabs most of the laughs with his hyperkinetic portrayal." Thomas O'Connor, writing for the *Orange County Register*, was not impressed. On December 12, he wrote, "Alan Sues roars about in a swishy, embarrassingly campy rendering of the film director."

On Christmas Day, the *Orange Coast Daily Pilot* reviewed the show during its one week engagement at Segerstrom Hall in Costa Mesa, California, "Alan Sues as the hyperactive director delivers a shtick-slathered series of over-extended sight gags that would have been too much even for his Big Al character in *Laugh-In*, and are out of sync with the more traditional tenor of the production."

Singin' in the Rain played the final week of 1986 at the Civic Center in San Diego. The *San Diego Tribune* reported, "Alan Sues furnishes some bright moments." The *Jewish Press Heritage* wrote, "Alan Sues strutted his stuff with flamboyant overkill melodramatics."

Alan was interviewed by the *San Diego Tribune* on December 26. "We've had a terrific time with it," he said. "The problems have come from the technical complexities, especially the rain machine, which takes up the entire stage and has to be shipped in pieces and reassembled. Most of the theaters we play in are old movie houses and have no backstage. Getting the rain machine set up has been a lot of trouble. Sometimes they had to knock down walls. Lack of backstage space creates other headaches, like having to suspend a piano on ropes and lower it on cue. In one city, some of the $14-an-hour stage crew could literally neither read nor write. We couldn't give them a list of costume changes and props so we had to work with colors. We were just praying they didn't pull the wrong colored rope and have the piano crash down on us!"

On December 31, the *San Diego Union* delivered Alan his worst review of the tour. "Alan Sues does much that is wrong, for which blame the director. Sues' comedy, as viewers of television's legendary *Laugh-In* will recall, tends toward the awesomely broad. Here, his braying and flouncing inflates the simple role of a film director to surreal proportions."

"Ah," Alan said, "Christmas and New Year's Eve reviews. Home for the holidays."

As the tour continued, Alan's reviews became more critical. Beginning January 5, 1987, *Singin' in the Rain* played one-week engagements in San Antonio, Austin and Houston, Texas. "Comedian Alan Sues makes a lot out of a small part," wrote Dan Goddard for the *Express News* of San Antonio. "But after a while, his vaudeville humor wears thin, and the first act seems needlessly long because of it."

On January 21, the *Houston Post* reported, "Alan Sues clowned absolutely outrageously as a harried and sycophantic movie director. But his overblown antics, which are really more suited for *Sugar Babies* than *Singin' in the Rain*, were skillfully executed."

The show opened at Saenger's Theater in New Orleans on January 27. Richard Dodds reviewed the musical for *La Gniappe* on January 30. About Alan he wrote, "Alan Sues ladles on the shtick as a film director but the results prove only sporadically amusing." The *Daily-Sentry News* reported, "Adding to the fun is Alan Sues who plays it with a broad comedy look and it works."

Singin' in the Rain spent the month of February in Florida, playing engagements in Miami, St. Petersburg and Orlando. On February 20, Porter Anderson wrote for the *Tampa Tribune*, "...jokes are shamefully milked by former *Laugh-In* star, Alan Sues."

The show traveled to Louisville, Kentucky, and Wilmington, Delaware, before fulfilling one week engagements at Bushnell Memorial Hall in Hartford and at the Shubert Theater in New Haven, Connecticut.

April 23, in the *New Haven Register*, Markland Taylor wrote, "The acting is mostly of the shout and scream school—Alan Sues

Alan in Singin' in the Rain.

is the worst offender." Alan was interviewed by Candy Williams for the *Tribune Review* on April 24. "Casting directors have a way of locking you into a specific role and it's very hard to break out," he said. "*Laugh-In* created that situation for me and it's difficult to get anyone to give me something different to do. It's a common complaint with everyone in the business. And I guess every clown wants to do something serious."

After a successful week at Heinz Hall in Pittsburgh, *Singin' in the Rain's* final performances were played in Baltimore, Maryland. The musical opened a three-week engagement on May 4 at the Morris A. Mechanic Theater.

"It's very tough on a long road tour away from home. Very lonely. There's no time for much socializing, and you're tired all the time. The only friends you make are the other actors—if you're lucky. We had a great company of actors and dancers," Alan recalled. "I loved the show, but by the time it was done at the Mechanic Theater, this old body *needed* a mechanic."

Alan spent two weeks in June resting at his Manhattan apartment before beginning rehearsals for an extended summer engagement in the musical *Sugar Babies*. Originally premiering in October 1979, and starring Ann Miller and Mickey Rooney, the burlesque-style musical revue conceived by Ralph G. Allen and Harry Rigby played for nearly three years on Broadway. With songs by Jimmy McHugh, Dorothy Fields and Al Dubin, *Sugar Babies* was a collection of risqué skits and variety acts much like a vaudeville show.

Alan was cast in the role of the Top Banana, created by Mickey Rooney. Wanda Richert (the Tony Award-nominated actress from the Broadway production of *42nd Street*) was cast in the Ann Miller role of the Prima Donna. "I so loved working with Alan," Richert recalled. "He was so kind. I was dealing with personal issues, and he was so patient, and easy to talk with. I knew him from *Laugh-In*, which I watched as a kid, and I really looked forward to working with him. I learned so much from him about comedy timing. Alan had an innate gift for making people happy. He couldn't help being funny, and it was twenty-four-seven. It seemed so easy for him.

"Alan's timing was impeccable. He was in the moment. And Alan was just being Alan. Of course the show was scripted, but Alan could read an audience in a minute, and he played to that. He could adjust his physical comedy and delivery to suit the audience. You can't teach that. I got lost performing on stage with him. He was hilarious.

"The audience loved the show," Richert said, "and it was a good production in a very good theater. The dressing rooms were very tiny. I spent a lot of time with him in his dressing room, telling stories and laughing. He was always funny but there was a quiet sadness about him offstage. We had an awesome time, and I had the time of my life."

Alan always downplayed his dancing skills, but *Sugar Babies* director Charles Repole said, "Alan moves very well, but it's his face that people are going to watch, and that face blends so well with all the rest of the talent on the stage. Alan's terrific."

Repole explained, "*Sugar Babies* depends on the two stars. I've directed Joel Grey in *George M.* and Anthony Quinn in *Zorba*. Alan has the same star quality. He has the speed, the face, and he dances through the dialogue. He's charming when he moves."

Sugar Babies began a three-month engagement on July 8, 1987, at the Evening Dinner Theatre in Elmsford, New York. The show was a smash and garnered rave reviews. On July 23, *Gannett Westchester Newspapers* wrote, "Though the top banana role is associated with Mickey Rooney, the twinkle-toed Sues brings it a thoroughly fresh approach and claims it as his own. Sues at first seems too fey for the role of a walking male libido, but his showbiz savvy quickly wins the audience. He rolls his eyes extravagantly, flings back his mane of flyaway straight hair, lets out a whoop, and the audience goes to pieces. He spices his delivery with plenty of schmaltz, and that's not the kind of thing you can learn in school. To look at *Sugar Babies*, an audience is made aware that the performers onstage are pros who know what entertainment is all about."

Alvin Klein gave Alan perhaps the best review of his life in the *New York Times* on July 26. "Alan Sues *is* the top banana. With his blasé, sometimes dour demeanor and a pained expression that threatens to erupt with tears, Mr. Sues is not one to conceal his disdain. Whereas most performers in such entertainments knock themselves out to win over the audience, something about Mr. Sues—it could be his understated coerciveness—makes the audience want to please him, perhaps fearing the consequences of his displeasure. In his various guises and wigs, as Judge Quackenbush or Madame Hortense Rentz, wearing a provocative, amazing Technicolor sequined gown and argyle socks, complaining that 'life is a drag,' Mr. Sues is a master (and mistress) of low-camp style. And with the cutting edge of his Tallulah-like inflections, the performer suggests that whenever high camp calls, Mr. Sues will have just the right wicked response. Mr. Sues puts his own imprint on *Sugar Babies*, proving that the top banana here doesn't have to be Mickey Rooney, for whom it was written, or a clone thereof."

Alan visited his parents in mid-November. They had moved to a condominium in Lompoc, California. "My father was all but comatose," Alan said. "My mother hired people to help her move him from the bed and clean him. It was a terrible situation. I knew that I had been cut out of their will years before. My parents intended to leave their estate to my brother and his kids. My eldest niece was a bit of a wild child and had run away with her guru. She called my brother and told him she was pregnant and wanted money. Because he didn't respond quickly enough, she made the mistake of calling my mother and asking her for money as well. And that was it. My mother cut all my brother's kids out of the will. I knew I had to work to get back in the running, and I called my mother all the time. I visited whenever I wasn't working. I sent her cards and letters all the time. It worked. She rewrote their will since she knew she would outlive my father. My brother and I would divide equally whatever was left when she died."

Before returning to New York, Alan taped an episode of the situation comedy *Punky Brewster*, titled "Tangled Web." The title character was played by a precocious, eleven-year-old child actress named Soleil Moon Frye. The story concerned an abandoned child who was raised by a foster father. "This kid was a pain in the ass," Alan said. "She might have been eleven, but she acted like she was thirty-five and ruled the world. When she wasn't on camera, she stood with her arms folded watching everything going on. She knew everybody's lines, and everybody's cues. When I did my first scene with her, we did one take and the director wanted another. I said to the kid, I thought that was pretty funny, and she said to me, 'not really and you got the line wrong.' I wanted to kick her like a football out the door.

In January 1988, Alan was cast in a concert presentation of the Jerome Kern musical *Sally*. Produced by the New Amsterdam Theater Company, and staged at the Academy Theatre on 43rd Street in New York, *Sally* was originally produced on Broadway in 1920 by

Alan as Chief Sitting Bull in Annie Get Your Gun.

Florenz Ziegfeld. The musical introduced three hit songs, "Look for the Silver Lining," "Wild Rose," and "Whip-Poor-Will." The Cinderella-themed story concerns a young lady who works as a dish washer in Manhattan, becomes a dancer in the Ziegfeld Follies, and eventually marries a millionaire. The production was represented as a "concert." There was a 29-piece orchestra on stage, and the actors worked with no props or scenery and carried their scripts in hand.

"This was never meant to be reviewed," Alan explained. "This show was rarely revived. We were just trying it out to see if it could play again. We had five performances, but they reviewed it, and killed us."

On January 22, Mel Gussow wrote in the *New York Times*, "The ancient jokes are disposable. It seems like a shaky run-through. There is one impeccable performance, and this is given by Sandy the dog, the co-star of the musical *Annie*. With the expertise of a seasoned trouper, Sandy enters and exits on cue."

"It really *was* a run-through," Alan explained. "And the fucking dog got a better review than any of us!"

In May, Alan returned to the Santa Barbara Theatre Festival to play the role of Sitting Bull in the Irving Berlin musical *Annie Get Your Gun*. The story concerns the adventures of Annie Oakley and her fanciful life in show business. Featuring one of the most popular show business anthems, "There's No Business like Show Business," *Annie Get Your Gun* was written by Herbert and Dorothy Fields. Presented at the Lobero Theater, the play starred Donna McKechnie, Lawrence Guittard, and Jm J. Bullock.

Don Shirley favorably reviewed the production for the *Los Angeles Times* on May 21. "The supporting cast is uniformly fine. And then there's Alan Sues as Sitting Bull, alternating between a deep, gruff voice for his more serious pronouncements and a nasally whine for occasional afterthoughts and punch lines, which bring down the house. The good-humored hokum is disarming. So is the big 'I'm an Indian, Too' musical number, choreographed by Murphy Cross."

As usual, Alan made the character of Sitting Bull "his own." As the Indians danced around him during the production number for "I'm an Indian, Too," Alan bumped into one of the male dancers. "Watch the moccasins, girlfriend," he snapped. The audience went wild.

Alan stayed at the Montecito Inn during the engagement, and was able to spend several days with his parents in Lompoc before the production moved to the Geary Theatre in San Francisco for the month of June. The show was well received and on June 15, Robert Hurwitt wrote in the *San Francisco Examiner*, "Alan Sues, unabashedly mugging in his best *Laugh-In* mode, makes Sitting Bull even more ridiculous than the script calls for."

On June 16, Gerald Nachman praised Alan's work in the *San Francisco Chronicle*: "Act I is largely in the hands of secondary characters, and to be sure, Alan Sues, with the only funny lines in the show, deftly rescues the chief from stereotype by kidding it."

Alan flew to Indianapolis in November 1988 to prepare for his appearance in an innovative new play called *The Three Musketeers*. Playwrights Tom Haas and Bob Gross dramatized a modern retelling of the classic Alexandre Dumas novel *The Three Musketeers* for the Indiana Repertory Theater. The playwrights tackled the conflict between old and new, and approached the tale with a freewheeling spirit. Their diverse influences included Greek mythology, seventeenth-century French farce, nineteenth-century British Music Hall, twentieth-century American Vaudeville, and the comedy of Monty Python and the Keystone Cops. To make the matters more zany, the actors mouthed the words to prerecorded songs including Romberg's "Stouthearted Men," Andrew Lloyd Weber's "Don't Cry For Me, Argentina," Michael Jackson's "Beat It," and the Shaker hymn "A Gift to Be Simple."

The show was a smash and Alan had one of the best times of his life playing the dual roles of Bonacieux and Estafania. On December 13, David McCann reviewed the show for the *Indy Today Newspaper*, "Everything about this production clicks. For me, Alan Sues was the ace in this deck. Mr. Sues is hysterical as he gamely switches between the deaf and blind Bonacieux and the mad lady of Argentina, Estafania. What a treat to see this wild comic talent on the loose." Charles Staff wrote in the *Indianapolis News*, "The success rests with the actors. There's the eye-rolling Alan Sues, who switches joyously from Argentinia's gift to femininity, the flouncing Estafania, to the ridiculous Bonacieux. In fact, his lightning changes would seem to strain even the fastest zippers and the best Velcro, not to mention the finest talent."

Alan's best review came from the local *Topics Suburban* newspaper. "There is no better reason to attend *The Three Musketeers* than to see Alan Sues—a one-time regular on *Laugh-In*," wrote Lori Sparger. "Sues plays the mostly deaf and rather blind Bonacieux, the drag queen Donna Estafania and Thalia the goddess of comedy, who is heard throughout the show and makes an appearance in the show's denouement. Some of the funniest scenes occur when Sues is on stage."

"I had the best time," Alan said. "I did everything but swing on a rope. The writers were so creative and inspired. They did a terrific job modernizing a classic story and making it relevant, sexy and hilarious. I loved it all."

Alan traveled to Palm Beach, Florida in March 1989, and reprised his role as Chief Sitting Bull at the Royal Poinciana Playhouse production of *Annie Get Your Gun*. He and Donna McKechnie were the only holdover cast members from the California production. Actor Joel Higgins joined them in Florida. The musical opened to good reviews on March 29, and closed on April 9. The shown then moved to two other Florida engagements but Alan was only contracted for the Palm Beach run. While he was performing as Sitting Bull, he was learning his lines for another play he quickly stepped into after *Annie Get Your Gun* closed.

After a couple of shaky previews, *The Gingerbread Lady* opened on April 14 at the Coconut Grove Playhouse. The reviews were mixed. Although the ensemble cast was praised, on April 17, the *Sun Sentinel* reported, "Friday's opening performance was marked by persistent dialogue problems."

Neil Simon wrote *The Gingerbread Lady* as a starring vehicle for Maureen Stapleton. The drama with comic overtones had opened on Broadway in 1970. The story concerns a has-been cabaret singer named Evy who suffers from alcoholism, and the equally flawed people in her life, including a lonely, middle-aged gay actor who has lost his bit role in a play.

The Gingerbread Lady was one of Simon's least successful Broadway plays. In 1981, Simon adapted his play to a film titled *Only When I Laugh*. Alan's friend, James Coco, played the role of the floundering gay actor in the film, and was nominated for an Academy Award for his performance.

"Jimmy died in early 1987 from a heart attack," Alan recalled. "He was fifty-six years old. He was also suffering from cancer of the esophagus. The last couple years of his life were very rough. I spoke to him whenever I could, but he was disheartened. He was lonely, but he always said things to cheer me up. He was such a funny man. He drifted away the last couple of years before he died because he got hooked on cocaine. I heard about his death when I was on the road in *Singin' in the Rain*. It broke my heart."

The part of Jimmy Perry, the gay middle-aged actor who faces the realization that he'll never be a star, was the most personal role Alan ever played. In a poignant exchange with Evy, Jimmy Perry worries about an impending audition. "I won't get this job tonight. They'll turn me down. I'm auditioning for some nineteen-year-old putz producer who has seventy-five thousand dollars and a drama degree from Oklahoma A&M. Some chance an intelligent actor has today... Oh, God, I want to be a star so bad. I want to be a big star with three agents and two lawyers and a business manager and a press agent, and then I'd fire them all and get new ones because I'm such a big star. And I'd make everyone pay for the twenty-two years I poured into this business. I wouldn't do benefits. I wouldn't give money to charity. I would become one of the great shit heels of all time."

"The role wasn't much of a stretch," Alan said, "which is probably what made it so hard to do. Janis Paige was the leading lady and I loved working with her. She was on fire all the time. It was like hanging out with a drag queen in a gay bar on two-for-one night. And she could throw darts and play pool! She was the best, and she got great reviews. They loved her! Me, they didn't even mention. Not one review mentioned me by name. That's worse than being panned by the critics. When I went home, I contemplated becoming a dog breeder. Or maybe Janis Paige."

To make matters worse, Alan's beloved dog, Lois Lane, died. "I couldn't *stand* it," Alan said. "It was one of the worst heartaches of my life. I immediately got another dog—a pedigreed black and tan dachshund I named Princess Amanda Der Sues. The commoners called her Mandy."

A short time later, Alan's father succumbed to Alzheimer's disease at home in Lompoc. "It was the slowest exit since *Camille*," Alan said. "It was such a relief when it was finally over. He had been absent for so long, the end was sort of anticlimactic. The sad

Alan and Mandy.

thing was that we just never connected. I didn't know how to make it right. He never gave a damn about me or what I did. Like any kid, I wanted him to be proud of me. I certainly admired his work ethic, and worked hard myself, but it didn't seem to matter to him. My brother asked me if I felt a loss. I told him I'd felt a loss since I was five years old."

For nearly a year, Alan took time away from performing and devoted his creative energy into the one-man show he had toyed with for years. He enrolled in a few comedy writing classes, and struggled to construct a workable format for his ideas.

In July of 1990, Alan returned to the stage to appear in the musical *Bye, Bye Birdie*. He assumed the role of Mr. McAfee, made famous in the film and original Broadway production by Paul Lynde. In an interview with the *Oakland Press* in Rochester, Michigan, Alan was asked mostly about his days on *Laugh-In*. "No matter what else I've done," Alan lamented, "that's the thing that people remember the most." He told the newspaper that he still took acting lessons and was working on his own material. "Stand-up comedy is great experience for whatever you want to do in this business. It teaches you discipline, concentration and the ability to work an

Alan in Bye, Bye Birdie.

audience. When I started out, there weren't all these comedy clubs. If you were good, you worked Las Vegas. Now I think I could do a great job in that situation."

Also starring Ann Reinking, Marcia Lewis, and Tommy Tune, *Bye, Bye Birdie* played a week at the Muny Theater in St. Louis, Missouri, and a week at the Meadow Brook Music Festival in Rochester, Michigan. The show enjoyed a good box office reception, and the reviews were good. Alan, however, was savaged by the critics. Horrible comparisons to Paul Lynde were made by the press. On opening night in St. Louis, Alan completely lost the lyrics for the star-making song "Kids."

"I was having trouble with the director," Alan said. "He wanted me to do it like Paul Lynde. I don't do impersonations. Paul created the role and was so associated with it. For anyone else to play it, they had to *recreate* it. They couldn't just *impersonate* Paul. Big mistake. I didn't think we had enough rehearsal time. I just blanked on stage. It's such a horrible feeling. Instead of helping me, those on stage just stared at me. It was disheartening."

Alan returned to Los Angeles to supervise repairs to his home in West Hollywood. The tenant who had occupied the house for

Alan in 1990.

a number of years had left the place in a shambles and destroyed Alan's gardens. He personally retiled the kitchen countertops, and wall-papered the small guest bathroom. Before he returned to New York, he attended his friend Charles Pierce's farewell engagement at the Pasadena Playhouse in August. "He was as great as ever," Alan recalled. "I saw a lot of the old classmates we had at the Playhouse, and we had a good time. *I* looked great, but they all looked like shit."

Always on the lookout for a venue for his work-in-progress one-man show, Alan considered his alma mater, the Pasadena Playhouse. "I called Charles and asked him about his arrangement with the

Playhouse, but he said he produced his own show. He told me to do the same. And he said, 'You've been talking about your one-man show since 1950. I don't want to hear about it again until you're doing it somewhere! I'd lend you a pair of pumps, but your feet are too damn big.' I wasn't sure if he was irritated or encouraging."

Later in 1990, Alan took a screenwriting workshop sponsored by the Writer's Voice Inc. at the 63rd Street YMCA in New York. The class was taught by an African-American playwright named Dr. Henry D. Miller, author of the critically acclaimed play *My Brother's Keeper*. Miller was also a well-respected director and was a veteran of the 1960s and 1970s black theater movement. Miller found Alan's material to be "pretty heavy," and not particularly funny. He thought the serious nature of Alan's writing would not be successful in its present form. In November, Miller introduced Alan to Arthur Kopit, a three-time Tony Award nominated playwright who wrote the book for the musical *Nine* and wrote the cult-favorite play *Oh, Dad, Poor Dad, Mama's Hung You in the Closet and I'm Feeling So Sad*.

"Alan enrolled in Arthur's playwriting workshop," recalled Kopit's assistant, Laura Castro. "Alan was very humble and seemed almost vulnerable to me. He actually asked me for an actor's discount for the class. I was a fan of his, and we became very good friends. Alan was very dedicated and Arthur loved some of his work, but Alan ultimately did what he wanted to do. He'd ask for input, and usually disregard it, but Arthur took Alan in stride and always encouraged him. Alan had great and funny ideas, but in terms of writing, he did have a tough time with structure. He wasn't a good *closer*."

Alan attended classes with Kopit for several months. He also enrolled in various comedy workshops, often accompanied by Laura. "We went to so many classes," Laura said. "Sometimes it was confusing. Each class had a different approach, and Alan would begin all over again what he had been working on. I think it would have been more productive to stay in one class and stick to it. Alan would go home and work on material and call me and ask me what I thought of it. He was very generous with his time. We'd almost always go see what the other students were doing outside of class. He was never critical, always encouraging. He even directed me in something I was working on. He was a good director, and he had a great sense of comic timing."

A few years earlier, Alan saw *The Kathy and Mo Show* at the Westside Arts Theatre on 43rd Street in New York. Written by and starring two young comediennes from San Diego named Kathy Najimy and Mo (Maureen) Gaffney, the two-woman comedy recital addressed the role of women in contemporary society. Playing many roles, including those of both sexes (most notably, Mo Gaffney in reverse drag playing the part of a homosexual man), Najimy and Gaffney won the 1989 Obie Award for their satirical performance. "The show was fresh and funny," Alan said. "Kathy reminded me of Lily Tomlin and the way Lily mocked feminism in her act. I saw Kathy's show a few times and loved it."

Paul Benedict, who starred in the hit situation comedy *The Jeffersons*, was the director. He and Alan were friends and occasionally met up for drinks at a nearby gay bar. "Paul was very smart," Alan explained. "And a very good director. I wanted to work with him. He had a strange sense of humor. He really made me laugh. That's how I met Kathy Najimy."

In 1991, Kathy and Mo went their separate ways professionally, and Kathy taught acting lessons. Alan worked with her for several months. "She had a great free-flowing style," Alan said. "She rolled with her material and her transitions were clean. I liked working with her. Her career as an actress really took off and she moved on to movies and TV."

The time spent in New York gave Alan the opportunity to ponder his professional future, and explore his creative side. He said he was determined to create a work that would most suit his comic abilities, but his subject matter usually concerned his family. The stories were humorous, but always had an edge that wore thin with repetition.

He had long suffered "trust issues," and he was uncomfortable talking with friends about very personal and painful subjects. His writing was the only way he knew to communicate the pain and paradoxes that consumed him. Writing is a solitary occupation, and, for Alan, was as therapeutic as the time he spent with a psychiatrist.

"Many times I thought he was writing just to work things out in his mind," Laura said. "He had great scenes and situations in his head, but no endings."

In spite of his own self-doubts about his abilities, Alan was very comfortable working with a live audience. "People used to say that stage actors somehow ranked below film actors," Alan explained. "That was such bullshit. Acting is acting. I liked working on a stage because, in spite of the risk of being rejected to your face, nothing could beat the instant gratification you could get. In my case, theater work was more consistent and more lucrative. And there was a privacy factor there, too. Audiences and the press were less intrusive in a stage actor's life than a film actor's life."

"Alan was a hard worker," Laura said. "We often had lunch, and we saw quite a few Broadway shows then, too. I think Alan was very lonely. He had his dog, but he was very solitary, even in a crowded place. He didn't talk to me about his sexuality. He didn't really want people to know he was gay. He was very ambivalent about that part of his life."

While *playing* a homosexual was happening with more frequency on television and in film, *being* a homosexual actor was still poisonous to a career. "There were more gay and lesbian roles on TV," Alan recalled, "but it had more to do with image. It was about *how* gays and lesbians were portrayed."

When it came to television, stereotyping was the name of the game. It applied to men and women, and heterosexuals and homosexuals alike. Of course, in the case of heterosexual stereotyping, a broad and thorough range of types was depicted. However, homosexuals were *defined* by their sexuality, and were usually limited to a few negative depictions, ranging from the maligned "sissy" or "nancy-boy" to the dangerous leather fetishist.

In 1991, the Gay and Lesbian Alliance Against Defamation (Glaad), a self-appointed watchdog for the ways lesbians and gays were depicted in the media, challenged producers and broadcasters. "We are tired of seeing gays represented only as buffoons or villains. We believe the time has come for television to stop promoting bigotry by marginalizing and denigrating lesbian and gay lives."

When it came to comedy, little had changed in the years since Alan starred on *Laugh-In*. Actors Damon Wayans and David Allen Grier portrayed two flaming-queen reviewers on the hit show *In Living Color*. Many people didn't know whether the characterizations should have been applauded or deplored. Recurring lesbian and gay characters were rare on series television at the time.

"There was nothing for me on television," Alan said, "except game shows."

"Alan was always interacting with people," Laura recalled. "He was easy to talk to and he was very interested in what other people were doing on stage. He was curious about gender identities—is this a man or a woman? He thought audiences had a preconceived idea about gender roles. He was very interested in that. He liked to test that."

Alan was always excited to see how experimental and how challenging a performer could be on stage. He was influenced by many shows and theatrical works. "In the summer of 1991, we saw a performance artist named Penny Arcade in a show she did called *State of Grace*," Laura said. "It was outrageous. She threw up on stage. Alan loved it. The trouble was, he would go home and try to integrate new things or routines that had impressed him into the piece he was working on. Consequently, his show never seemed to have a definite forward motion. He was writing laterally. He tried to cram everything into the show with little consideration of where he ultimately wanted to go with the story. And many of his ideas *were* funny."

Alan had originally seen Penny Arcade in a show she had written called *Bitch! Dyke! Faghag! Whore!* at P.S. 122 a year earlier. Penny presented a performance that combined an exuberant blend of humor, satire, cabaret, exotic go-go dancing, improvisation and audience participation. "I saw her show a few times," Alan recalled. "It was exactly what I wanted to do, except for the go-go dancing, even though I look good in metallic hot pants."

Alan attended a couple of the infamous "drag balls" at the Elks Club in Harlem. Rather than a conventional ball, the happening was more of a parade of elaborate, hand-crafted costumes worn by men dressed as women "voguing"—which was a series of exaggerated fashion-model posturings inspired by pop music. Alan was attracted to the flamboyant effeminacy of the drag queens and their enviable sense of freedom. They embraced their identities with a verve that confounded Alan. He had lived a guarded public life, and felt like an exile in a conservative-dominated society. Still, the freewheeling display of newly "liberated" homosexuals presented certain problems.

"I felt like I was in limbo," Alan explained. "Drag, camp, and the snide remarks that defined that style were all features of gay life. But there was malice in the bitchy dialogue, and that type of conversation usually ended up a game of 'can-you-top-this.' After a while, it all got to be monotonous. Paul Lynde often slipped into that type of situation. What started off as very funny turned into something very mean and malicious. It was hard to know where to draw the line because there would always be someone laughing."

Alan had seen the British raconteur, author, and "professional homosexual" Quentin Crisp perform his one-man show several times in New York. Crisp sat comfortably on the stage in a simple spotlight and explained how it was to be a homosexual in a comedic discourse on manners and style. "I loved Quentin," Alan said, "his purple hair and Carnaby Street silk scarves. He used fingers to punctuate what he was saying. He was terrific." But what Alan found ingratiating about Crisp—particularly his out-of-date flamboyance—was the thing many young gay men found dislikable and even embarrassing. "It was such a confusing time," Alan said. "Where does a guy fit in? There were different schools of thought, but it was mostly about young versus old."

Drag queens and cross-dressers had fascinated Alan all his life. He was especially intrigued by the few actors who regularly performed in drag and were able to work on the legitimate stage outside of the more common drag clubs. He was influenced by Charles Ludlam who played several characters of both sexes in his hit off-off Broadway play *The Mystery of Irma Vep*. Alan saw the show many times.

In 1984, Alan saw another "drag" performer named Charles Busch in a satirical play he had written for himself called *Vampire Lesbians of Sodom* at the Limbo Lounge, a gay bar in the East Vil-

"This was a good look. I could have done a lot of made for TV movies if I'd started earlier." Photo credit Michael Lamont.

lage. "That was one of my favorite places," Alan said. "It was very popular and they had some great shows there. They called it Theater in Limbo. It was really on the wrong side of the tracks unless you were a homeless, drug-addicted, cross-dressing pedophile who beat puppies. You had to step over lifeless bodies on Avenue C to get there."

Charles Busch had also been influenced by Ludlam, however, Busch managed to raise the bar a bit and write material that was less about exaggerated camp, and more about the glamorization of feminist heroines. He specialized in playing the part of a femme fetale. Busch's approach of appearing in meticulously coifed drag, and playing it less for shock value and more as an homage to strong women appealed to Alan.

A few years later, Alan and I saw British comic Eddie Izzard, who exercised transvestism rather than "drag" by performing comic monologues while dressed simply as a woman. "That was perfect," Alan explained. "Dressing like a woman had nothing to do with his act or his material. He just walked onto the stage wearing a frock, earrings and lipstick. And he acted like it was perfectly normal. It had all come around full circle."

Alan's disjointed approach to writing and his inability to edit himself had led him to seek the assistance of a young writer he had met earlier in 1990. After several intense months of collaboration, Alan sent his newly-titled one-man show, *Changes*, to Emanuel Azenberg for consideration. Azenberg was a successful Broadway producer who often backed Neil Simon's plays. Peter Lawrence, Azenberg's production supervisor, rejected Alan's script and said, "There's an element of desperation in the familiar sketches that seems to work against the humor. I was hoping for more of a plot."

Alan and the young man worked throughout the fall, but over time, their working relationship soured. When they submitted the work to agent Joyce Ketay, the script was summarily rejected. Ketay wrote, "While I had great hopes for your script, I am sorry to say that I was disappointed. My recollection of your talent is that you are funnier than this vaudeville routine which is more reminiscent of 1940s Borscht Belt humor."

After years of crafting this acting vehicle for his solo performance, and being rejected repeatedly, Alan decided to reclaim the property and rework the material again. The more he was influenced by others, however, the farther away he found himself from his own core of comic-storytelling. Unfortunately, Alan's writing partner felt he was entitled to an ownership share of the script, and asked to be "bought out" of the property in exchange for his contributions.

"It was impossible," Alan said. "He helped me a lot, but he demanded a lot of money which just wasn't worth it. I thought we were both working on spec, and if the work didn't get sold, then we were out our time. When he demanded money, I threw my hands up. I had to hire an attorney. I'd had enough. I gave up my New York apartment and moved back to my house in West Hollywood. My days of living in New York were over."

Act 3
Scene 3

1991–2011 "This is no fun."

Charles Repole, who had directed Alan in *Sugar Babies*, called him in August 1991 with an intriguing offer to appear in an "updated" production of a classic musical. Television comedy legend Steve Allen wrote a new libretto for *Cinderella* to accompany the musical score originally written by Richard Rodgers and Oscar Hammerstein II for the 1957 television broadcast. "The book of the show was—now that Mr. Hammerstein is dead," Allen told the *Houston Post*, "just terrible. There was nothing really funny about it—and nothing much good about it at all, in fact."

In the new production, former Miss America Susan Powell played the title role of Cinderella. Ruth Buzzi played her mean stepmother, and Alan and Leonard Drum (an actor who had starred on Broadway in *Whoopee*, and appeared with Alan in *Sugar Babies*) played the evil stepsisters, Mercedes and Portia.

"Charles was a very good director," Alan said, "and I liked him. And working with Ruth sounded great."

"Actually, it was the first time we worked together in a play," Ruth recalled.

Alan arrived in Houston on November 16 to begin rehearsals. On November 27, he took a bad fall and twisted his knee. He was taken to the hospital, but refused to let the injury stop him. The doctor wrapped his knee and he returned to work the same day.

Previews began on December 7, and the Theatre Under the Stars holiday presentation of *Cinderella* officially opened on December 12 at the Music Hall in Houston.

"Nothing is as unfunny as an attempt at humor that doesn't succeed," Steve Allen told a reporter for the *Houston Chronicle*. The reviewers couldn't have agreed more. Everett Evans panned the show in the *Chronicle*, writing that "Alan Sues and Leonard Drum contribute broad, intentionally vulgar clowning as the stepsisters."

Writing for the *Houston Post*, William Albright called the material "leaden," and about Alan wrote, "Sliding his head back and forth across his shoulders like a Burmese court dancer or kitschy doll in the back window of a car, Alan Sues played step-sister Mercedes as a cross-dressing cross between Bert Lahr's Cowardly Lion and a basso profundo truck driver."

Alan with Steven Allen and Jayne Meadows and the cast of Cinderella.

Alan had been especially interested in the offer because it gave him the opportunity to explore working in drag. But what attracted him to the role proved to be his undoing. He drew upon the many "drag" artists he had admired in New York. But like the problem that plagued his writing, he tried to integrate many different styles into one portrayal. "I had fun," he said, "but it was hard to find the right balance. I thought about doing it like I was a woman to begin with, but that wasn't right. And the stepsister was a bitch, and the play was a comedy, so there was a fine line between playing it sinister or with humor. And Steve's libretto wasn't that great. Plus I was on pain pills and the fucking heels killed me."

To soften the sting of the bad reviews, Alan's cast mates presented him with a "joke" acting award created at a local trophy shop. Except for the "Flying Fickle Finger of Fate" statuette from *Laugh-In*, it was the only acting-related object he kept at home on his desk.

"To top it off," Alan said, "Steve kept hitting on me backstage. He just wouldn't take no for an answer. I did look good in that dress. Orange worked for me."

Alan had a wonderful time working with Ruth. "We always worked so well together," he said. "We always cracked each other

Alan and Leonard Drum, the wicked stepsisters in Cinderella.

up. It seemed like *Laugh-In* was yesterday and we just picked up where we left off."

"I loved working with Alan again," Ruth recalled. "He was hilarious, as always. His timing, which was always good, was even better. He was so at ease and comfortable, and we had a wonderful time."

Alan fulfilled his engagement, but was plagued with severe knee pain. When he returned to Los Angeles in January 1992, he consulted with a doctor who diagnosed a partially torn ACL in his right knee. Surgery was not necessary, but he required rest and physical therapy for four months.

I asked him how he was able to continue to perform in *Cinderella*—and in high heels—with such a painful injury. "The shoe must go on," he shrugged.

On February 7, 1993, Alan appeared in the two-hour NBC television special called *Rowan & Martin's Laugh-In 25th Anniversary Reunion*. Executive Producer and Director George Schlatter recorded some of the material used in the special at a party he had hosted on January 25 at Loews Hotel in Santa Monica. Dick Martin, Gary Owens, Dave Madden, Goldie Hawn, Lily Tomlin, Barbara Feldon, Henry Gibson, Ruth Buzzi, Chelsea Brown and Judy Carne gathered to reminisce at the press reception and dinner.

People magazine printed a cover story about "the happening" in their February 8 issue. The four page feature was packed with photographs and updates on all the cast members. "Bachelor Alan Sues," the magazine reported, "who was *Laugh-In*'s campy Uncle Al and has since worked steadily in touring productions, ambles over to ask Goldie Hawn, 'So, what have you been up to since the show?' Goldie giggles."

The special was a ratings bonanza and garnered great reviews. *Daily Variety* wrote, "Two-hour compilation of clips of the innovative comedy series helps support the claim that *Rowan & Martin's Laugh-In* may have been the funniest series in the history of television. Certainly, the anniversary special is as laugh-provoking as anything that's been on the tube in the last several years. Viewers will be thankful for commercial breaks, giving them a chance to catch their breath."

The *Hollywood Reporter* wrote, "Once upon a time there was no *Saturday Night Live*, no *In Living Color*, but there was *Laugh-In*. *Laugh-In* prevails not just as a generator of pop phrases (e.g. 'here come da judge', 'veddy interesting', and 'sock it to me'), but as memorable television that holds up after all these years. Here is comedy that continues to cut and slice with a sharp point of view."

Henry Gibson, Jo Anne Worley, Alan, Ruth Buzzi and Arte Johnson, Laugh-In Past Christmas Present.

"It was fun to see everyone again under one roof," Alan said. "It just goes to prove that everything old is new again, especially after a few belts of booze."

Rowan & Martin's Laugh-In 25th Anniversary Reunion was so well-received that George Schlatter and Ed Friendly produced a follow-up special for NBC titled, *Laugh-In Past Christmas Present*, which was broadcast months later in December. The show consisted of more clips, archival footage and current interviews with Alan and his *Laugh-In* cast mates.

Alan returned to the stage in July 1993, when he presented his one-man show, re-titled *No Flies on Me*, for the Simi Valley Cultural Association's annual Summer Festival of the Arts. The three-night engagement was uneventful, and the audiences were not responsive. I accompanied Alan back and forth to the small theater in Simi Valley. After his final performance on July 11, we drove back to his home in silence. When we pulled into the driveway, he said, "It still needs work, but this was good. Right? It gave me some new ideas."

After years of being told by critics that his work was reminiscent of vaudeville, Alan accepted a lucrative offer to headline Breck Wall's production called *Bottom's Up 1993 Revue*. For nearly thirty years, Wall produced a "floppy shoes and baggy pants" vaudeville-style revue including blackout sketch comedy, dancers, singers, magicians, and strippers. His *Bottom's Up Revue* originally began at Jack Ruby's Dallas night club, and moved to Las Vegas in 1964 where it ran successfully for years. Breck was an old-style comic who purloined most of his material from other shows. He was a flamboyant character in real life, and appeared in most of his own productions, often stripping to his underwear, or appearing in drag. *Bottom's Up 1993 Revue* began a two-month engagement on November 23, 1993, at the Park Cities Playhouse in University Park, a suburb of Dallas, Texas.

Interestingly, the premiere of the show was thirty years almost to the day of the assassination of President John F. Kennedy in Dallas. Breck Wall had been a friend of Jack Ruby and was in Dallas the day the President was shot. Wall spoke to Ruby, with whom he also had a business relationship, the day before Ruby shot and killed Lee Harvey Oswald. Wall was also one of the few people to visit Ruby in jail, and helped arrange for his attorney. In 1964, Wall testified about his relationship with Jack Ruby for the Warren Commission investigating the assassination.

"Breck was quite the guy," Alan said. "When we were getting ready to open the show, one late night we were talking and he spoke about the Kennedy business. He said Jack Ruby was gay, like him, and had a lot of connections to the Mafia. He also said Ruby knew every cop in Dallas because he was running a strip club and always wanted *in* with the law.

"He made it sound like there was some kind of secretive cover-up, but I didn't want to hear it. For the rest of the time I was in Dallas, whenever I heard a car backfire or any loud noise, I'd throw myself on the pavement. Great exercise."

While Breck Wall's shows were a throwback to the days of burlesque, so were his self-promotional skills. "He had an organ grinder with a monkey and two tap-dancing strippers on the sidewalk in front of the theater," Alan said. "This guy was a real class act."

To help promote the show, Alan agreed to be interviewed on a local radio station. He didn't realize the radio program was geared to a gay listening audience. He was sand-bagged during the interview when he was asked about his own personal life and sexuality. "I couldn't really get out of it," Alan recalled. "I mumbled something about it and tried to change the subject. But I was appearing in a strip show in a musty old dive in Dallas produced by Jack Ruby's onetime partner, so I thought, what the hell can I lose. I'll take it to go, please."

After his appearance in Dallas, Alan was professionally inactive for about a year, except for his appearance in another George Schlatter-produced television special, *Rowan and Martin's Laugh-In: A Valentine's Day Special*. Broadcast on February 14, 1994, the one-hour special included new interviews, film clips and bloopers.

"If you live long enough," Alan said, "you start getting invited to all kinds of things. People just want to see what you look like anymore." Alan attended numerous award shows for the Academy of Television Arts and Sciences, and the American Comedy Awards. "I called those the Awards I Don't Win banquets," Alan joked. "George produced a lot of those. You just sat at these tables and watched each other get older. And I hate watching film clips of myself that are twenty years old!"

One evening in early 1995, he had dinner with his friend, actor/playwright George Furth. Furth had won a Tony Award for writing the book for Stephen Sondheim's musical-comedy *Company*. He was currently working on another play with Sondheim called *The Doctor is Out*. It was a comic thriller about seven patients of a murdered psy-

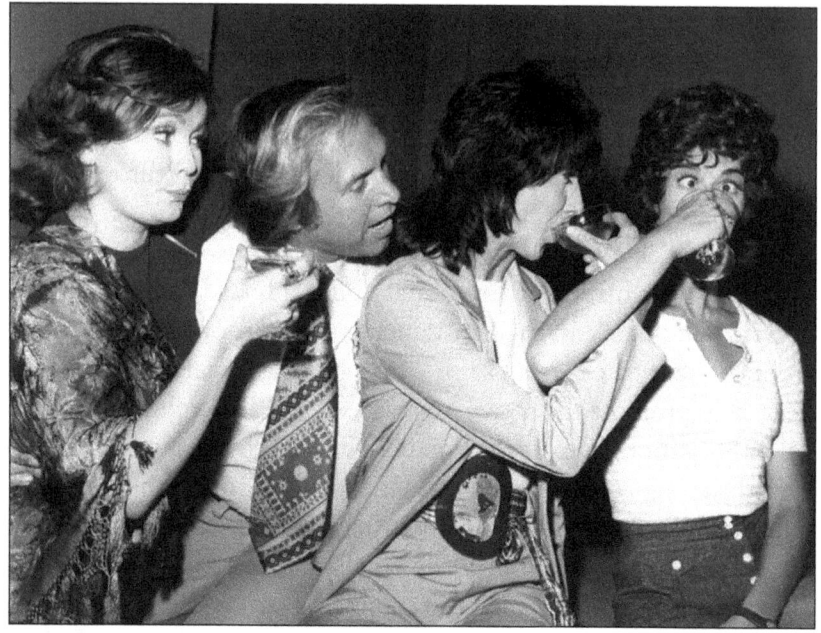

Barbara Sharma, Alan, Lily Tomlin and Ruth Buzzi. "Any excuse for a group martini."

chiatrist who decide to conduct their own investigation of the crime. The Doctor is Out premiered a few months later at the Old Globe Theatre in San Diego. The play was re-titled Getting Away with Murder, and opened and closed on Broadway in early 1996.

The idea of a comedic mystery intrigued Alan, consequently his one-man show took another creative turn. Alan asked Furth for help. Furth was too busy, but he suggested his friend Randal K. West as a directorial candidate. West had worked with Sondheim and Furth on their musical *Merrily We Roll Along*, and was working with Furth on a rewrite of his musical *The Act*.

Under the direction of West, Alan's one-man-comedy-murder-mystery, now called *Show Stoppers Revue*, became the second production at the newly renovated Butte Theatre in Gridley, California. *Show Stoppers Revue* began a three-week engagement in the Northern California town on May 12, 1995. "We were in the middle of the redwoods," Alan said. "They were all gold-miners or lumberjacks. They came to the theater armed with a gun or an axe. Tough crowd. I knew I was in trouble when I saw all the ashtrays in the lobby were replaced with spittoons."

Before reprising the role of Roscoe Dexter in a new summer tour of the musical *Singin' in the Rain* a month later, Alan filmed the small but memorable role of an effete art buyer in the Showtime Cable Network horror movie titled *Bucket of Blood*. The film was a remake of Roger Corman's 1959 film of the same name about a psychopathic artist who murders people, covers their corpses in plaster, and passes off his creations as fine art. The cast included some wonderful comic character actors including Will Farrell, Paul Bartel, Mink Stole, Jennifer Coolidge and Patrick Bristow.

Singin' in the Rain, under the direction of Charles Repole, opened at the Music Hall Theatre in Dallas, Texas, on June 20. The show was well-received and played for two weeks. The musical then played to sold-out audiences at the twelve-thousand seat outdoor Muny Theatre in St. Louis, Missouri. On July 19, the *St. Louis Post-Dispatch* wrote, "Veteran Alan Sues adds the comic relief." After a week at the Pittsburgh Civic Light Opera and then at the Starlight Theater in Kansas City, *Singin' in the Rain* played its final performances in August at the landmark Fox Theater in Atlanta, Georgia.

While Alan enjoyed a burst of work in 1995, his mother's health took a turn for the worse. Following the death of Alan's father, Alice Sues had sold their condominium in Lompoc and moved to Lutheran House, an assisted-care facility in Solvang, California. Years before, Pete Sues helped finance the project with the promise that he and his wife would have complimentary accommodation if the need ever arose. Alan and his brother and sister-in-law visited Alice whenever they could. She developed dementia, and died in September 1995. Alice's million-dollar estate was bequeathed to Alan and his brother John.

Yvonne Sues recalled, "John and Alan were always respectful of their parents. I heard John assert himself with his father only once, about work. I never heard Alan argue with them. In spite of how they treated him, he was always polite."

During the months it took to settle his mother's estate, Alan labored on his solo show. He filled his newly remodeled koi pond with fish, and hired a gardener to help him landscape the backyard. However, his boredom got the best of him. "How many roses can

The backyard at 9014 Dorrington.

you prune?" he pondered. "I plant tomatoes and the raccoons eat them! They show up wearing bibs!"

Alan reached out to many theaters across the country to find a venue for his one-man show. Flush with his inheritance, he considered producing the show himself, and entered into negotiations with the Herberger Theater in Phoenix, Arizona. Once a budget was completed, he decided not to risk his own money on an untried theatrical venture.

On Memorial Day weekend in 1996, Alan attended a comedy-sketch writing class taught by Mary Willard. Mary was actor Fred Willard's wife. There, Alan met a writer/director named Todd Lampe. "Mary said a friend of hers was coming in to try out some material for his one-man show. Alan Sues from *Laugh-In*. I was very impressed," Todd said. "I was a big fan and it was really thrilling to meet him. He was still hilarious! Alan had a certain style that drew me in. No matter what he did, I was immediately on 'his side' and felt for him, even if he was the brunt of the joke. Vulnerability was the key to his humor. Very Chaplin and Stan Laurel-esque.

"After the class, we spoke and I asked if he had a director. In that familiar and unique lilt that only he had, he said, 'Well, I *did*, but he had a job opportunity and he moved just far away enough to be inconvenient ... oh, nothing ...' The next day we had lunch together and a friend of Alan's came to the table. Alan introduced me, 'And this is my friend Todd Lampe. He's my director.' And that's how I started working with him."

Alan had never been a "Hollywood Player," and did not effectively "network" with show business associates. He admired that quality in others, however, and always expressed regrets that he couldn't seem to bring himself to be so professionally aggressive. He certainly had his talent to promote, but he didn't have the drive and, more importantly, he never had the confidence it took to be a self-promoter. He credited Fred Willard's wife with her husband's success. "I wanted her to manage me," Alan said, "but she wasn't interested at all. She said she had enough to do with Fred."

Alan traveled to St. Louis in June 1996 to prepare for a special two-day engagement in a concert version of *The Desert Song* at the Muny Theatre. He reprised his role of Benjamin, which he played in the theater's 1979 production. "I was interested in this because through the years all the controversial elements of the show were taken out—sexual innuendo, lewd dialogue and all the references to homosexuality, all the *good* stuff—and the producers put all that back in for the first time in years. They had some wild times in the desert, you know what I mean? So, they asked me back and I wanted to do the restored show for the fun of it."

When the proceeds of Alice Sues's estate were finally dispersed, Alan hired a contractor to add a second story to his house. A room with a balcony that overlooked the backyard was built directly over his bedroom. The second story was accessed by a rickety, lighthouse-style, circular metal staircase. The project took more than a year, and two different contractors to complete. At the same time, he had central air conditioning and heating installed, and he hired another contractor to rebuild a "garden-style" room that connected the living room with the terraced backyard patio.

On October 7, 1996, Alan appeared in a special one-time performance of *Aardvarks to Zebras*, a gala benefit for PAWS/LA (Pets Are Wonderful Support for People Living With HIV/AIDS/ Los Angeles). Produced and directed by David Galligan, and with mu-

Alan with Jo Anne Worley.

sical direction by Ron Abel and Jerry Sternbach, *Aardvarks to Zebras* was staged at the Pasadena Playhouse. Hosted by Jo Anne Worley, the cast also included Jane Carr, Loretta Devine, Nancy Dussault, Earl Holliman, Dale Kristien, Charlotte Rae, and Gretchen Wyler among many others.

Alan took the stage in the person of "that totally unknown canine behavioral scientist, Dr. Gork." He smiled, furiously itched himself for a moment, and said, "Good Evening everyone. I'm Dr. Gork. Well, I *am*! I'd like to thank you all—ladies and gentlemen of the Pasadena P.A.W.S associated women's section for the protection of our wandering canine four-footed friends club! Wow! Does that fit on the membership card? Anyway, thank you for inviting me to this festive raw meat dinner! The thought that all over this nation tonight dog lovers have gathered to celebrate poodle day makes me want to lie down and roll over. So to speak. Easy that's *my* joke. Ever since they invented the French poodle I have devoted my entire life to French dogs, French perfume, and French fries. And

I have found that the more dogs imitate humans the more they become human."

Alan smiled nervously, and itched himself again before continuing.

"The celebrated Professor Pavlov was the first to discover this. Everyone thought him crazy. *Nearly* everyone." Alan pointed at himself and shook his head to show his disapproval. "I was just fascinated by his problem and determined to make the dogs that I work with as human as possible. Everyone has seen dogs go after flies. And incidentally, nothing so annoys dogs as flies. By always hitting flies with my hand, I soon found dogs were imitating me and hitting flies with their paws. They would stalk a fly just like we do, and hit it with their paw." Alan suddenly swatted at some imaginary flies around his head. "I know that sounds unbelievable but it's true. Could I have a glass of water please? Oh, to hell with it, I'll let it go until my walk.

"They say dogs don't have a sense of humor. Well, dogs *do* have a sense of humor. For instance, this whistle [Alan took a whistle from his pocket] which you cannot hear strikes a dog very funny." Alan blew the dog whistle. "If a dog was here, he would smile and giggle." Alan started to laugh. "Oh, I wish you could hear this!" Alan blew the dog whistle again, and broke into hysterical laughter. "Oh, that *is* funny! There is *nothing* like a good dirty dog joke! Now I would like you to concentrate with me while I hammer home an important point." Alan pointed one arm and one leg like a dog. "Dogs get neurotic just like humans. And I *know* about neurosis. Dog's neurosis is caused by humans. We cause neurosis by saying something to a dog and not waiting for it to answer. For instance, we will ask 'How do you like your dinner?' And just as the dog gets ready to answer, we pay no attention to it. Obviously the dog develops neurotic tendencies."

A siren was heard off stage. "In closing, I would like to say I'm Dr. Gork. Well, I *am!*" Alan blew the dog whistle again, and laughed loudly. "Oh, yes. One of the worst things we do is pretend to throw a stick in one direction and hide it behind our back." Voices are heard off stage, and suddenly two men wearing white coats walk on stage. "The dog starts to look for the stick and can't find it and finally goes out of his mind!" The two men in white coats gently took Alan by the arm and escorted him off stage while he threw his head back and loudly howled.

On October 10, Robert Osborne reviewed the show for the *Hollywood Reporter*. "There was only one thing wrong with last weekend's PAWS/LA benefit—it only lasted for a single performance. This show was good enough to have tied with Carol Channing's *Dolly!* record, or at the very least to be repeated for a few months. Good show? An understatement. Good cause? You bet, since these annual parties for PAWS continue to raise big bucks to feed and care for the pets of people who are HIV-positive. All in all, a whale of a show! The cat's meow! Dog-gone good! Owl drink to that!"

The Museum of Television and Radio (MT&R) presented the Thirteenth Annual Television Festival in Los Angeles. As part of the festival, the MT&R hosted a tribute to producer George Schlatter on October 8 at the Director's Guild Theatre on Sunset Boulevard. The evening program included a screening of filmed highlights from Schlatter's career, and an onstage panel discussion featuring Henry Gibson, Goldie Hawn, Arte Johnson, Gary Owens, Lily Tomlin, Jo Anne Worley, and Alan.

When Alan was introduced, he said, "I'm so thankful that you asked me to be here this evening to honor George Schlatter. After all, he discovered so many talented people who went on to superstardom . . . like the go-go dancer who went on to win an Academy Award, Goldie Hawn . . . the hysterical Tony and Emmy and Grammy Award winning Lily Tomlin . . . and me! You know, I don't think George recognized me when he saw me this evening. I've had a facelift. So, basically, I'm talking out of my ass right now. George, where has the time gone? Where's my hair? Where's my teeth? Seriously, whoever has them, give them back! No questions asked. I got to work with so many legends on *Laugh-In* like Sammy Davis Jr., John Wayne, Jack Lemmon, Kirk Douglas. And Richard Nixon. Whatever happened to *him*, anyway? George, I'm ready to do *Laugh-In* all over again, but this time I get to wear the feather boa."

In the fall, Alan formed his own production company with Todd Lampe called Precipice Productions. "He made a big push to get his show out there, which he worked on all the time," Todd recalled. "We sent out packages to many theaters and producers. I was trying to get a theater in Denver that had expressed some interest." Alan reached out to Dallas Summer Musicals where he had worked before, but the theater rejected his play, now called *The What If? Revue*.

Alan reprised his role of Roscoe Dexter in the 5th Avenue Musical Theatre Company production of *Singin' in the Rain* in Seattle, Washington. The show opened on November 29, 1996, and played through December 22. On December 6, *The Seattle Times* wrote, "In an eccentric turn, Alan Sues (formerly of TV's *Laugh-In*) hams it up as an old-time movie director."

Alan said, "Long ago I should have changed my last name to *Laugh-In*." The Seattle engagement exhausted him. "It poured rain every night on stage, and it poured every day outside." He was disheartened because he struggled with his lines—lines very familiar to him after more than a year on the road playing the same role. When he returned home at Christmas, he said he didn't want to travel anymore. "Living out of a trunk is only glamorous in the movies," Alan said. "I wanted to work in the garden, lunch with the ladies, and visit friends once in a while. I think they call that *life*."

In August 1997, Alan finally had the facelift he had often joked about. Years earlier he had rhinoplasty surgery in Chicago. He was never happy with the proportions of his nose, but he told his friends he had the "nosejob" done to fix a deviated septum. Following his cosmetic surgery in the summer, he was confined to his home for six weeks to recover.

Alan called me to say that his ex-wife Phyllis, with whom he had reestablished a friendship, had stopped in to see him. She told him she hated his "new face."

"She said I look like Mitzi Gaynor," he complained, "or was it Janet Gaynor?"

I said, "Let's go with Mitzi."

"Yeah, that's right," he said, "she can sing and dance. And we've both got great legs." Then he hung up on me.

While he was recovering, Alan concentrated on "fine-tuning" his solo show. The trouble was, although he was genuinely funny when he was talking about his family and life experiences, the bubbly spontaneity was missing when he tried to construct a humorous work of fiction. He didn't trust his instincts, which made him rely on other contributors and his own samplings of other peoples' writing and jokes. As a result, the show took many turns and was eventually re-titled *Two for the Show Review.*

Alan did not return to work until October 1998 when he appeared in a special Halloween episode of *Sabrina, The Teenage Witch* titled "Good Will Haunting." The story had the title character attending a Halloween party in an asylum. Alan played a mad doctor named Bellevuedere, and was joined by other *Laugh-In* alumni Ruth, Jo Anne, Dave Madden, and Gary Owens.

In private, Alan had always been rather soft-spoken. Professionally, he was uninhibited. His wild alter-ego emerged when he had a few glasses of wine. One evening, we had dinner at a nearby restaurant, which we often frequented. Alan flirted with the waiters, and always requested one stunningly handsome waiter named Johnny to attend to us. Alan had a little too much to drink on this occasion, and suddenly grabbed his bread plate and threw it on the terracotta tile floor. It shattered, startling the other patrons in the dining room. The waiter hurried to the table.

"I'll have another glass please," Alan said, tapping his wine glass.

The waiter asked, "Why did you throw the plate on the floor?"

"It's so rude to snap your fingers for the waiter," Alan said. "Just put it on the tab." Alan looked at the people who were seated at the next table and said conspiratorially, "It's very cheap dinnerware. No big deal." Then he looked at our waiter and said loudly, "Look at that precious face ... so pretty ... and he's got a tiny Renaissance peepee."

It was difficult for Alan not to personalize any professional failure, and it was impossible to get through to him when he was depressed. If you spoke niceties and encouraged him, he accused you of being a patronizing asshole. But if you didn't try to make him feel better, he said you were an idiot. Ultimately, it was his enviable ability to turn hardship into humor that drew him out of any emotion funk.

Alan had sought psychiatric help throughout his life. One day, after returning home from his bi-weekly visit to his psychiatrist, he grumbled to me, "I've been doing this for years. Have you noticed any effects?"

"Just to your bank account," I answered.

"Well, fuck you, Freud," he snapped, but after nearly forty years of seeing a "shrink," he abruptly and permanently quit.

"What better way to get over depression than being in a parade," I exclaimed.

"I hate parades," Alan grumbled. But in November 1998, Alan and Ruth Buzzi were celebrity guests in the 67th Annual Hollywood Christmas Parade. Many celebrities rode in classic convertibles amid floats and marching bands in the holiday spectacle.

"I ran into Mickey Rooney at the party before the parade began," Alan recalled. "He was bobbing for candy canes in the punch bowl. I said, 'Hi, Mickey! How are you?'

"He didn't know who the hell I was. 'Who is it?' he croaked, squinting into my belt buckle.

"I said, 'It's Alan Sues.' 'I don't *know* you,' he snapped. I told him we worked together on *Rudolph and Frosty's Christmas*, and he asked me when. I said about twenty years ago.

"'Jesus Christ!' he yelled, 'Move on! Get on with your life! Jesus, get over it!'

"'Nice to see you again, Mickey', I said as he stomped off.

"I stood under the mistletoe until the fire department cleared the tent. Nothing, absolutely nothing. Just another Hollywood party."

Alan was shocked when his old friend Charles Pierce died on May 31, 1999. He had retired several years before, but he and Alan had stayed in touch. Alan took Pierce's death very hard. They had known each other for fifty years. "The clock is ticking," he told me.

A few months later, Holly Hester, the executive producer of *Sabrina, the Teenage Witch*, offered Alan a role in a short film she had written and planned to direct titled *Lord of the Road*. The story concerns the problems Jesus Christ encounters when his car breaks down in the town of Sweetwater, Florida. Alan played the role of a small town pastor who helps Jesus shop for a more suitable wardrobe. The film screened at a number of film festivals, and won a Special Jury Award at the 1999 Kudzu Film Festival for "Best Use of Blasphemy."

Alan renewed his friendship with Patty (Eng) Faure, his model friend from New York. While he had established a show business

Todd Lampe with Alan at a screening of Artificially Speaking.

career, she had stepped behind the camera and had become a noted fashion photographer, and later a respected art gallery owner in Los Angeles. We attended opening receptions at her gallery, and socialized with their mutual friends, Peggy Moffit and her husband, Bill Claxton, and photographer Helmut Newton and his wife, June, when they were in Los Angeles. One night we were all having dinner at Chateau Marmont, and we were joined by Barry Humphries, the Australian actor whose professional alter-ego was Dame Edna, a character he played in drag.

At Humphries's invitation, Alan and I attended a performance by Dame Edna at the Ahmanson Theater in Los Angeles. We sat with Don Rickles and his wife. At the intermission, as we were making our way to the lobby for a drink, Alan tapped Don on the shoulder and said, "That's a good part for you."

Don laughed and shot back, "What happened? You didn't make the cut?"

"Shoes didn't fit." Alan shrugged.

Alan recorded his final acting role in a film in 2000. *Artificially Speaking* is a short film written and directed by Todd Lampe. Alan played the role of Sparky Schlosser, the gardener at an artificial fruit farm that is under investigation following the poisoning of a young boy who ate tainted artificial fruit. "There was a script," Todd explained, "but Alan improvised most of it. And whatever he did was funnier than what was on the page." The "mockumentary" was screened at numerous film festivals.

Todd continued to work closely with Alan on his one-man revue. The script called for Alan to play almost a dozen characters, change costumes, accents, dance and prance, jump on chairs and a steamer trunk, and waltz with a coat rack. Todd directed and video-taped Alan's special invitational performances of *Two for the Show* on July 7 and 8, 2001, at the Chandler Studio in North Hollywood.

Nearly a year passed before Alan ventured into the public eye. On April 8, 2002, *Rowan and Martin's Laugh-In* was inducted into the "Broadcasting Hall of Fame" by the National Association of Broadcasters. George Schlatter was joined by Alan, Ruth, Jo Anne, Lily, Gary Owens and Henry Gibson at the presentation ceremony. They were then interviewed by Katie Couric on the NBC morning program, *The Today Show*. When he brought home the handsome plaque memorializing the honor, he put it in the closet. "Why don't you hang it up," I asked. "You should be proud."

"Ancient history," he muttered.

In May, Charles Nelson Reilly's acclaimed one-man show, *Save it for the Stage . . . The Life of Reilly*, opened at the Canon Theatre in Beverly Hills. Alan wanted to see the show, so we attended an evening performance. Afterward, we visited with Reilly in his tiny dressing room backstage. As we entered the room, Alan suddenly stopped in the doorway and joked, "Jesus, Charlie, you're back in the closet!"

Reilly barked his "nyuck, nyuck" laugh and said, "Yes, but they get smaller as I get older."

Alan asked, "How much smaller can they get?"

Reilly clucked. "You know the punch-line. I'd offer you a drink, but there's not even room in here for a bottle." He looked and me and asked, "Who's your shadow?"

"My man servant," Alan answered. "Want your shoes shined?"

"No," Reilly said, "but I need my pipe cleaned."

"That'll cost you," Alan snapped.

The two comedians first met in New York City in the early 1950s. They both attended acting classes with Herbert Bergoff, and collected milk bottles to sell for subway fare. Alan was enchanted by Reilly's show, and praised his writing and stamina on stage. We talked for nearly an hour. During the conversation, Alan lamented the fact that he abandoned Hollywood following his years on *Laugh-In* to pursue theatrical work. Although it had provided him with steady income, he wondered aloud if he had sacrificed a potential career in movies and television by moving to New York.

Reilly answered him quickly.

"You did the right thing," he said. "You wouldn't have gotten a series after *Laugh-In*. None of you did after the show ended. The audience associated you with the character you played on the show and you wouldn't have been able to act your way out of that. It happened to all of us. *Match Game* was a steady job for eight years, but killed me. Just killed me. Most of my work has been on stage. And I'm directing and teaching, too. You had a public face after *Laugh-In*, and you used it to your best advantage."

As Alan and I drove back to his house, he reiterated how much he enjoyed Reilly's terrific performance. Like much of Alan's *Two for the Show*, Reilly's show centered around his dysfunctional family. "Thank God for them," he had said to Alan. "I wouldn't be here without them!"

Alan was more determined than ever to make his show a viable act. "I can do that," he said. "I can do what he did. I need to tighten it up a little."

"You know," I ventured, "his show is not a work of fiction. It's an autobiographical performance. And it's endearing. Your stories are more edgy."

"Yeah, yeah," Alan said dismissively. "His timing and reactions are perfect. I can *do* that."

On May 30, Alan and I attended the opening night performance of a special fortieth anniversary production of *Spoon River Anthology* at Theater West. The haunting musical, based on the poetry of Edgar Lee Masters, had been conceived by Charles Aidman. Naomi Caryl wrote the music for Aidman's lyrics. The show had premiered at Theater West in 1962. The new production starred Lee Meriwether and Bridget Hanley, and was directed by Alan's friends Betty Garrett and Joyce Van Patten. The performance was enthralling. At the reception after the show, Alan approached the theater's director and pitched *Two for the Show*. Ultimately, Theater West passed on Alan's proposal, but after seeing *Spoon River Anthology*, Alan decided his piece needed more music and singing.

A few months later in September, Alan presented a few performances of *Two for the Show* at Theatre Unlimited in North Hollywood, California. I accompanied Patty Faure on the first night and we took Alan out for a late snack at Bob's Big Boy restaurant in Toluca Lake after the show. "Oh, honey," Patty said to him, "why are you working so hard?"

After so many rejections, and indifferent audiences, Alan felt defeated. He shelved plans to find a venue for his show, and after more than twenty years of work, finally set the script aside.

"He really had some great routines and characters," Todd Lampe said. "It's too bad that he didn't trust himself enough to just be secure as a performer to let go and enjoy it, because some the most funny moments were when he was his natural self. He was such an engaging soul. If he had just done characters or told stories that would have sufficed."

For years, we tinkered with Alan's self-penned comic monologues, and with a humorous, murder-mystery screenplay he conceived titled *White Vinegar*. Todd worked on the screenplay, as well. Initially, Alan wanted to star in *White Vinegar*, but little interest was expressed by the few producers who read the material. Alan then

Alan on stage for Pacific Coast Dog Rescue.

thought he could produce the film himself, but that was impossible. He seemed satisfied that he had at least *finished* the screenplay about a policewoman who was investigating a perplexing murder and moonlighting as an interior decorator.

With no work to occupy his time, Alan found boredom to be a dangerous state of mind. He tried to get an extended booking as a guest-star in the long-running *Palm Springs Follies* in Palm Springs, California. Other friends of his had appeared in the show and told him they had a wonderful time. He worked on a demo reel to send to the producer, but the popular show had guest-stars booked a year in advance.

On June 1, 2003, I produced a fund-raising event at the Silent Movie Theater in Hollywood to benefit Pacific Coast Dog Rescue, a non-profit organization, which was then chaired by actress Linda Blair. Alan was the special guest entertainer. He extracted some material from *Two for the Show*, and put together a stand-up routine. The sold-out crowd loved him.

"I know what you're thinking," he said when he stepped up to the microphone. "He's *fat*. What's he been doing since *Laugh-In*, eat-

ing? Well, I'm on a new diet. It's a liquid diet. This morning I put a ham in the blender."

Alan was always tinkering with a creative project. He was never lacking for ideas. We enrolled in a screenwriting class at the Gay and Lesbian Center in Los Angeles. On the first night of class, he leaned over to me and said, "If the class is no good, it's not a complete waste. Maybe we'll find a date here."

He frequently called me to say he had heard an item on the news or found an interesting tidbit in a magazine or the newspaper that he thought could be worked into a comedic story. But performing was never far from his heart. He was an earnest entertainer whether he was playing to a full house or an audience of one. His eyes would twinkle and a smirk would tug at his mouth, and the performer emerged from his shell. He liked my sister very much, and whenever she visited, he sang a couple of silly songs and danced a soft-shoe routine. Sometimes he threw in a bump-and-grind. It made him happy to make people laugh.

On August 4, 2004, Alan joined Ruth, Gary Owens, Dick Martin and George Schlatter for a *Laugh-In* reunion on the first annual *TV Land Convention Special* televised on the TV Land cable network. Later that year, Alan signed a contract to license his image and voice to be used on slot machines. George Schlatter had worked on the deal for more than a year. The plan was to place *Laugh-In* themed slot machines in Indian casinos across the country. Alan, Ruth, Jo Anne, Gary, and Arte Johnson made a personal appearance at an Indian Casino in Connecticut to promote the new machines. Alan hoped George Schlatter's business venture would be successful because the actors' potential royalties would have been considerable. Unfortunately, the plan was never realized.

With no professional obligations, Alan was restless and at times melancholy, but he enjoyed being retired from road shows, and he was content to be close at home. He was heartbroken when Mandy, his beloved dog, died suddenly. To assuage his grief, he bought a tiny golden dachshund from a breeder, and named her Doris. Though small in size, Doris was a loving companion and fierce watchdog. She was also determined never to become housebroken. Every time I scolded her and tried to train her, Alan would

Dick Martin and George Schlatter with Alan at the TV Land Convention Special.

scold me. "Oh, leave her alone, you big bully" he'd say. "It doesn't matter. Just look at that little face. She's cute as a button."

Alan enjoyed watching films and we often attended screenings at the Director's Guild and the Motion Picture Academy's Goldwyn Theatre in Beverly Hills where he was always over-run by fans and autograph collectors. He grumbled, but secretly reveled in the attention.

We also ventured out to the theater whenever we could. He loved Joyce Van Patten's performance in a stunning production of *Dead End* at the Ahmanson Theatre, and Jo Anne Worley in *Wicked* at the Pantages Theatre in Hollywood. He didn't want me to tell Jo Anne he was coming, and when I offered to help him backstage to see her after the show, he opted to go home. He didn't want her to see him because he thought he looked fat, and he didn't want her to see him leaning on me for assistance. "She's really busy, you know," he said to me. "It'll be crowded back there and I don't want to bother her." On the drive home, he was reticent. He complimented Jo Anne's work and said he envied the determination that drove her successful career. "She works all the time," he said. "She's a real go-getter."

Alan loved going to the theater. When he was in New York, he'd often call me to tell me about a show he had just seen on Broadway. "It was *great*!" he'd exclaim. "It was *fucking* great!" Then he'd say, "Why am I wasting money calling you long distance? What do you know about theater?" And he'd hang up the phone.

Alan enrolled in comedienne Judy Brown's Stand-Up Comedy Workshop. Upon completing her course, he performed his routine at the Improv in Los Angeles, and had several bookings at the Ice House in Pasadena. I drove him to the theaters, and tape recorded his performances, which he carefully listened to later in the quiet of his office.

One night following a performance in Pasadena, Alan complained to me on the drive home. "They hated me," he said. "This isn't going anywhere." I knew enough not to say a word of assurance since that would only set him off on a tirade. Alan was a tall man, but that evening, when we got back to the house, he looked deflated when he slowly walked in front of me toward the patio.

He turned and said, "What did you think?"

"I'm not a good judge of this Alan," I sighed. "I've told you before I don't like stand-up comedy."

"You're stupid," he barked.

"Yes, I am," I said. "I answered your question."

"Hey," he snapped, "just open the door. *I* tell the jokes here!"

A short time later, Alan's home fitness-trainer called me surreptitiously. She said she was concerned about him, and found empty wine bottles in the trash can outside his kitchen door. When I mentioned this to Alan, he became enraged. I don't know if he was more angered because she rifled through his things, or because she revealed his drinking to me. He fired her at once.

His longtime housekeeper (who was a bit of a chatterbox) said something to him that he found offensive. Upon a friend's recommendation, he hired another housekeeper who was cheaper, but more importantly, spoke little English. "I don't want to listen to other people's problems all day," he said. "I'm paying her, she's not paying me!"

"Your advice isn't good enough to pay for," I joked.

"Neither was her cleaning!"

Alan decided he needed someone to take dictation, and to transcribe some material he was tape-recording. Alan's old friend, Jerry Jackson, recommended a young woman who was "in recovery." The first time I met her, I told Alan she was under the influence. "No, she isn't," he snapped, but he told me to lock up the booze before I left the house that day. Several days later, she drove off in his fifteen-year old blue Toyota pickup to run errands, and did not return. I discovered she had wrecked his truck in a traffic accident and was jailed for drunk driving. We never saw her or the truck again, but over the next few weeks more than a dozen parking tickets charged to the Toyota's license plate number were mailed to Alan's house.

He never liked to deal with "confrontations" or "complications." He grunted, shrugged it off, and said he didn't want to talk about it. However, he seemed to realize that he could or would no longer be bothered with running a household or administering his own affairs. "You just take care of this stuff," he demanded, as if I had been to blame for what happened with his truck. "Sure," I said. And I did.

John and Yvonne Sues had traveled from their home in Connecticut to visit Alan for a few days in 2005. At the time, John was suffering from Lewy Body Dementia, a form of Parkinson's disease that caused tremors and hallucinations. His condition worsened, and Alan flew to Connecticut to see him in 2007. He was very disheartened to find John in a delicate and confused state. When Alan returned home to California, he was morose. "That's what happened to my father," he said. "John has the same thing, and he's younger than me. And I'm sure it's going to happen to me. It's a nightmare. It's terrible. At least he has Yvonne to take care of him."

Alan was overcome with worry about how he would care for himself when what he thought was a medical inevitability would happen to him. He had begun to suffer brief blackouts.

I knew it was important to keep him occupied. Phyllis Sues visited and spoke with Alan frequently on the phone. He agreed to be interviewed by her at her home. She was working on recording content for her professional website. The interviews had a casual, conversational style that was very charming, and best represented the Alan that we all knew and loved. He was quick-witted and sharp, and the give and take between the couple who had known each other for more than fifty years was delightful. He enjoyed reminiscing with her. "We always ended up arguing, though," Alan said. "Who had the best managed stock accounts and who wore the best age-defying foundation. Estee Lauder versus Chanel. The usual things."

In June 2007, Alan had a pacemaker implanted. The doctors thought his dizzy spells were caused by an irregular heartbeat. His physical recovery was quick, but the psychological effects were severe. He felt compromised and vulnerable, and to make matters worse, the pacemaker didn't seem to make a difference.

He was determined to maintain his mobility. One day, he was walking the dog in his neighborhood. He felt faint, and crumpled to the ground. Comedienne Carole Cook saw him outside her window, and came to his aid.

"Alan, are you all right?" she asked.

"Yes," he said.

"What are you doing on the ground, darlin'?"

Alan gently brushed his hand over the grass and said, "Checking to see if this grass is real. It's *too* green, don't you think?"

Carole said, "Alan was such a funny person. Quick on his feet . . . and on his ass! He was a funny and complicated man. But all comics are complicated."

On another occasion, Alan collapsed on a walk to the grocery store, and hit his head on the curb. He had to spend the night in the hospital, and was diagnosed with hypotension. He was a terrible patient. He called me repeatedly, and ordered me to take him home. When I picked him up at the hospital, a nurse helped me get him into the car. "Did you see that?" he asked indignantly as we drove away. "She was trying to pick my pocket!"

"I don't want to go to a fucking nursing home," he lamented one day when I was preparing lunch. "You'll be fine," I assured him. "You'll never go into a home. I promise we'll make it work here. You're not going anywhere." My assurance seemed to calm him, but he was rocked when his brother John died on April 11, 2008. He barely spoke for days.

Alan was not a religious man. It always irked him to hear someone say, "God bless you," when something terrible had happened. "What's that supposed to mean," he wondered. "It's a little late for that. Why do people thank God when things go right, but don't blame him when things go wrong? There's no logic in religion."

He had no belief in an afterlife, either. The idea of Heaven and Hell was silly to him. "When you're dead, you're dead," he'd say. "That's it. It's over."

Then, Dick Martin passed away on May 24, 2008. Alan had had a testy relationship with Dan Rowan, but was always fond of Dick. And he loved Dick's wife, actress Dolly Read. He attended a memorial for Dick at the Martin home in Santa Monica. Alan was very embarrassed when he fainted and collapsed at the gathering. He was taken away in an ambulance. To put him at ease, Jo Anne joked with him, "Oh, Alan, you're always doing a bit!"

Each personal appearance, though fewer and further between, became burdensome for Alan. He refused the use of a wheelchair to expedite mobility, and shuffled with assistance. The *60th Annual Prime Time Emmy Awards* program was broadcast on September 21, 2008. The producers of the special reunited many classic television show casts to appear as presenters on the show. Alan joined Ruth and Jo Anne, Lily and Gary Owens to recreate *Laugh-In*'s iconic "Joke Wall." Following a quick comedy bit, they presented the Emmy Award for "Outstanding Variety, Music or Comedy Series."

Although we requested a golf cart to transport him through the labyrinth-like backstage area of the Nokia Theater, the producers did not provide assistance. Alan was exhausted as he walked the endless halls during the dress rehearsal the day before. On the afternoon of the live telecast, Alan was overwhelmed and suffered several fainting spells. The dressing room he shared with Gary was a twenty-minute walk from the stage. We had rewritten the few lines of script he was expected to deliver on camera. During the performance, he needed assistance to stand behind the "joke-wall" set and maneuver the door that he had to throw open in order to reveal himself to the audience and deliver his lines. He dropped the prop bell he was supposed to ring, which unnerved him, and he subsequently "tripped" over his few lines. He was mortified.

Alan with Jo Anne Worley, Lily Tomlin, Ruth Buzzi and Gary Owens onstage for the 60th Annual Emmy Awards presentation.

When he and the other *Laugh-In* cast members walked to the microphone to announce the winner of the Emmy Award, Alan corralled every ounce of strength to remain upright and not collapse on live television.

Following the show, Alan attended the Governor's Ball at a nearby hotel. He sat with George Schlatter and his wife. He was so disoriented that he didn't recognize actress Sally Field who walked over to praise him. "I can't believe it," he repeated for days, "I couldn't see her with all the lights in my face and I didn't know who she was, and I *really like* her!"

Alan could not be consoled regarding his awkward appearance on the Emmy telecast. His friends called to say they had seen him on the show, and were kind to him, but he was terribly embarrassed. "That's it," he said to me. "I'm finished. I'm not going to work again. I can't."

To make matters worse, a year earlier Alan had consented to laser eye surgery to correct his cataract eye disease. Unfortunately, not only did the surgery not improve his vision, it worsened his eyesight to the point of making it nearly impossible for him to read. Alan had been a voracious reader, and this other disability was devastating to him. I sometimes read to him, but it only frustrated him more, and he took to directing my readings.

Alan fell at home and badly broke his leg in early December 2008. A pin was implanted, and he spent a few weeks at the Rehabilitation Center of Beverly Hills near Cedars-Sinai Hospital. I stopped in to see him every day. He was ill-tempered and very impatient with the staff and his recovery. I brought him a box of See's candy which normally would have cheered him up, but the next day he told me the nurses had stolen the candy. But he didn't want a replacement. "Bring me a bottle of Cabernet. I can hide it under the sheets between my legs. Nobody will look for it there."

When Alan returned home in early January 2009, he reluctantly agreed to have a caregiver move into the house to assist him. "I only want young, good-looking guys," he told me. "No Nurse Ratched!"

With the help of a physical therapist and his caregiver Zac, Alan was able to walk with assistance in a few months. During the summer he regained his strength, and later in October, he felt well enough to appear at an Autograph Collector's Show in Burbank, California. Dozens of stars who had appeared on the legendary television series *Twilight Zone* filled a section of the banquet room. Hundreds of fans lined up for hours to buy their autographs. Originally, Alan agreed to appear both Saturday and Sunday, but he could only fulfill the Saturday engagement. This would be Alan's final personal appearance. A few celebrities, who were personal friends, visited with him that day including Ruta Lee, Earl Holliman and Jackie Cooper.

Ruta Lee cheerfully greeted him, "Oh, Alan, you look great!"

Alan laughed, "I can't walk and you can't see! We should do the *Miracle Worker* on ice!"

One gratifying result of Alan's appearance at the autograph show was the realization that his time on *Laugh-In* had been appreciated by so many fans. Many gay men stood in line to meet him that day. They told him he was one of the few gay men they saw on television when they were young, and his gay visibility, though myopic in style, made a difference to them. Alan was shocked, and genuinely overcome. One fellow told him that he had looked forward to Monday nights just to watch Alan on the show, and it was the

Taylor Negron, Alan and me.

only way he got through his problems. Alan posed for photos with many of the guys, always looking a little coquettish, flirting and saying something to make each person laugh.

"And I thought nobody knew I was *gay*," he said to me as he rolled his eyes. He was genuinely touched.

For the next couple of years, Alan lived quietly at home. We established a routine that occupied his time with watching television, fiddling with his writing, and perusing every design and garden magazine we could find. Occasionally he hosted a guest for lunch, or dinner. I found a couple of dusty boxes filled with Christmas ornaments on a shelf in the garage one day. For the first time in years, we livened things up and decorated the house for the holiday.

Alan had lived alone for so long, he had convinced himself that he didn't like the festivities – but he did. I hung a leather strap covered with sleigh bells to the front door. It jangled whenever the door was opened. When I came in, he looked up at me and grumbled, "Here comes Santa Claus. I heard your annoying bells."

Alan's old friends Walter Finley and Laura Castro traveled from the east coast to visit him a couple of times, and stayed at the house for a few days. With the housekeeper's appearance once a week, the gardener working in the yard, and the caregivers living in the house, Alan said to me, "I've never had so many people in my house! Are they paying me rent? Kick them out!"

Alan's circle of friends tightened by attrition as they began to pass away, and as his own physical condition limited his mobility. Alan was shocked when Teresa Graves, who appeared on *Laugh-In*, perished in a house fire at the age of 54. Henry Gibson's beloved wife Lois passed away in 2007. "Henry won't be able to live without her," Alan lamented. Henry died two years later.

Comedian Taylor Negron had met Alan at one of the many American Comedy Awards Shows produced by George Schlatter, and they became friends. Taylor visited Alan whenever he was in town, usually with a couple of quarts of Haagen Daaz butter-pecan ice cream or a bag of cookies which Alan complained about—but always ate.

"Alan was a complete original," Taylor said. "He was funny to the core. It was not an act. His presence was comical. I thought he was hilarious. He was a true blue cornflower in a field of bright yellow tulips. Alan's approach was rooted in an old-fashioned theatrical style of storytelling. Each moment with Alan was full of his organic and enormous passion for the craft of comedy. He was wildly feline, like few humans have ever seen. He waited to tell a joke. He sensed the listener and could hear the audience and delivered the material accordingly. The result was explosive and always surprising. Sometimes when he finished telling one of his blithely shaggy-dog stories, he would fold his hands elegantly, stare right at you, and serenely he would whisper, '... lights down ... slow curtain ...'"

Barbara Sharma visited with him, as did one of his *Laugh-In* costars, Johnny Brown, and Alan's dear friend Ruth. Jo Anne and

George Schlatter spoke with him often on the phone. Joyce Van Patten remained in close contact, too.

In 2009, Alan was diagnosed with Parkinson's disease. He began to suffer occasional tremors. Though the episodes were brief and painless, the illness was one more discouraging burden for him. The new round of medication prohibited him from having even one glass of wine. This was actually more disturbing to him than the Parkinson's diagnosis. It was difficult to deny him a drink since it was one of the few temporal pleasures he entertained. His self-imposed dieting ended, though, and he allowed himself to eat whatever he craved. He enjoyed hearty meals and decadent desserts. Often, he gauged what he wanted for dinner upon what we had planned for dessert. His favorite evening at home consisted of eating banana pudding and watching *The Judy Garland Show* on DVD.

Like his brother and father before him, Alan began to experience visual delusions that confused and frightened him. He often told us he saw his mother standing in the corner of his bedroom. Sometimes he couldn't be dissuaded or consoled. Other times we could coax him back to reality.

He cried one day, convinced his dog had died. We tried to reassure him to no avail, and finally put Doris in his lap, which eventually soothed him.

One afternoon I walked into his room and told him I was going to cook dinner for the household that evening. "What would you like?" I asked him.

It took him a moment to focus on me before he said, "My mother's here. Is there enough for her?"

"Your mother's here?" I asked. "No, I think you were dreaming, Alan."

"Oh," he mumbled. He looked at me blankly, then smiled slyly and said, "I couldn't have been dreaming. There were no dancing boys."

"This is no fun," Alan said to me numerous times about his worsening health. He was bored and frustrated with his frequent visits to various doctors. "More pills," he grumbled. "Every time we go, more pills. They're all pushers."

Alan with Doris in his backyard. I took this photo in November, 2009. This was Alan's last portrait, but he loved it. "Doris and I look so young!"

One afternoon, Zac drove Alan to Beverly Hills to have his hair cut. He dropped him off at the curb in front of the salon, and drove off to park the car. Alan's hairdresser, Tad, met him outside and helped him to the door, but Alan felt lightheaded and slowly crumpled to the ground.

"I tried to hold him up," Tad said, "but he's a big guy and we both sort of gently went down to the sidewalk. I asked him if he was all right, and he looked up at me and said, 'Don't just stand there, kiss me!' So, I kissed him and helped him up. I went to the house to cut his hair after that, but he was so funny. I admired that about him. No matter what was going on or how shitty he was feeling, he could make a joke."

After that episode, Alan's trips away from home were restricted to doctor appointments.

Whenever we could, we served him lunch outside on his front or back patios for a change of scenery. For a short time, he was interested in a tiny garden of herbs, tomatoes and strawberries we planted in the backyard. One of his favorite programs was the medically-themed talk show, *The Doctors*. He watched it religiously and self-diagnosed, asking for new vitamins and herbal supplements daily.

Even though his short-term memory began to erode, he always surprised us with his sense of humor which remained quick and sharp. Although Alan feigned indifference, and actually objected to my plan, I decorated the entrance hall in the house with framed photographs, theater programs and other memorabilia from his career. There were few show business mementos in the home. When I was finished, Alan's caregiver Zac helped him into the hall to review the new décor. Alan carefully looked around the entry. He studied the newly framed photos and other memorabilia, which he hadn't seen in years. After a minute, he simply said, "Okay." He began to walk back to his room, but stopped and turned to me with a half-smile on his face. He said, "Can you rig the hall light switch to play *There's No Business Like Show Business* when we turn the light on?"

One day I found Alan on the backyard patio with Peter, another one of his caregivers. Peter had stripped to his gym shorts and was doing calisthenics while Alan watched. His hands were folded demurely in his lap.

I said, "What's going on here?"

Peter huffed, "We're doing our exercise."

"Really," I said. I looked at Alan and asked, "What are *you* exercising?"

Alan slowly turned to me and said, "My imagination."

In late 2010, George Schlatter produced a special program for PBS called *The Best of Laugh-In*. Alan was not invited to participate in the show. Alan knew, as did Schlatter, that he was physically unable to work. Nonetheless, he was very hurt by his exclusion. Following the television taping, Jo Anne and Ruth stopped at his house for a nice visit. They reminisced, had a glass of wine, and laughed a lot. Jo Anne assured Alan that he was well represented on the show with many clips. Still, he felt he had been left behind.

We decided to have a little party one evening. After a lobster dinner, Alan's caregivers and a couple of close friends gathered in his bedroom to watch a videotape of *The Charles Pierce Show*, which had been recorded in 1982 when the female impersonator performed at the Dorothy Chandler Music Pavilion in Los Angeles. Phyllis, Alan's ex-wife, owned the rights to the show and provided us with the recording.

While we watched the show, Alan laughed loudly, and periodically remarked, "Now, *that's* an act."

He cried when the special concluded. We had all laughed so much, I was a little taken aback. I asked him, "Why are you crying? I thought you liked it. You were laughing. What's wrong?"

"It's over," Alan muttered. "It's all over."

From November 2009 until April 2011, Todd Lampe recorded Alan at home while he recounted funny stories about his life. The audio recordings were edited and packaged in a special CD titled *Oh, Nothing . . . An Audio Collection of Stories and Memories from Alan Sues* to be marketed on Alan's website, which Todd maintained. The project had been a healthy diversion for Alan, and provided him with a purpose. Todd recorded him in different settings in the house a couple of times each week for many, many months.

In early November 2011, Todd brought the cover artwork for the CD and a booklet to be included in the package for Alan to approve. Alan had a hard time focusing, but he seemed satisfied with Todd's work. Todd hadn't seen Alan in a couple of months. He was disheartened by Alan's appearance. "Even in his final days,

The living room at 9014 Dorrington.

Alan would call me, eagerly asking when we were getting together to work, he had new ideas. It was an admirable quality that is not common with people these days," Todd remembered.

A few days later, we had a couple of friends over for an early-evening Thanksgiving dinner. I had had a premonition about Alan's mortality, so we festively decorated the living room for Christmas. Zac and I hung fresh evergreen wreaths in the windows and placed poinsettias by the fireplace. Alan grumbled to me that he wasn't the slightest bit interested in Christmas, but he loved to sit in the living room by the fireplace and look at the colored, twinkling lights on the table-top tree. He always waited for me to leave the house before being helped into the living room. His caregiver Andy told me that Alan warned him, "Don't tell Michael."

Alan struggled through our turkey dinner that evening, but we did have a long and wonderful conversation about his youthful days working in nightclubs and trying to make ends meet in New York. The present was often muddled in his mind, but I always coaxed chats about his past which remained very clear and memorable in his head. We laughed a lot that night.

During the next week, Alan continued to fade. He lost his interest in eating and conversation, and spent daylight hours asleep in his recliner in front of the television. We noticed that he had begun to lose his will to fight a couple of months earlier.

On Friday morning, December 1, I arrived at Alan's house to check on him, peruse the mail and pay some bills. He was sitting in the recliner in his bedroom. His eyes were half closed. I wasn't sure if he was awake. "Good morning," I said softly. "How are you doing today?"

He looked up at me and said, "I don't like your decorating habits."

I was a little surprised by his cognizance. "Really," I answered, "why not?"

"You put the Christmas tree in the middle of the room," he said, pointing toward the living room. "You can't do that. People can't see each other. Move it in front of the window."

"Okay," I said, "it sounds like you might like to have some company for Christmas. Do you want me to make a dinner? It's just a few weeks away."

He looked at me for a moment, and without emotion stated, "I think I'm dying."

"Oh, Alan," I said, "why do you say something like that? You'd do anything for attention."

He slowly looked me up and down, pointed at me, and said, "Yeah, well, I wouldn't wear that shirt."

Early that evening, Alan suffered a heart attack while watching television. His beloved dog, Doris, was sitting in his lap. Zac called for assistance and tried unsuccessfully to revive him. I was watching *The Nutcracker* on stage at the Dorothy Chandler Music Pavilion in downtown Los Angeles when I received the first frantic telephone call. Perhaps appropriately, I was made aware of Alan's fatal seizure in the middle of the "Dance of the Sugar Plum Fairy."

Alan would have rolled his eyes and said, "Perfect. Put that on a cracker."

Alan at the "Joke Wall" onstage for the 60th Annual Emmy Awards.

Alan Sues, Playwright

Alan in 1980.

The following works were created and written by Alan Sues. They are included here to show Alan's comedy writing skills. He aspired to be a writer, and wrote song lyrics, jokes, skits, sketches, plays and screenplays during his life. These works are not available for use, recording, performing or production in any form. Each work included here is copyrighted by Alan Sues, and remains the sole property of the Estate of Alan Sues.

"THE JAIL VISIT"

Alan with Edie Adams on Here's *Edie.*

"The Jail Visit" comedy sketch was written by Alan, and originally performed on the comedy/variety television show *Here's Edie*, first broadcast on March 19, 1964. Edie Adams played the role of "Ethel." Alan played the role of "Harry."

The sketch was performed again on the variety television show *Hollywood Palace*, broadcast on February 1, 1969. Ruth Buzzi played opposite Alan on the program.

HARRY

What did you say, guard? I've got five minutes to see my wife? Great. Let her out of the chute.

THEY COME AT EACH OTHER BOTH HANGING ON TO THE IMAGINARY FENCE SEPARATING THE PRISONER FROM HIS VISITOR.

HARRY

Ethel!

ETHEL

Harry!

HARRY

Ethel!

ETHEL

Harry!

HARRY

Slip me a kiss between the screen.

THEY KISS. HE JUMPS BACK.

HARRY

You bit my lip!

ETHEL

I'm sorry. I have a plate now.

HARRY

Gee, have I been in prison that long?

ETHEL

Harry, I was talking to Mr. Goldoften down at the supermarket…

HARRY

I hate him!

ETHEL

…and you can get your old job back! But you'll have to start as a bag boy.

HARRY

Bag Boy!?

ETHEL

Then, it's back at the cash register.

HARRY

That's how this whole thing started!

ETHEL

Watch yourself this time.

HARRY

Ethel, I don't want my old job back.

ETHEL

I was talking to mother.

HARRY

How *is* Captain Hook?

ETHEL

Well, she's a little worried about me living with an ex-con. But we found the most wonderful dream house with this wonderful high picket fence. Oh—I wasn't thinking when I did that.

HARRY

Listen, I don't want to be an *ex*-con. I like it here.

ETHEL

What are you talking about?

HARRY

You know how you always said I could never do anything with my hands?

ETHEL

That's right, mittens.

HARRY

Well, you should see me in bead craft! Yesterday, when I started with those beads, I couldn't stop "Over Under," "Over Under," "Over Under." I got so excited, I went to my loom! I've taken up weaving! You know what I'm weaving? I'm weaving the front of the penitentiary for over your mantle! I don't even want to finish the sky now ...

ETHEL

What are you saying?

HARRY

You know how you always said I was tone deaf?

ETHEL

That ear is tin.

HARRY

Oh, yeah? Well, I happen to be chairman of the penal chamber music society. I play the electric organ. Plugs in right next to the "chair." Just as their walking the last mile, I hit them with "Toot, Toot, Tootsie, Goodbye."

ETHEL

Oh, Harry . . . our song!

HARRY

I know. They wanted "Zippity Doo Dah," but I wouldn't let 'em have it.

ETHEL

You're so considerate.

HARRY

I just don't want to get out!

ETHEL

You've got to!

HARRY

I can't!

ETHEL

What's this all about? Tell me why you don't want to get out of prison!

LONG PAUSE

HARRY

I'm in the play. I've hit the big time at the big house!

ETHEL

Play? This is nuts! How did this happen?

HARRY

Oh. Well, it's all so crazy. We were planning a break. I took my tin cup, and I'm running it back and forth across the bars. Break out! Break out! Break out! Break out! And pretty soon I got bored out, and I went, Break out! Boom boom! Break out! Boom boom! Break out! Boom Bah! Break out! And from the jail came a wail. And all of a sudden, the warden said, "Don't break out, we can put on a show! We got that solitaire cell out back. Judy, you could do the costumes! Mickey, you could do the directing! We have some old search lights we're not using. We have some wigs we're not using. And the next thing you know, we're in a full production of *Annie, Get Your Gun*! And guess who's going to play "Annie"? You don't think I'm too tall, do you? My solo, "You Can't Get a Man With a Gun," is cracking! It's got a lot of snap and pop! It's a cellblock hit! I'm thinking about doing it as a sing along! The boys will love it!

ETHEL

What will I tell your mother!?

HARRY

Tell her I've gone on the stage.

ETHEL

What about the kids?

HARRY

There's no business like show business!

ETHEL

But Harry, what about me!?

HARRY

I'll leave you two tickets at the gate.

"CATER TO MURDER"

Alan in 1976.

In 1976, Alan wrote a treatment for a television pilot titled *Cater to Murder*. Alan wanted to co-star with Ruth Buzzi in the situation comedy, and he wanted his other *Laugh-In* co-star, Johnny Brown, to play the role of the police detective. No script was ever completed.

SETTING

"Mom's Catering" is located in a cozy building that resembles an old fashioned thatched cottage. Inside, a receptionist dressed in an Old English costume and a grey wig greets clients. The interior décor is done in European antiques, decorative framed needlepoints, and delicate white doilies. Tea is always served to perspective clients from a large, antique silver teapot. The kitchen in the rear, however, contains all the latest industrial equipment. "Mom's Catering" ("Whether a party or dinner for two, no one brings it home like Mom.") is owned by a brother and sister, Alan and Ruth, who inherited the company from their mother, who was a chef of the highest reputation.

CAST

ALAN: Alan is a hypochondriac and a compulsive eater, who, to his sister's envy, never gains any weight. He loves his sister, and wants the business to succeed however, he is always in heated arguments with the current chef because he manages to eat the last of the supplies at crucial moments. Alan's dream is to design his own party favors and wedding cakes, but his sister won't let him, mainly because he has no talent for it whatsoever.

RUTH: Ruth is hyperactive, a workaholic and a compulsive dieter who fantasizes about every male client who walks through the front door. She relies on her brother because, although she has a great business head and wonderful creative skills, it is Alan who manages the serving staff and always charms the clients into paying the highest fees. Alan and Ruth have not inherited their mother's talent for cooking. In fact, they can't boil water. The business is not doing very well. Both Alan and Ruth hate needlepoint and doilies with a passion. Their respective apartments are decorated in chrome and lacquer.

JENKINS: Detective Jenkins is a pleasingly plump, single black police inspector who will help Alan and Ruth solve future crimes. Alan and Ruth pay him with pastries. They hire his teenage nephew to make deliveries, and cater his daughter's wedding in return for Jenkins running down license numbers and other legal favors.

GLADYS: A mousy, shriveled woman with a bad perm that matches her bad attitude is the catering company receptionist.

CHEF JEFF: The company chef with a nervous stammer.

CHARLES GRANVILLE: A very handsome bakery customer.

EDNA: Edna is Alan and Ruth's new receptionist. She's a car thief and auto mechanic who has recently been released from prison. Edna studied martial arts, weaponry, and obscure art forms while in the joint.

SHORTY: Shorty is Alan and Ruth's new chef. He is Edna's friend. A Spanish short-order cook, he studied gourmet cooking in prison, and speaks several languages.

THE STORY

Chaos reigns in the main office. Gladys, the receptionist, is having an emotional meltdown, screaming about wearing an unflattering uniform and itchy grey wig. Chef Jeff has just followed a trail of empty maraschino cherry bottles to Alan, who is trying to present his sister with his latest wedding cake design. Two biking enthusiasts are about to get married. Alan has designed the top of the cake to show the woman with one leg braced on a Harley and the other leg planted in the middle of the back of a man who is laying face down in the cake. The woman sports a tattoo, muscles, a leather mini-dress, and a veil made out of chains. Ruth patiently explains they are bicycle enthusiasts, not bikers. Alan is crushed. The chef is frantically searching Alan's pockets to see if there are any maraschino cherry jars left. Gladys pulls off her wig, and begins to strip out of the old-fashioned costume right in the middle of the office. Ruth is hurriedly searching her desk for an aspirin when a bell rings which signifies that someone has entered the shop.

Charles Granville is greeted by Gladys, whose wig is askew and whose dress is improperly buttoned. As she shows him into the office, he is passed by the chef triumphantly holding aloft the one remaining full jar of maraschino cherries. Granville is greeted by a very serene Alan and Ruth.

As Granville shakes Ruth's hand, she immediately fantasizes about him. He is polished, handsome, obviously old-school wealth. He shakes her hand, kisses it, kisses her arm while murmuring words like, "I knew you had the best crumpets in town." With a swoop of his arm, he clears off the desk and lays Ruth down on it, devouring her with kisses while Alan calmly asks, "Would you like a cup of tea?" Suddenly, Ruth snaps out of her fantasy, realizing Alan has indeed offered their potential new customer a cup of tea.

Gladys brings in folders containing cake designs. Granville explains that he wants them to cater his wedding. He has a special request. He wants the caterers to bake a fabulously expensive diamond necklace inside a specially marked section of the cake. When he cuts the first piece of cake for his bride at the reception, the jewels will be a surprise for his new wife. He assures Alan and Ruth that the necklace will be insured, and they shouldn't worry. No one else knows about his plans, so the necklace would be quite safe. Alan and Ruth agree to accept the job.

On the day of the wedding, Chef Jeff stands in front of an enormous wedding cake that is he is in the process of frosting with white icing. He shows Alan and Ruth how he marked the designated section of cake that contained the jewels, so that when the cake tier was baked and ready to be added to the top layer of the cake, he would know where to frost the spot with a red fondant heart, a signal to the groom that he should cut that section first to reveal the necklace. He tells Alan and Ruth that everything at the business is under control, and they should go to the groom's home to oversee the decorations. The chef tells them that he will deliver the finished cake on time. Alan and Ruth agree, but on the way out, they are confronted by Gladys who is throwing a fit. She throws her wig at Alan, screams that she has quit, and storms out the door.

Alan and Ruth become frantic at the groom's home because there is no sign of the cake or Chef Jeff. Alan decides to drive back to his bakery to find out what has happened, but when he walks out the front door, he sees the catering truck parked near the back door. The wedding cake is inside the truck, but there is no sign of the chef. Alan rolls the huge cake (it is on a trolley due to its size) out of the truck and into the reception, sneezing uncontrollably.

The groom lovingly cuts the first slice for his bride, being careful to find the spot decorated with the fondant heart. There is no necklace in the cake. He screams out to the wedding crowd that he baked a diamond necklace into the cake and he cannot find it. The crowd rushes toward the cake, using their bare hands to claw apart the cake and cram it into their mouths. The groom calls the police.

Once the police have taken control of the chaotic situation, they question Alan and Ruth, and release them.

On the way home, Alan points out that the center of the cake contained a blueberry filling, which he is allergic to, hence the sneezing. The original recipe called for a raspberry filling. Something is fishy, he surmises. It is not the same cake, or if it is, the chef made a mistake. Alan and Ruth agree that the theft will hurt the reputation of the business so they must find out what happened. When they return to the shop, they find Chef Jeff has been murdered, drowned in a vat of batter. They frantically call the police. A rotund black detective arrives who they constantly bribe with pastries. He informs them the police have returned the catering truck that they have dusted for prints. He asks them not to leave town. Not only are they needed for further questioning, the detective has an anniversary he wants them to cater.

Putting their heads together, Ruth and Alan decide to find out more about the necklace and the background of the groom. But first, they need to hire a new receptionist as quickly as possible to watch the shop while they look for clues. This task is undertaken by Alan.

Ruth makes a quick trip to the insurance agent and discovers that the necklace was over-insured. When she returns to the shop, Alan introduces her to the new receptionist. No employment agency would work with a company under investigation for murder, so Alan has hired Edna from the local prison release program. She is a dour looking woman who never smiles and obviously knows her way around the tougher parts of town. The next morning, they leave her in charge of the office as they go to interview Granville. Ruth worries that the silverware will be missing when they return.

Granville agrees to answer some questions, and shows them into the library. Alan raves about the décor, since there is not an antique or doily in sight. In fact, there are so few personal possessions that the house looks "unlived in." There is nothing in the house to indicate a wedding reception had ever taken place. Unfortunately,

Alan sits near a vase containing sunflowers and has a violent allergy attack. Granville tells him where the bathroom is and Alan heads for it, sneezing constantly. He inadvertently ends up in the wrong room and finds the wedding cake intact. He quickly backs out of the room and returns to Ruth, meaning to make an escape. However, once in the room, he sits next to the sunflowers again and starts sneezing. Ruth asks Granville for a glass of water for Alan. When Granville leaves the room, she quickly ransacks his desk. Alan is still sneezing so hard that he cannot explain they are in danger. She finds a picture of Granville and his bride, but they are wearing different wedding attire. An earlier date and a nearby town is written on the back of the photo. Alan and Ruth quickly leave before Granville returns.

Alan tells Ruth about the wedding cake he found hidden in the room. They drive to the nearby town written on the back of the photo where they look up the wedding announcements in the newspaper files. Sure enough, they find the same scam took place five years previously. The bride and groom have been married to each other before, claimed to have been robbed of a diamond necklace hidden in their wedding cake, and collected an insurance settlement.

Alan and Ruth return to the shop and find that it has been totally ransacked. When they enter the office, two gunmen, one of them being Granville, are holding Edna. Granville explains he examined the original cake and the necklace was not hidden in that one, either. He admits he murdered Chef Jeff when he saw him switch the cakes, so he and his cohort drove the catering truck to the party. Now it seems someone has switched cakes before he got there and he wants the necklace back. Alan has an asthma attack, Edna hits the groom with the silver tea pot, and Ruth hits the second gunman with a rolling pin. Ruth, Alan and Edna escape in the catering truck. The gunmen follow in their car. Edna drives while Ruth and Alan pelt the Granville's car with pies until the windshield is covered allowing them to disappear around a corner in the catering truck.

Alan congratulates Edna on her skillful driving. She explains that driving getaway cars is her forte. While driving, Alan and

Ruth try to figure out who else knew about the jewels. They come to the same conclusion at the same time ... Gladys.

The trio bursts into Gladys's apartment in the nick of time. Gladys has dyed her hair orange and is packing her bags. She swears she doesn't have the missing diamond necklace, but Ruth finds it in the bathroom, stuffed into a toilet paper tube and covered with a knitted rendition of a poodle. Gladys admits that she switched the top tier before it was frosted when Chef Jeff went to answer a phony telephone call that she had arranged. She took the cake tier containing the jewelry and left the shop before the cake was ultimately switched by the bad guys.

Just then, the two gunmen burst into the apartment. Before they can grab the jewels, Edna cries out, rips a curtain rod from the wall, and with the kendo skill of a master, knocks the guns out of both of their hands and renders them unconscious. When Alan asks her how she did that, she says it was a hobby she took up in prison to pass the time. She has earned Alan's undying admiration.

Life has now settled down somewhat for the catering duo. The police have the culprits in hand. Edna now answers the phone with a new greeting, "This is your mother, and if you don't order a party now, I better hear a damn good reason why not." Edna explains that most families are dysfunctional and everyone relates better to an abusive Mom. Business is looking up, but Ruth and Alan must now find a new chef. "No problem," Edna says. She opens the door and introduces Shorty, a short Latino man with a cigarette dangling from his lip and tattoos on both arms. Shorty had a lot of time on his hands in prison so he studied gourmet cooking. The first thing Shorty says is, "Oh, you have doilies. I just love them doilies." Alan knows he will hate him. Ruth looks at him appraisingly and says, "How well can you make pâté de foie gras?"

THE END

"NO PARTY IS COMPLETE WITHOUT AT LEAST ONE"

No Party is Complete Without at Least One is an outline for a proposed television situation comedy written by Alan Sues in the early 1980s. The story involves the misadventures of a middle-aged couple who realize that they are the only ones in their social circle who do not have a homosexual acquaintance, and set out to find one.

Episode 1. The wife invites her beautician home, but he's straight and tries to seduce her.

Episode 2. The husband goes to a gay bar and encounters a hustler—who is actually a vice cop, and is arrested.

Episode 3. The couple answers an advertisement in the "Free Press," and are invited to a strange, orgy-type affair.

Episode 4. The couple go to a drag show, and the clueless, overdressed wife wins first prize.

Episode 5. The couple visits a psychiatrist.

Episode 6. The couple has their house redecorated – by two feuding twin sisters who each make a play for the husband.

Episode 7. The couple attends an art gallery opening, and is talked into buying a very expensive painting.

Episode 8. The wife visits her dress designer.

Episode 9. The husband visits the local florist.

Episode 10. The couple attends the ballet.

Episode 11. The couple's son arrives home from college. He's very gay. Problem solved.

Two for the Show
A One-Person Play by Alan Sues

Alan worked on this play for many years. The work slowly evolved, and was influenced by a number of people he hired or asked for help. Several different versions of the play were performed. This most complete version was written as a homage to 1940s film noir. It was part autobiography and part "bugle beads and baggy pants" vaudeville style. Alan played all the roles.

Alan in 1990. Photo by Michael Lamont.

SETTING: PERFORMANCE AREA IS SMALL. A LARGE PROP BOX, A HAT RACK WITH VARIOUS HATS, WHICH HE USES TO REPRESENT THE VARIOUS CHARACTERS. A CHAIR, AND SEVERAL OTHER PROPS ARE DOWNSTAGE, STAGE LEFT. AN OLD FASHIONED CHANGING SCREEN IS STAGE RIGHT. THE STAGE IS DARK. AS ALAN (MELVIN BOND) SINGS "THE FLYING SAUCER SONG" A SPOTLIGHT GRADUALLY ILLUMINATES HIM, STANDING CENTER STAGE.

MELVIN BOND (SINGING)

'Five little men in a flying saucer, flew around the earth one day. They looked to the left and they looked to the right, but they didn't like the sight, so one man flew away.'

MELVIN BOND (WEARING A WORN FEDORA HAT. THERE IS A YELLOW FLOWER PRESET—PINNED TO HIS HAIR—UNDER THE HAT)

The name is Bond. Melvin Bond. My outside persona—I'm tough, hard, smart! (slams chair on the floor) Inside, oh God . . . I'm a mess! My last name isn't Bond. Oh, God, to be one of those 1940s detectives. Here's lookin' at you kid. You look hot. Did I say that or did you say that? I get the two of us mixed up. Come on, tough, hard, smart, in a classy upscale restaurant, like Denny's or Norm's. They take one look and say, "Any seat that's available." In good stores—the other day in Pic 'n' Save, this guy said, "Before you put that in your pocket, let me help you." That's service. Enough about me. You're here to see Miss Frankie Walters and her partner, Donny, in "Two For The Show." There is no show. Thanks for coming. I'm sorry. I'm really sorry. I'm the producer. I produced it. I'll give you your money back . . . no, that's a lousy idea. I'll keep the money because it makes me feel more secure. I'll tell you what's up. There's been a murder, (sound of thunder crack O.S.) now the killer is after me! Why?! I'm in show biz. Everybody is basically good. If I believed that, I'd be in plastics. Aren't we here on Earth to help others? What are the others for? This killer is evil. Evil spelled backwards is live. And that's what I'd like to do. I finally get a hit on my hands and the star, Miss Frankie Walters has been murdered! Murder can change your mood faster than killer bees at a nudist camp! (pointing to an audience member in the front row) You'll vouch for that, right Miss? What a terrible weekend for you. Okay. All right. Focus. Six months ago, down on my luck, broke, miserable ... I had to do something, so I taught myself to dance the limbo. Not for pleasure or fun, so I could sneak into pay toilets—sitting there thinking, "How stupid. I just busted my ass for a nickel." You're thinking they're a quarter, now where was I? It all started on a bad-ass Monday. (MELVIN SITS ON THE PROP BOX ON STAGE AND MAKES 'JAZZ HANDS' AND SAYS) Flashback, flashback, flashback ... Here I am across the street from the theater, in my favorite greasy spoon. Hot. Steamy. Hung over. That's another story. I slide into my seat. (MELVIN QUICKLY SLIDES TO THE END OF THE PROP BOX) Well, I said it was greasy! Fern, my waitress slid to the table.

MELVIN BOND REMOVES HIS HAT REVEALING THE YELLOW FLOWER PINNED TO HIS HAIR.

FERN

Melvin, baby, honey, sugar, sweetie pie. Sausage and flapjacks, Mr. Producer?

MELVIN BOND COVERS THE FLOWER WITH HIS HAT.

MELVIN BOND

Nah ... Hey, Fern, you got ringworm?

MELVIN BOND REMOVES HIS HAT REVEALING THE YELLOW FLOWER.

FERN

Just what's on the menu, honey. Mr. Producer, heard you got the pink slip. John Tesh fired you. That's bad, sweetie. Listening to him, you start thinking, My, God, maybe I should have seen *Cats*!

MELVIN BOND TOSSES THE YELLOW FLOWER OFF STAGE AND PUTS HIS HAT BACK ON HIS HEAD.

MELVIN BOND

Fern, cancel that side of sarcasm. Hit me with some coffee. Hey, you hit me with the coffee! Now you listen to me? Damn it, dame, scram.

MELVIN BOND (CONTINUED)

Good. Now I won't have to tip her! Got her for the nickel for the toilet. So, I'm polishing off a gallon of java, waiting for my rent to say hello.

SOUND CUE: HIGH HEELS CLICKING

MELVIN BOND (CONTINUED)

All of a sudden, she's coming straight for me.

SOUND CUE: HIGH HEELS CLICKING. MELVIN BOND'S EYES FOLLOW THE IMAGINARY STEPS AS IF THEY HAVE WALKED AROUND HIM.

MELVIN BOND (CONTINUED)

With a strut like that she don't want to see my sensitive side. I haven't seen it in about thirteen years. I'm saying, Hi, 'cause I'm a guy's guy. Your beehive hairdo would make a bumblebee's stinger get tense!

MELVIN REMOVES HIS HAT WHENEVER HE SPEAKS AS FRANKIE WALTERS AND REPLACES IT ON HIS HEAD WHEN HE IS SPEAKING AS MELVIN BOND.

FRANKIE WALTERS

Oh. Tense, huh?

MELVIN BOND

Yeah, I get your buzz all right. That strong cheap perfume could make a banana turn brown, yet you got that little girl quality that really gets to a guy.

FRANKIE WALTERS

I'm lookin' for a producer. I want to be produced.

I strongly suggest you watch me rehearse.

MELVIN BOND

Yeah, doll, your hips are winkin', sayin' FREE RENT.

I can produce, you thrombotic thespian.

FRANKIE WALTERS

Say... who's talkin' dirty! I'm lookin' for a producer. I'm Frankie Walters, and I got a new partner named Donny!

SOUND CUE: A MAN'S FOOTSTEPS. MELVIN TURNS THE BRIM OF HIS FEDORA UP WHEN HE SPEAKS AS DONNY.

DONNY

Like my outfit? I think I look like an albino penguin with a two picture deal! Yo, I'm the masculine part of the show! (grabs crotch) Well, Madonna ruined that move for us guys, she made it so feminine!

FRANKIE WALTERS

That's my new partner Donny. My old partner, Ci Ci, had very bad manners and wound up in the slammer. So I said, "See ya sailor!" Now nothing's in my way. I'm going to the top. Want a piece of pie? Just remember you're the statue and I'm the pigeon.

Ta-ta bambino!

SOUND CUE: HIGH HEELS CLICKING AWAY

MELVIN BOND

Spank Papa, was she controlling, and on a Monday, Tuesday! I'm seeing dollar signs.

MELVIN BOND TURNS THE CHAIR BACKWARDS AND SITS FACING THE AUDIENCE.

MELVIN BOND (CONTINUED)

Frankie and Donny are dynamite. I fell into her big baby blues, like a fat lady falls off a diet. Thinking, us making love. Bells will ring, lights would flash. Then thinking, how am I going to get her on top of a slot machine. Frankie and Donny look alike, but they worked different. The perfect yin and yang. Frankie's got some yin, maybe I don't need yang? I don't have any yang, but I could nose dive into a yin and tonic right about now. Maybe I'm still crawling out of those big baby blues, maybe love is blind, but a guy's guy knows a little girl quality when he sees it.

MELVIN BOND STANDS, WALKS DS. PLACE DONNIE DSL

MELVIN BOND (CONTINUED)

When Frankie took off for the ladies, I asked Donny, "How'd you two meet up?"

PLACE MELVIN BOND DSR.

DONNY

My story? Me? You want my point of view? My POV? Only if you insist. I'm in a market. Three in the morning. Working the graveyard shift. Waiting for my big break. Haven't you all heard that before? In comes this whirlwind ...

SOUND CUE: HIGH HEELS CLICKING. FRANKIE COMES DSC AND MOVES DSL. ADDRESS SL ANGLE, TRACKING FRANKIE ACROSS THE STAGE.

DONNY (CONTINUED)

Yo, doll. Closing time. Don't care if you are dressed to the nines!

THE FEDORA STAYS ON DONNY'S HEAD THROUGHOUT THE SCENE. ADDRESSES SR ANGLE.

FRANKIE WALTERS

It's more like the sevens. I'm on a budget. This Chanel knock-off put me on a liquid diet. I stuck to it. Yesterday, put a whole ham in the blender. Let's see now...Oreos? No. Ho-hos? No.

DONNY

Lady!

FRANKIE WALTERS

Twinkies? No. Oh, cabbage only three calories! Here cutie, ring it up.

FRANKIE GOES THROUGH THE MOTION OF TOSSING THE CABBAGE OVER HER RIGHT SHOULDER.

DONNY

There's a bite out of it!

DONNY TOSSES BACK THE CABBAGE.

FRANKIE WALTERS

Who could wait? An old superstition, "Eat in the market and it doesn't count calorie-wise." I'm eating whole barbecue chickens in here. Cutie, ring me up.

DONNY (LOOKING INTO THE BAG)

Nothing but bones in your bag!

FRANKIE WALTERS

The draft was so bad in the back of the market it blew all the meat off my bird!

DONNY (APPLAUDS)

Hey, you're funny!

FIRST TIME FRANKIE APPEARS TO ACTUALLY LOOK AT DONNY.

FRANKIE WALTERS

Don't give me a hand, a finger will do. What's your name and where are you from?

DONNY

Me?

FRANKIE WALTERS

Well, I'm not talking to the sale rack, sweetie.

DONNY

Donny. I'm from Oklahoma. Named after the musical.

FRANKIE WALTERS (LAUGHS)

Yeah, right . . .

DONNY

Got in a coma, so I left Oklahoma. Now I'm a Californian!

FRANKIE WALTERS

Sugar, hit me with the giggle juice. Beaujolais. Two cases.

DONNY

I'll get it in the back.

DONNY GOES BEHIND THE CHANGING SCREEN AND STEPS AROUND THE OTHER SIDE IN THE PERSON OF FRANKIE.

FRANKIE WALTERS

You Californians are so marvelous. Gotta get my ass on TV, damn it. When I do . . . first, my own place. Waiting for my name in that rag, National Enquirer, "Frankie Walters keeps her socks on having sex with alien." A lie. I don't do casual sex. Me probed by a stranger . . . well, there's a ring to that.

FRANKIE GOES BEHIND THE CHANGING SCREEN AND STEPS AROUND THE OTHER SIDE IN THE PERSON OF DONNY, CARRYING A CARTON TO DSR.

DONNY

Here's Beaujolais.

FRANKIE WALTERS

Forget it, sweetie.

DONNY

But I rang it up.

FRANKIE WALTERS

Unring it, you silly thing … ring a ding ding … "Baubles, bangles and beads."

FRANKIE RAISES HER RIGHT ARM FOR A BIG FINISH, SWITCHES TO HER LEFT ARM TO CHECK HER WATCH, SWITCHES BACK TO HER RIGHT ARM.

FRANKIE WALTERS (CONTINUED)

Screw Sarah Vaughn. Did very well with that in Fresno. I killed in Fresno.

DONNY

Hey, I know that song!

BANGS ON THE CARTON, CREATING A RHYTHM, AND SINGS. SR OF CHAIR.

DONNY (CONTINUED)

"baubles, bangles and beads …"

FRANKIE WALTERS

You're an artist. Talent, but for God's sake honey, slow it down. You're not drilling teeth. "Baubles, bangles and beads," what, what the hell are you doing? Dirty little pervert, get away from me. Slimy, disgusting degenerate … oh, wait. Oh, oh my. Oh, my God! Oh, you're lifting me? A dance move! I'm back on top! Lover! Baby cakes! What's your suit size?

DONNY

42 short

FRANKIE WALTERS

42 short? Put me down! Ci Ci's costume will fit you fine! And you got your own hair! "Sketches Together." That's it, Denny!

DONNY

Donny

FRANKIE WALTERS

If I only had something to read. Wait a minute. Now don't look. The other day a guy shoves this at me. "Wrote this for you!" I looked at the envelope. I'm not Gwyneth Paltrow, I said. You look a little different, but I'd know that voice anywhere, he croaked. I get that all the time. But this is called, "The Home Surgery Club!"

DONNY

You mean "The Home Shopping Club."

FRANKIE WALTERS

No, sweetie! "The Home Surgery Club." Here, doll face, read Dr. Soaker. You can make it funny, right Dougy?

DONNY

Donny. Okay, I'm Dr. Soaker. Welcome to the "The Home Surgery Club." Got Alzheimer's disease? Pay in advance.

FRANKIE WALTERS

Oh, another voice ... Not in my show. I can fix it. Now, howdy you all, I'm nurse Nancy Dimple! See, I do voices, too! I decided to operate on myself, 'cause I'm such a cut-up! Broke out the "T.T."—tit-tuck kit—at three in the afternoon. Five had time to make chili in the sterilizer. Yum, yum! And sterile, too! Nine tonight? Hittin' them bars! New around here? So are these! "Operate on yourself, it's so cheap!" Anything left over, just spray it white and make some summer jewelry. Got Alzheimer's, pay in advance!" Took that line 'cause it's better for me. Yes, we can work. Now I'll take that Beaujolais, charge it!

DONNY

We don't have charge on account here.

FRANKIE WALTERS

Slip me a couple of jugs! When the show hits, you'll get your dough, Danny.

DONNY

Donny! Just this once, or I'll get canned.

FRANKIE WALTERS

I'm Dr. Soaker! Welcome to "The Home Surgery Club"... ha ha ha ... see? You get all the funny lines! A very famous 42 short, Davey.

DONNY

Donny. Famous? Don't you lie to me!

FRANKIE WALTERS

Lie? Never! We resemble each other. Brother and sister, your younger sister, of course. Family, partners, close, like two people in the circus, making up one horse. Me in front, you behind. Lie? Never! Where am I getting a better horse's ass than you with timing like that? Miss Frankie Walters and her partner. Look. Wanna be on a marquee? Quit changing your name all the time.

DONNY

Melvin worked in that market for five years. I just got canned. My POV? I'm ready to go!

FRANKIE WALTERS

My POV! Do what you do best, Dicky. Go hail us a cab. Now Melvin, your call. When's the first day of rehearsal? Then maybe you can get a six pack of something. So the statue and the pigeon can play in the park after dark. Ta-ta, bambino!

MELVIN BOND

My POV. Is she coming on to me? Sure. It's my exterior persona. Tough, hard, smart. What the hell am I gonna do? I'm flat broke. Blew all my greenbacks on booze, gambling, and cheap sex. But the cheap sex should've been cheaper ... Nothing's left. Hocked everything. I got two suits, and they're both pending. Now to get dough for the show? There's only one way left, and it's a killer. Taking my life in my hands. They're organized and they're tough, bloodthirsty, ruthless killers—your average hairdresser. The hairdresser's mafia can get you, can kill you. Wednesday, off to Mr. Marmalade's Beauty Salon. I hooked up with a guy named Druff. First name, Dan.

MELVIN TOSSES HIS HAT SL AND MAKES "JAZZ HANDS"

MELVIN BOND

Flashback...flashback...flashback...

DAN DRUFF

Who keeps calling dandruff? I'm here! Oh, Melvin? So busy! My eyes look bloodshot. You should see them on the inside. The salon is just teeming with celebs—my regulars. Don't stare, for God's sake. Wanda, ready? My special shampoo. Rinsey, rinsey. Well, close your mouth. Melvin, you need a loan? Our Don—Spit Curl—I'm his left hand man. He don't have a right hand. You're lookin' funny. That other ain't my voice. I figured it out. Higher voice, bigger tips. Dames. I ain't no barber. I'm a stylist. So busy. I'm shampooing. Okay, Wanda? Is Rosie O'Donnell still wet? I guess so! Get her under the dryer. Get Meat Loaf out of the dryer. Oh, my God, his hair has fallen on the floor. Sell him a hat. Charo's ready for nails. With those claws, I thought you only hung from trees. I'm so kidding. Love you! Teensy, teensy shampoo Amy. Tomorrow she's getting married. Amy, sweetheart, who's giving the bride away? I know 247 men who could. I'm so kidding. Love you! Edwina, Edwina, Edwina, my best impersonation. Remember me, Marweena Dietrich. I'd like to pin up my blonde face, your facial, darwing. Only $12.95. Nothing's $12.95 except my cousin Twixy. She was before your time. You don't look forty. But you used to. I'm so kidding. Love you, Wanda! More special shampoo rinsey, rinsey. Melvin, you launder our money through your show? Once a week, secretly, $300,000 cash in a bag is dropped off. Where? In the prop box. Perfect, didn't even have to tease you, a little salon humor, get it? Red neck or faggy—I'm funny, right? Steal from the prop box, Spit says you're a bald spot. You won't come back. Spit is not kidding. Welcome to the Hairdresser's Mafia. Our slogan, "Dye job has a whole new meaning!"

MELVIN BOND (MAKING "JAZZ HANDS")

Present day...present day...present day...

MELVIN BOND (CONTINUED)

Dandruff is Spit Curl's left hand man? His special shampoo? What's in that crap that makes you come back and back and back? Their own secret handshake. Watch a woman tip in the salon. "Thank you, Bobby, see you next week take it, take it!" Cash and more on the way. Yes, those hair benders came through. The pigeon and the statue started nesting. Our eggs were making omelets. We had pet names. I called her angel wing and she called me cement. Opening night, boffo, a big hit! Everything was great! Wrong. It all went wrong after last night's show. Max, our sound man who's deaf, played music loud, heavy on the drums. Last night, drums so loud the walls sweat. Then the lights went out. Someone whispered, "put this in your pocket." They did. Who's paying attention? Just thinking, did I pay the electric bill? The lights come back on. Me all alone. That's when it really hit the fan. Closing up, all alone, just thinkin'. A gun shoved in my pocket. Just thinkin'. I'm laundering money! Caught! It's twenty years! Just thinkin' was the back stage door locked, or can someone come in and slash my throat to ribbons? Just thinkin' ordinary stuff.... That's not ordinary! The prop box lock is gone!

MELVIN STANDS BEHIND A LARGE PROP BOX CS. HE OPENS IT AND FEELS AROUND INSIDE THE BOX. ONLY THE AUDIENCE CAN SEE A LARGE LETTER "W" PRINTED IN BLOOD ON THE INSIDE OF THE PROP BOX LID.

MELVIN BOND (CONTINUED)

The money's gone! I'm in a mess!

MELVIN CLOSES THE PROP BOX.

MELVIN BOND (CONTINUED)

Frankie's dead! Deader than fried rabbit. Unrecognizable, except for her cheap wig, her trademark. Shot by a man or a woman—I nailed it! It's a man, or a woman! Frankie was the mule? The Marmalade goons double-crossed for 300,000 cold cash? Talk about extensions! No, Donny's yang got in the way? Frankie caught him and he shot her? Murdered for money! Cooked for coins! Wait, the facts. The money's gone, Frankie got lead poisoning. The suspects? Donny or the Hairdresser's Mafia. Me solving this alone, which would be by myself?! My shrink says, "Ya Muter Kinder, mama's boy, codependent." Although I did dress myself this morning. Yes, I go to a shrink! Do you? Do you pay? I don't. He won't take money, something to do with tax breaks. Dr. Kline isn't Freudian, his method is "Cyber-Browse." Deal with your problems by shopping! For him! I know it sounds nuts, but look what he did for Pia Zadora! Is she still working? I'm running all over town trying to make that man happy. Kline says, "za more you buy for me, za healthier you get." Can I deduct my Bloomingdale's bill for medical expenses? Dumping Kline, right after his garage sale, that should be a blow out. Does he like me? Won't let me talk in my sessions! Right, sir?

MELVIN DROPS HIS HAT SR OF CHAIR.

DR. KLINE (SITTING IN THE CHAIR)

Calling me sir, I like, but no talking in za session! Za healing is in za silence! Vhat's with zhis Frankie? Superstitious. Got a rabbit's foot? Other one is okay, ya? Get laid? Just slap her and get on vith it! Finish something, dummkopf. Think you're a loser. Vhat's the problem? That's what losers think. Guilty? You should . . . za couch, zhat's vere I lie down. Get up! Now get me a cookie and my blankie so I can look at zhat new Neiman Marcus catalog, and find vhat you can buy me. Oh, a tiny Gucci bathing suit for me . . . Oh, Gucci, Gucci, goo. Zhis shirt you bought, it's not real silk. Zhat's a rayon-poly blend! Start expecting bargain basement therapy, vhat does zhat say about za vay you feel about yourself? No talking!

MELVIN PUTS HAT ON HIS HEAD AND STANDS.

MELVIN BOND (WHISPERING)

Here's bargain basement therapy. Solving two problems for the price of one. Keep the show going, or, two, find the killer's "M.O.M"—motive, opportunity, means. Three hundred thousand in cold cash, that's a motive! Opportunity—here's one.

Last night drums, loud, made the walls sweat! A perfect time to shoot Frankie. And means—she's dead from second hand smoke! Frankie was borrowing big hunks of dough from those Marmalade goons.

FRANKIE WALTERS

I gotta borrow, or I'll go in debt.

MELVIN BOND

Conning the Mafia, planning her own funeral, digging her own grave! Talk about multi-tasking ... I told you she was controlling. Wait! What! I missed a clue! Dan Druff tricked me? That hair bender knew who did it!

MELVIN MAKES "JAZZ HANDS.

MELVIN BOND (CONTINUED)

Flashback ... flashback ... flashback ...

DAN DRUFF

Melvin, your hair! What a desperate cry for help!

MELVIN BOND

So, Druff, what's the dope?

DAN DRUFF

Don't say dope. It's dandruff. Wait! Oh, God! Seventy-five bucks right on the floor!

MELVIN BOND

Frankie's dead!

DAN DRUFF

Oh, God. I didn't ... I'll send funeral flowers. Candy flowers have been done to death.

MELVIN BOND

I'm closing the show.

DAN DRUFF

Closing the show!? Stop laundering money? That killed Mr. Marmalade!

MELVIN BOND

When did he die?

DAN DRUFF

Tomorrow morning.

MELVIN BOND

You just made up a joke at a time like this?

DAN DRUFF

Yeah. She's sitting right there. I'm so kidding. Love you! Don and Frankie play hide the salami. He thinks you got jealous and killed her. He left this. An invitation to your funeral. Spit's favorite kind of party. You don't have to bring a gift and you get to complain.

DANDRUFF TAKES A LETTER OUT OF ONE POCKET AND HANDS IT TO MELVIN.

MELVIN BOND

I'll put this in my pocket.

DAN DRUFF

Don't open it. I know what it says, "Get ready for your last comb out!" That's kind of funny. Now, run, run fast!

MELVIN BOND MAKES "JAZZ HANDS."

MELVIN BOND

Present day ... present day ... present day ...

MELVIN BOND (CONTINUED)

He don't know anything. But I gotta run, and run fast! Someone is setting me up so the Don will give me a permanent permanent! Putting me six feet under in the bone orchard, permanent! Fat chance! I'll get myself cremated, get a friend to flush me down the toilet. I've got my pride. Frankie having an affair, catered by the Don? She was going with me? This statue wanted the pigeon all over him! Knocked on her door so much I would have made a great Jehovah's Witness, except she wanted me to come in. Got along great, nothing nutso like twin tattoos. You know what I think is strange? Body piercing. Here, here, and here. I guess it's not weird if you like polishing silver with your tongue! The last time I saw her before before she got whacked, I had great news! "Pidgie, this show's going to Broadway!"

FRANKIE WALTERS

Broadway!? Me on Broadway? The Great White Way? Don't blow it!

MELVIN BOND

Gotta get some cash…

FRANKIE WALTERS

Broadway! Sell your nest egg! That shitty swamp in Thailand!

MELVIN BOND

If it dries up, I could make a…

FRANKIE WALTERS

Sell! Make your ulcer pay off! What? You feel insecure? If I feel insecure, I wear false eyelashes. They're making them for men, now.

MELVIN BOND

No! Bond in eyelashes?!

FRANKIE WALTERS

The latest! "Exec-u-lash!"

MELVIN BOND

Exec…

FRANKIE WALTERS

…u-lash…get 'em, and close the deal! Go out a statue, come back a monument. Making piggy wanna get on top of you… Dump that swamp!

MELVIN BOND

My prayers were answered. Frankie really cares... my guiding light... my L. Ron Hubbard. Showing me the way! Yes! I got those lashes!

MELVIN BOND REMOVES HIS HAT.

MELVIN BOND (CONTINUED)

Miss, those big thick black power lashes? The industrial size! I feel more secure! Hey guy! Invest in the next American resort city! Do you know where it is? Thailand! Got everything Las Vegas had forty years ago. Nothing! Know what Thailand's capital is? Four dollars and twenty-two cents. Got all the plastic temples and rubber elephants we need to open up Thailand Land. Zen Land. Commie Land is iffy, too bad, 'cause the kids got to swing around on a sickle and get hit on the head with a hammer. Cute as these things are, Democracy Land is red, white and green. They can't get blue paint down there, I don't know why?! But we have a little Coca-Cola lake, kids swim around and drink. They mess it up, it's just another flavor! Hey mister, mister, wait, your complimentary happy coat? It comes in extra large. Damn those power lashes. What the hell, so we don't have Broadway. What is important is that the shy, vulnerable Pidgy and the statue have each other.

MELVIN BOND PUTS THE HAT BACK ON HIS HEAD.

MELVIN BOND (CONTINUED)

Frankie, Frankie, I'm sorry, but I know you'll understand. I killed Broadway! My nest egg...

FRANKIE SLAPS MELVIN.

FRANKIE WALTERS

...is a rotten egg. Look, life is a vaudeville turn. You're turning out to be nothin' but an opening act, flash act, dog and pony.

MELVIN BOND

Well, I'm not a dog...

FRANKIE SLAPS HIM AGAIN.

MELVIN BOND (CONTINUED)

Oh, nothing …

FRANKIE WALTERS

Who told you to wear those, anyway?

MELVIN BOND

You told me …

FRANKIE COVERS HIS MOUTH.

MELVIN BOND (CONTINUED)

I don't know …

FRANKIE PINCHES MELVIN'S CHEEK.

FRANKIE WALTERS

I'm going to help you get me on Broadway.

MELVIN BOND

Thank you, Frankie.

MELVIN KISSES FRANKIE'S HAND.

FRANKIE WALTERS

I'll see those villains at Marmalade's.

MELVIN BOND

That would be great.

FRANKIE WALTERS (WHILE COVERING MELVIN'S MOUTH)

Ta, ta, bambino …

MELVIN BOND

She's standing by me. Dames dump guys that screw up. She's helping me. My little Pidgy with that shy vulnerable quality, I can still hear her saying …

FRANKIE WALTERS

Bet your sweet ass I'll be a star, damn it!

MELVIN BOND

"Star" spelled backwards is "Rats." Those hairdresser rats will get me! They got ways to kill a guy. I'm safe here. You're the witnesses... wait, I've got that gun. Damn, no bullets. Anybody got any bullets? You mean in this neighborhood without bullets? Are you a crazy person? I know what you're thinking, could things be worse? "Worse" spelled backwards is "Esrow." I have no idea what that means. I had a minimal education as a kid. Dad had attention deficit disorder. He used to say, "God's country! This is God's country! This is where I want to live and die!" Two weeks later we moved. When I was a kid we moved 32 times. Mom gave up! Had all her linens and sheets monogrammed "U-Haul." Dad would have made a great gypsy, but he was too straight to wear an earring. I could pack my room in 17 minutes. "God's country! God's country!" He's doing it again. He forgot to take his Ritalin. We moved all over. Once, on a ranch. A ranch? In California, that's any place where the mailbox isn't attached to the house. Ranch life stinks. The 4H Club stinks. You raise a pet, get a prize, and kill it. "Hey, mom, what's for dinner?"

MOM

Elsie!

MELVIN BOND

Elsie, my best friend, surrounded by peas and carrots. Dad once moved us onto a boat, to impress us with his nautical terms.

DAD

Ahoy! Ahoy! Okay? Okay? Son, you'll have your own room. It's in the basement.

MELVIN BOND

What an old salt. He really had those nautical terms down.

DAD

Ahoy! Ahoy! Okay! Okay! Mount the boat! Okay! Okay! Everybody to the starburst side! Okay! Okay!

MOM

I made this little hors d'oeuvre. It's a cheese puff. If you don't like it, just throw it overboard. The fish seem to love it. I don't know why ...

DAD

Ahoy! Ahoy! Okay! Okay! I'm going to unpark the boat. Okay! Okay!

MOM

I made this little hors d'oeuvre. It's a piece of liver dunked in chocolate. It tastes just like eggplant. I don't know why ...

DAD

Okay! Okay! First activity! Smell the air! Okay! Second activity! Fishing! We're smelling, we're fishing! Okay!

MOM

I made this little hors d'oeuvre. It's an apricot and a shrimp. All you do is take the apricot and shove it up the shrimp, but you might get an aftertaste. I don't know why ...

MELVIN BOND

Speeding up the Sacramento River, our hooks skipping on top of the water. Here's an old guy in a little boat, up since five, clinging to a fishing pole ... our big waves splashed his little boat, scaring the fish ... Whamo! Flips Dad the bird. Dad says, "See that? Everybody up here knows me! Me, nothing but a poor salesman." I saw him sell, he was poor. Dad died of food poisoning. I don't know why ... If I'd been able to tell Dr. Kline this, I'd have had a break through! So it has nothing to do with the murder, but I do worry about myself. Okay. Frankie wasn't poisoned. She was shot. Not Donny. Not the Hairdresser's Mafia. Who? Okay, we got Max the deaf sound man, he hated Frankie. Marlene? Frankie's understudy Marlene Magatelli? Caesar Magatelli, that two bit dress designer in wardrobe? Maybe Ci Ci, her ex-partner? Remember she said, "My old partner Ci Ci had very bad manners, wound up in the slammer, so I said, "See ya, sailor!" She wouldn't have double-crossed him. He'd have more motives than Imelda

Marcos had bunions. Off to the slammer to spill his beans, wag his tongue, and splat his guts.

MELVIN MAKES "JAZZ HANDS."
MELVIN BOND (CONTINUED)

Flashback... flashback... flashback...

CI CI STANDS GRIPPING IMAGINARY JAIL BARS.
CI CI

Melvin, spill, wag, splat. Who writes your dialogue, James Ellroy? Kill Frankie? Why? I just love prison! Why? I'm in a play! Back in show biz! I know, show business is full of thieves and crooks! They're all in here! I already got an agent! Should have gotten arrested years ago! Hey, Swifty! I'm getting new headshots. My head shots will do? Great! I've hit the big time in the big house! It's so funny how it happened. We were planning a break, see. Had my tin cup. Did you hear what I said? Tin cup! Can't wait until Martha Stewart gets busted, we'll get some style in here. So, back to me. We're going (SINGING AND DANCING) 'Break... out... break... out... ba zing... break out... boom boom... ba zing... break out' And from a cell comes this wail. A downhearted frail old voice singing 'Y.M.C.A.' And the warden said...

WARDEN

Stop! Hey (HIGH KICKS AND CLAPS HIS HANDS) kid! You've got talent! Don't break out, I'll give you a break! Hey (HIGH KICKS AND CLAPS HIS HANDS)   , we'll put on a show! Got those old solitary cells for dressing rooms. Hey (HIGH KICKS), old search lights for spotlights! Mickey, you direct! Judy, make the costumes! Hard Time Follies! Hey (HIGH KICKS), we'll break it in on the road—gang! Then the big time Leavenworth (SINGS) 'If I can get there, I'll make it anywhere..'

CI CI

Hmmm... I think the warden is missing a few keys on his ring. But the next thing you know, a full production of *Annie*. A few changes. But we got great writers! You've read their ponzi scheme proposals! A bunch of sensitive guys who just scream prison! But no dog for Sandy, 'til the warden gave us his Doberman Pinscher. He wouldn't come when we called him Sandy, but when I said 'Kill,' he did a hell of a job! But now, no Annie. The problem is there's too damn many kids in here, and they're all talented! Truth... am I too tall to play Annie? (SINGING), 'Tomorrow, tomorrow, a gang bang tomorrow, it's only a day away!'

CI CI (CONTINUED)

Kill Frankie? No, yes, no, yes, no yes... it'll be a huge opening. I'll leave you two tickets at the gate.

MELVIN BOND

Ci Ci, what an alibi! In the slammer! Starring as Annie! But I know you got someone to kill Frankie. Stop sucking on a lollipop. Spill the beans, wag your tongue, splat your guts, talk!

MELVIN BOND (MAKING "JAZZ HANDS:)

Present day... present day... present day...

MELVIN BOND (CONTINUED)

I didn't say that, I couldn't. I got no proof. It's as lousy as a fire-eater with hiccups. Wait, I forgot about Frankie's understudy, Marlene! Anorexic, schizophrenic. Her brain missing in action. Marlene. Tried to put her on one night... what a mess!

MELVIN BOND (MAKING "JAZZ HANDS")

Flashback... flashback... flashback...

MELVIN BOND (CONTINUED)

Frankie's not here! Call the cops! Call the hospitals! Try Marmalade's, maybe she's getting a tint and a toot! Damn it! Marlene! You're going on, Marlene, you ready?

MARLENE

I'm only 26. Already I've seen five flying saucers. Why did I tell you that? Because Virgos never confide. (LOOKS UP AND THEN OFF TO ONE SIDE) Oooh. Six. I start every day with organic vitamins and potatoes. (HOLDS UP A BOTTLE OF VODKA, THEN LOOKS UP AND OFF TO ONE SIDE) Oooh. Seven. Wait until they hear me sing tonight! (SINGING) 'Five little men in a flying saucer, flew round the earth one day. They looked to the left and they looked to the right, but they didn't like the sight, so one man flew away.'

MARLENE (CONTINUED)

It's like dating. (TAKES A SWIG OF VODKA)

MARLENE (SINGS)

'Four little men in a flying saucer, flew round the earth one day. They looked to the left and they looked to the right, but they didn't like the sight, so one man flew away.'

MARLENE (CONTINUED)

My God, this is a ballad. I'm a torch singer. But it misses something without the accordion. Melvin! I'm ready! Curtain up!

FRANKIE WALTERS

Marlene, someone locked me in my dressing room. You're not going on, you scheming tramp! You back-stabbing bitch!

MELVIN BOND

That little girl quality really gets to a guy. Marlene had murder in her eyes. Dames... when their blood sugar gets low and their hormones get high...

MELVIN BOND (MAKING "JAZZ HANDS")

Present day... present day... present day...

MELVIN BOND (CONTINUED)

But killers leave clues. Something's got to be in that box! (MELVIN OPENS THE PROP BOX LID REVEALING THE LETTER 'M' WRITTEN ON THE INSIDE OF THE LID) I didn't see that! Dried blood! Ah-ah, Frankie wrote 'M.' The killer's initial must be 'M' (CLOSES THE LID AND TURNS THE BOX AROUND) Hmmm...let me think. Marlene! Max the sound guy! Magatelli, Caesar Magatelli in wardrobe! They all hated Frankie! Why? My little pigeon Frankie. Frankie was never frank with me, only Frankie. Why do women like to be called men's names? Andie McDowell, Drew Barrymore, Stevie Nicks. Very few men want to be called Betty...What about Magatelli? Caesar Magatelli in wardrobe. Me telling him Frankie's been murdered. He wasn't surprised. He was nervous, like a goose at a Christmas dinner. I missed a clue? Watch!

MELVIN BOND (MAKING "JAZZ HANDS")

Flashback...flashback...flashback...

MELVIN BOND (CONTINUED)

Hey, wardrobe! Wardrobe!

CAESAR MAGATELLI (SEWING A PIECE OF BLACK CLOTH)

Not *wardrobe*. I'm Caesar. Caesar Magatelli. Named after the great Caesar...salad. My brother's name is Waldorf. What can I tell you, mama was into greens. But I'm very secure. You can call me 'Betty.' (STICKS HIS FINGER WITH THE NEEDLE) Damn it to hell! Me kill Frankie? I have no time to kill Frankie! Ah...Frankie, she had it all, I'm glad she didn't give it to me. 'I'm a star! I'm a star!' I don't wish to speak ill of the dead, but one drug bust does not a star make. Melvin, you're stuck with a dead pigeon. Depressed? No, it takes imagination to be depressed. I have a great imagination! I no do fashion shows in Roma. Roma, the eternal city, is over. No one goes there anymore, not even for the food. Domino's pizza is passable. And they deliver! This year my collection previews in Oxnard, the strawberry capital of California. Who doesn't like strawberries?

MELVIN BOND (INSPECTS CAESAR'S FINGER)

Ah-ha! Your finger is burned. I call it a powder burn! What do you call this?

CAESAR MAGATELLI

Painful is what I call it. You figured it out, right, Melvin? (CAESAR PULLS OUT A GUN) You caught me, you caught me! The pressure is too much. I'm crazy! I did it! I did it! I can't stop! (PUTS A CIGARETTE IN HIS MOUTH AND LIGHTS IT WITH THE GUN—WHICH IS A LIGHTER) I smoke! I can't quit! I can't! I'm an addict, and a Texan. Mama says I'll go to Hell. Of course, that's where the action is, it's so hot. I didn't kill Frankie. But what about Donny? She wouldn't let him use his name in the program! Miss Frankie Walters and partner Donny. But Donny who? Marlene told me. Martin. Donny Martin. But how did she know? This year I do two collections. One for the rich and influential. The other for you. For the rich and influential, making a woman feel more like a woman. Panty hose for nuns! Who could be richer? They're married to God! They do marvelous things with knits. And they have certainly proven that black flatters *any* figure. Their hubby's picture—a little cross at the ankle. J.C. at the knee all in knits. We call it 'Rosary Hosiery.'

MELVIN BOND (MAKES "JAZZ HANDS")

Present day ... present day ... present day ...

MELVIN BOND (CONTINUED)

Wait? Marlene knew Donny's last name? She's the killer! In dried blood, the killer's initial 'M.' Oh, no! She'll try to kill me! (A BOTTLE ROLLS ACROSS THE STAGE) She's here! No! (HE PRODUCES A CELL PHONE AND DIALS A NUMBER) No, she's got to be home. Answer the phone! Answer the phone! Hello? Marlene? I got some bad news. The pigeon's dead. The show is cancelled. You're canned.

MARLENE

I know. Donny said she was murdered. The show's cancelled? But Frankie was ...

MELVIN BOND

Did I wake you?

MARLENE

No. I'm a compulsive mumbler. Why did I tell you? Because Virgo's never confide. On the freeway, I don't even use my directional signals. Everyone doesn't need to know what I'm doing as long as I wind up where I'm going. Damn, I just lost my contact lense! My dumb luck. Oops, I found it! Ouch! It's a toe nail clipping. My dumb luck! Can you keep a secret? Me and Donny are getting married! He got the money for our own show! Too bad your show pays peanuts—no offense, Melvin. I'll be starring in a new independent film. For the audition, I'll wear your favorite dress. I'll spray it with scotch guard so if I get nervous and throw up, I can just wipe it off and keep on singing. I'm starring as Madame Curie, you know the famous scientist. I've got this part! Finally, type-casting is working for me! (MARLENE UNFOLDS AN ENTERTAINMENT NEWSPAPER) Right here. In the casting column. It says, 'highly intelligent, inner beauty, must know chemistry, full nudity required.' Oh . . . I didn't read that part. I flunked chemistry. My dumb luck. (MARLENE LOOKS UP AND TO THE SIDE). Oooh . . . Nine . . .

MARLENE (SINGS)

'Nine little men in a flying saucer, flew round the earth one day. They looked to the left and they looked to the right, but they didn't like the sight, so one man flew away . . .'

MELVIN BOND

Donny's ying yang got in the way! Stealing dough! He snuffed Frankie. You're an accessory, and I'm not talking earrings, sister. Cinderella, you'll be in the Big House. Sneaking butts for her Prince Charming named Ethel. I didn't say that. Did I say that? I gotta have proof! I need to close this case tight. Tight as weightlifter's thong. Someone must have seen or heard something. Why the hell was that music so damn loud last night? Max? You up there? (DRUMS START TO SOUND) Not now! I'm coming up, Max! The letter 'M' written in dried blood . . . the killer's initial! (MELVIN CIRCLES THE CHAIR AS IF IT'S A SPIRAL STAIRCASE. STAGE LIGHTS CHANGE TO REFLECT A SOUND BOOTH. THE SOUND OF WIND

BLOWING IS HEARD) Max! What the hell! You're buck naked, except for the raincoat! (ASIDE TO THE AUDIENCE) I've seen this movie before ...

MAX

Hello, Melvin? I can't see good.

MELVIN BOND

And you think being naked brings back your sight? It's wrecked mine, I'll tell you. And by the way, your birthday suit doesn't fit anymore. Needs to be taken in ...

MAX

No! Bumped my head real bad on a tree. But I learned something. Now when I open my raincoat, if nobody screams then I know it's a tree. Old age. I hate it! People say, 'he smells funny. Did he poop? I think he made a poop.' Well, they're not talking to a baby!

MELVIN BOND

Why the hell was the music so loud last night?

MAX

Donny started yelling, 'Turn the music up,' he yelled. Strange. First time he ever yelled.

MELVIN BOND

Max, put your teeth in.

MAX

See! You don't say that to an old lady. Give me respect! People pay attention to an old lady. The minute they see smeared makeup, wrinkles and a shopping bag, something makes them say, 'sit down, dear ...' 'Take a load off dear ...' 'Let it spread it out dear ...' 'Dear ...' Do they say that to me? Nooooo! 'Did he make a poop?' Really? I hate being an old man!

MELVIN BOND

Everyone thinks you're a cute old man.

MAX

Oh, yeah! (MAX GOES TO THE WINDOW, THROWS IT OPEN, AND FLASHES) Cute! Cute! Cute!

MELVIN BOND

For God's sake, Max! (MELVIN SHUTS THE WINDOW) For my sake, Max!

MAX

See, nobody likes an old man. I'll be an old lady! No. No sex change ... Medicare doesn't cover that, does it? They barely remove warts. Call me by my favorite name, Misty. Misty of Saks Fifth Avenue. I'll start my new life as a saleswoman, ready to greet the public graciously saying, 'We're out of that. We used to have it, but we don't anymore. It's simply discontinued. Sorry. Or maybe I'll just mumble. (MUMBLES GIBBERISH) They'll just think I'm a crazy old lady, smelling good! In a dress, I can get away with murder.

MELVIN BOND

Wait ... you'll be an old lady? Disguise yourself as a woman? No one will know who you are! So you'll get respect as a man. I've fallen off the page here! The lights went out. He could have put the gun in my pocket, so I'd take the rap! He killed Frankie. Is he deaf, missing sound cues? He ain't deaf now. See ya, Max. Have a nice day.

MAX

Nice day ... I play jacks ... just too old ...

MELVIN BOND

Buck up, Max, You're still in the loop!

MAX

Well, fuck you, too. I didn't make a poop!

(MELVIN BOND WALKS AROUND THE CHAIR AS IF DESCENDING THE CIRCULAR STAIRCASE)

MELVIN BOND

Yeah, you got it. Donny lost control and started yelling.

(A BOTTLE ROLLS BACK ACROSS THE STAGE)

MELVIN BOND (CONTINUED)

Of course! I know who did it!

DONNY ("APPEARS")

Yo, Melvin! I'm here! Frankie Walters murdered? Oh, God, no! No, no no! So we're starting late? I've got a great idea for the show! It just came to me! It will work! I'll do both parts!

MELVIN BOND

That's crazy! I'll use Marlene.

DONNY

No! Save the salary. She's not reliable.

MELVIN BOND

What? Aren't you two getting married and doing your own show? I'm baffled. Baffled as a transvestite getting a Mother's Day card!

DONNY

'The Japanese Legend' act that me and Frankie did—I can do the whole thing alone! Watch!

(BLACK OUT. MUSIC. LIGHTS UP)

DONNY

Once upon a time on the tiny island of Japan (CLAPS HANDS AND SNAPS OPEN A PAPER FAN). God, I gotta get off the Prozac... Long before Sony or Subaru, long before robots made fortune cookies in the image of fortune cookies... we tell a very old and very serious Japanese legend, about Little Red Riding Kimono.

LITTLE RED RIDING KIMONO

What are you looking at? What are you looking at?

DONNY

And the Big Bad fiery dragon.

DRAGON

How would you like to be in show business?

LITTLE RED RIDING KIMONO

Show my business? What for? You think I drop my fashionable panties for every dragon that crawls along? Sex with a dragon is sleazy, cheap and dirty.

DRAGON

With the right dragon, Red. Let me buy you a bowl of wonton soup.

LITTLE RED RIDING KIMONO

Wonton spelled backwards is 'not now.' What are you looking at?

MELVIN BOND

Okay, stop, Donny. I got it. Sorry, but it was better with two people. It's funnier with a dame. I'll get Marlene.

DONNY

No! No! I'll have none of that Marlene talk! I'll star alone!

MELVIN BOND

I need a doll. A tootsie. I'm bankrolling a big publicity campaign. Frankie wasn't bad on the talk shows, but Marlene will slay 'em! She'll pull a younger crowd!

DONNY/FRANKIE WALTERS

(DONNY'S VOICE) No! Nooo! Don't get Marlene! (FRANKIE'S VOICE) No! No! I'm the best, damn it! Me! Frankie Walters! Yes, I pretended to be Donny, and convinced you. That's Donny in the box, you sucker. Frankie Walters can do the whole show alone! Marlene will pull a younger crowd? Gang members don't buy theater tickets! (FRANKIE FLIPS OPEN THE PROP BOX LID, POINTS AT THE LETTER 'M', AND THEN SLAMS THE LID DOWN) Not 'M,' Sherlock. It's upside down. I wrote 'W.' 'W' for Walters! Frankie Walters! They say there's no such thing as bad publicity! Frankie Walters . . . ripe off the vine, freshly squeezed, a star!! Why did I snuff Donny? So sad... I couldn't afford to hire someone to do it. Those lousy hit men have gone union. With health insurance, dental plans—not to mention retirement accounts. Donny thought he could get away with it! I had to do it. Dressing him up to look like me. Getting him in that box was a lot of work. And the worst part? The worst part, my best wig on his dead head. I had to make it look authentic. Once I figured out he was the bag man, the rest was a snap. Thinking he could get away with it... Doing a new show without me! Dumping Miss Frankie Walters for that space alien, Marlene?!

(POLICE SIREN HEARD OFFSTAGE)

FRANKIE WALTERS (CONTINUED)

So, Broadway's out, but I will survive! Because I'm tough, hard, smart. You're not looking at the softer side of Sears here. Maybe it's shallow optimism, but I think $300,000 will get me to Bangkok's Thailand Land! I'll star alone at U.S.A. Land in the Doctor Laura Pavilion. The building is shaped like the head of Doctor Laura—between her ears, an empty theater. In her eyes—two revolving restaurants and 140 cars can park in her mouth! I'm off to Thailand Land to live. Ta-ta, bambinos!

(FRANKIE LEAVES THORUGH A REVOLVING DOOR)

MELVIN BOND (SITS ON THE PROP BOX)

Across the street from the theater in my favorite greasy spoon, hung over again, but that's another story. I just came to say, hi, 'cause I'm a guy guy. And you've got a beehive hairdo that could make a bumble bee's stinger get tense. I'm getting your buzz, all right. I'm a producer... I'm a producer... I'm a producer...

(LIGHTS SLOWLY FADE AND MARLENE SINGS V.O.)

'Two little men in a flying saucer, flew round the earth on day. They looked to the left and they looked to the right, but they didn't like the sight, so one man flew away.'

THE END

Acknowledgments

I would like to thank Alan's caregivers; Andy Curry, Peter DiVito, and Zac Morris. They worked very hard to provide Alan with a good quality of life until the end of his days. Andy's wife, Maytal, was very helpful and supportive, and cooked a few great meals for him. Zac's girlfriend, Amy Johnston, often stayed at the house with Zac and watched over Alan when Zac went to the store or ran errands. Although Alan griped about all the people in his house, and complained about his lack of privacy, he loved all "the boys and girls" who helped him. They were all as close to him as family. It was a loving household. When Maytal faced a critical medical emergency, Alan was very concerned about her. In spite of his own failing health, he asked about her progress all the time. Thanks to Tad Dowell and Cheryl Augustine who tended to Alan's personal grooming needs.

Thank you to Walter Oleziak, Alan's neighbor. Walter was a very good and attentive long-time friend.

Alan loved and cherished his oldest friends who graciously contributed to this book. Thank you to his ex-wife Phyllis Sues and Jerry Jackson, who graciously shared wonderful stories and photographs. Thank you to Jack Gilbert, and Joyce Van Pattten for their wonderful Alan tales. Thank you to Walter Finley for his support and constant encouragement. Alan's friends loved him, and he loved them, too.

Thank you to his sister-in-law, Yvonne Sues, who provided wonderful stories and access to Alan's scrapbook. Alan was very fond of Yvonne.

Thank you to those who worked with him and shared their stories: Laura Castro, Jane Connell, Carole Cook, Phyllis Diller, MacIntyre Dixon, Nancy Dussault, George Furth, Jackie Joseph, Sid Krofft, Jack Larson, Paul Mazursky, Henry Miller, Karen Morrow, Charlotte Rae, Charles Nelson Reilly, Doris Roberts, Wanda

Ritchert, Paul Sand, Rip Taylor, Tom Troupe, Breck Wall, and Fred and Mary Willard.

Thank you to Todd Lampe who worked tirelessly with Alan on a variety of creative projects. Todd gave Alan professional purpose in his last years.

Thank you to Taylor Negron, who loved Alan and always made him laugh. Thank you for the butter-pecan ice cream, Taylor.

And special thanks to all the kids from *Laugh-In*—George Schlatter, Digby Wolfe, Dolly Martin, Gary Owens, Ruth Buzzi, Jo Anne Worley and Barbara Sharma. Alan loved Ruth, Jo Anne and Barbara like sisters.

All the photographs included in this book were culled from Alan's personal collection. Every effort was made to identify the photographers. Alan was very fussy about photos. If any photographer was not properly credited, it was simply an oversight.

Finally, thanks to Lois, Mandy and Doris. Alan adored the dachshunds! His dogs were his most constant companions and traveling partners.

About the Author

The author's portrait by actor/artist Thom Bierdz.

Michael Gregg Michaud is the author of the critically acclaimed, Lambda Book Award nominated *Sal Mineo, A Biography* (Crown Archetype, 2010). Michaud is the co-author, with actress Diane McBain, of *Famous Enough, A Hollywood Memoir* (Bearmanor Media, 2014). He writes about Hollywood history, and has contributed to numerous books about show business. He is also an award winning poet, and photographer. Follow him on Facebook.

www.ingramcontent.com/pod-product-compliance
Lightning Source LLC
Chambersburg PA
CBHW071649160426
43195CB00012B/1399